Published by CelebrityPress®, Orlando, FL

CelebrityPress® is a registered trademark.

Printed in the United States of America.

ISBN: 978-0-9907064-4-1
LCCN: 2014953345

Most CelebrityPress® titles are available at special quantity discounts for bulk purchases for sales promotions, premiums, fundraising, and educational use. Special versions or book excerpts can also be created to fit specific needs.

For more information, please write:
CelebrityPress®
520 N. Orlando Ave, #2
Winter Park, FL 32789
or call 1.877.261.4930

Visit us online at: www.CelebrityPressPublishing.com

CELEBRITY PRESS®
Winter Park, Florida

CONTENTS

CHAPTER 1

THE DOMINO EFFECT

BY MATT CRAVEY

The difference between a successful person and others is not a lack of strength, not a lack of knowledge, but rather a lack of will.
~ Vince Lombardi

SETTING THEM UP

Back in the late 1980's, the real estate business almost completely tanked in Texas. You couldn't give real estate away. At the same time, the savings and loans and banks were closing and the oil and gas business had just about fallen apart. I was not unscathed by this downturn of the real estate market, and even though I saw myself as a rather intuitive businessman, I was really kicking myself, wondering why I didn't see all of this coming. I was treading water, but just barely. Only a few months prior, I thought there would be no end to the fountain of money that ran from my commercial real estate company I had started in the 70s. After I had established that company, I had invested in a telephone and security company. As my assets grew, I expanded and collaborated with a licensed commercial interior designer and created an interior design and supply company.

The next logical step from the real estate company was forming an investment company, in which we acted as the general partner in limited partnerships that purchased commercial real estate. We grew so quickly and were so successful that we decided to form a securities company that was licensed to sell shares in the limited partnerships that bought the commercial properties. I had created a closed circuit in which each of my companies did business with each other. This was a huge mistake, because it actually created a line of dominos, once one business fell, it toppled the next one.

I saw myself as a savvy businessman, but in hindsight, this seemed like such a rookie mistake. I listened to my own press as people called me a business genius, and I believed I was invulnerable, that is as long as the money fountain flowed. The first six years of the eighties were amazing. I was so caught up in all the meetings and the growth, I did not realize what was about to happen.

THE DOMINO TIPS

The federal government passed into legislation a new tax law that not only allowed the IRS to stop a particular tax incentive being used by the oil and gas and real estate industry, but they made it retroactive for a number of previous years. It was the tipping of the first domino for us, as the limited partners that invested with us were not going to receive the reduced taxes they thought. They were going to have to pay the IRS more money. As the domino fell, the investors looked to the investment company for their money back or were not willing to pay any more money into the partnerships.

MOMENTUM BUILDS

The dominos began falling fast and hard on top of me. Because the banks were having their own problems, they would not renew our loans because they needed money to keep their doors open. Tenants in properties we owned, and we never dreamed would be a problem, were filing Bankruptcy or going out of business, leaving us with back rent and angry partners. The closed circuits I had created between the companies I owned were becoming increasingly problematic, because each company had one customer – me.

The one domino that was outside this circle, the real estate management company, kept me from total annihilation. As the banks were foreclosing on properties, they needed my services to manage their ever-increasing corral of unoccupied properties until they could decide how they could unload them.

People in my companies were being laid off, and most of my time was being spent, speaking with limited partners, bankers, and attorneys. As the final dominos fell, I was forced to move from my beautiful offices to my home, which was not a problem, because I was the only one left. I sifted through the rubble of my life and made some major decisions concerning my business and personal affairs. This whole episode was embarrassing and heart-wrenching. I felt I had let my employees, agents, investors and lenders down but most of all, I let my family down.

THE AFTERMATH

For a time, I became depressed, and put some distance between others and myself. I was not sure what people were thinking about me and my situation, and I was embarrassed. I only had a real estate company left and almost all of my real estate assets were either gone through foreclosure or traded to partners if they would agree to let me off the hook of having to pay them back.

I listened to motivational tapes, and began going to the library in order to read financial magazines and the Wall Street Journal. I began to notice stories about people who were making quite a bit of money amidst this financial disaster. I became focused, and wrote down some short term goals. My real estate company started making enough money that I was able to put some money away. During this reconstruction phase, I visited my relatives in my hometown, which stood just north of San Antonio. It was quite the healing experience as I ran into people who did not care who I was or what had happened to me. One of these people was a local banker who approached me to buy a large warehouse they received from a recent foreclosure. I told him I wasn't sure how I would pay for it but I would go with him and look at it. Once I saw this large warehouse, my mind began to swirl.

A NEW DOMINO

As I drove around, I noticed the recycling collection centers were buying aluminum cans for half of what they were paying in larger cities. I figured I could take away most of their business if I would pay a higher price for the cans. I had never run that type of business and I didn't see how I could buy enough cans to make the payments on the building much less pay for the electricity.

I quickly figured out that I needed to be processing more than just aluminum cans to make this work. I asked around and found a man in the area that told me that many of the small towns north of San Antonio had to upgrade their landfills or construct new landfills because the existing landfills were not lined and could contaminate the groundwater. One of the ways to keep the landfills from filling up too fast was to recycle. I took this information to some large scrap dealers that dealt with buyers in San Antonio. The dealers told me they were not set up to accept the small towns bringing in their unprocessed recyclables. I could help them with the space, but I had no equipment, and I did not have a plan on how to buy ones that could process aluminum cans, newspapers, glass and corrugated boxes.

THE NEW DEAL

My Dad reminded me that a friend of ours worked at a large scrap dealer in San Antonio and that I should go see her. Turns out she not only worked there, she was a manager. She listened to my situation and came back with a proposal for the processing equipment.

She knew there was no way I could get the equipment with a loan or lease. I just didn't have the money. She offered to let me use some of their used equipment and in return I would sell them the aluminum, brass and copper I received exclusively. I would pay a penny per pound of processed material as a way to lease the equipment. For instance, if I sold her some brass for $1.00 a pound, she would pay me $.99. This seemed like a terrific deal, except the exclusivity part. In this type of arrangement, she could pay whatever rate she wanted.

Even though I was in no position of strength in the deal, I blurted out that I would only accept their terms if they were competitive with their pricing. She chuckled and assured me they would be fair in their pricing, and encouraged me to check other dealers' prices if that would make me feel better. The economy was hitting everyone during this time, so the equipment had been repossessed by her company, and it was just sitting in her yard rusting. This type of deal created some cash flow to pay for the equipment, but would be used and maintained by me, and she now had a great source of raw materials her company could process.

SMASHING, BAILING, AND SORTING

I purchased the building and upgraded the electric in the warehouse to accommodate the new equipment. I converted some of the offices to living quarters to give me a place to stay when I was in town and a place for my children to stay as well. It was time to let the world know what I was up to, and so I contacted the local newspaper who agreed run a story about this crazy venture.

The response was unbelievable, and for the first time since the toppling of my world, I found I was at the right place at the right time. People everywhere were looking for ways to make a couple of extra dollars, and I now provided a place for people to bring their recyclables and make a little extra income.

The word of the new recycling center traveled quickly to other smaller towns in the area. They wanted to bring in their recyclables by the truckload because the distance to San Antonio was cost prohibitive. This posed a new challenge. I needed a large truck scale, and those were not cheap. I called the only people in the area that had one, the local feed store. They agreed to weigh the trucks with a full load, and then after we off loaded the product, the empty truck would return to the feed store to be weighed again. I would pay the feed store a small amount for each truck that they weighed. I agreed to mail the township a check for their recyclables, but they were less concerned about the check and were relieved they had a place to unload the material without having to truck it to San Antonio.

MOVING FORWARD AND MOVING BACK

My little recycling center experiment was a hit, and soon it grew larger than I could handle. This recycling center was a three-hour drive from my real estate company in Corpus Christi, and real estate was coming back. I was itching to concentrate on the commercial real estate game, but I could not hope to do that while running a large scale recycling plant. I got help running the plant and eventually sold it for a tidy profit. I returned full time to my commercial real estate business, but this time I was not setting up a row of dominos, rather I am building on a stable foundation that I can build upon in the future, layer by layer.

As smart and clever as we might think we are, there are always new things we can learn, and sometimes it is the toughest and most painful lessons that are our greatest learning opportunities. Here is what I learned during my journey from the top to the bottom and back to the top.

1. Thinking about a goal is not enough. You MUST write your goals down in order to remind yourself daily what they are and the steps to achieve them. It may need to be in writing in several places. You may even need to write each goal separately so they are not bunched together and lost. I have some of them taped on my wall behind my computer monitor.

2. Be present and up to date in the world. Be aware of events that are going on around you. Contemplate ideas that arise after reading books, newspaper, or magazine articles. Write down these ideas and review them often. You never know when some idea that may not be relevant today, can be a game changer tomorrow.

3. FOCUS, FOCUS, FOCUS. Avoid becoming scattered. Find a few things that you are passionate about and prioritize what it is you need to be focusing on. However, do not get so focused that you do not see approaching challenges or opportunities sitting right in front of you.

4. Build a network of people that you can share and discuss ideas and issues you may be facing. Make it a point to meet new people. Begin by asking questions and then stick a lollipop in your mouth and listen. You will be amazed at the people that will want to help if you truly are sincere and appreciative.

5. Increase your value whenever possible through learning new skills or improving on the ones you already possess. Never stop learning until the day you leave this earth. People have a tendency to want to stop and rest. Stick to your strengths. You can waste a lot of time trying to improve your weaknesses, but your strengths will keep you going and get you out of bad situations. Even if you are not the brightest or quickest, you can eventually pass those who stop. I am proof of that.

6. Maintain the support from your family and/or partner. You will need their support to generate and refine new ideas, and they will be there when you need help being dusted off should you fall. The issues of losing my companies lead to my divorce because my wife at the time could not handle it. After my divorce, I found a wonderful woman whom I am happily married to now. She shares my vision and supports me moving forward. She is a Godsend, and I cannot overstate how important it is to have those closest to you, support you.

7. Be honest and straight with everyone. People will be impressed when you are transparent, and authentic, and those same people will be an unexpected support when you need one. People judge you more heavily on your actions and your ethics than promises you make. You will be surprised at the people that come to your aid because of how you have handled yourself during interactions with them and others. Your reputation is worth more than gold.

8. Jump in and get to work. People have the tendency to overthink things. If you feel you have the pertinent facts, and are still passionate about your decision, just do it. Sometimes you will have to figure out the details as you go, but I am sure I would not have done many of the things I did if I had thought through the situation more. Success, real success, is not without risk. Sometimes you just have to take the plunge.

About Matt

Since 1974, Matthew Cravey has been involved in real estate marketing, sales, leasing, management, investment, and development. As President of Cravey Real Estate Services, Inc., one of the largest Commercial Real Estate Companies south of San Antonio, Matthew holds two of the highest designations in the commercial real estate industry: Society of Industrial and Office Realtors (SIOR) and Certified Commercial Investment Member (CCIM).

Matthew is known for his proficiency in problem-solving, as well as his tenacity, focus and passion, intensity and desire. Matthew and his firm have cultivated a reputation for reliability and prudence in providing clients with real estate leasing and sales, investment counseling, asset management and real estate marketing services. He has helped court trustees, creditors and debtors negotiate and resolve problems involving properties in bankruptcy, and has testified as an expert witness in legal cases involving lenders vs. borrowers, offering his expertise on both sides of the equation.

Background and Career Progression

Raised in the Texas Hill Country, Matthew began his career in the real estate industry in 1974, selling ranch land and large commercial tracts in the Kerrville-San Antonio region. He continued selling ranch property when he moved to Corpus Christi in 1975, but the scope of his professional involvement quickly expanded to include marketing commercial buildings, retail centers, apartment complexes and developer tracts, as well as income property and asset management.

Although working primarily in Texas, Matthew's real estate expertise extends to out-of-state clients in markets including New York, Atlanta, Memphis, Santa Fe, Oklahoma City, Tampa and Jacksonville, Florida. His experience with large, complex properties has allowed him to build a network of investors, owners and brokers in Mexico, Germany, Japan, Korea, Canada, the U.K., Netherlands, Belgium and Switzerland.

Matthew has been recognized for his expertise in real estate and has won the prestigious NAI Global Elite award several times and is a contributor to national trade journals across the country.

You can connect with Matthew at:
Email: matt@craveyrealestate.com
Web: http://craveyrealestate.com

CHAPTER 2

WHY BE AVERAGE WHEN EXTRAORDINARY IS AN OPTION?

BY ALANA MCKINNEY

What I love about the run-away hit reality show "Shark Tank" is seeing the initial meeting and possible collaboration of Investor and Entrepreneur. Entrepreneurs had better come to The Tank with more than a great 60-second infomercial. Time and time again, I see those that cannot back up their pitch with salesmanship, proof of perseverance, a business plan and a strong work ethic, only to hear the unanimous , "I'm Out!"

What the true Entrepreneur has going for them is that the Sharks were once struggling Entrepreneurs and know what they had to do to be successful. The questions are more revealing if you remember the person asking probably has a back-story of why it is so important for them to know the answer. That's it! There is a process and payment every Entrepreneur must go through to be successful. It is the survival of the fittest.

Thomas Edison once said, "Opportunity is missed by most people because it shows up in overalls and looks like work."

Here are five principles I have found that have helped me change the course of my life from average to extraordinary:

1. EXTRAORDINARY ENTREPRENEURS DO THEIR HOMEWORK.

Malcolm Gladwell, in his book *Outliers*, states that it takes roughly 10,000 hours of practice to achieve mastery in a field. I would like to tweak that statement a bit and say it takes roughly 10,000 hours of "perfect practice" to achieve mastery in a field. Notice I did not say perfect results or outcomes, but "perfect practice." One should strive for progress and not perfection.

"Perfect Practice" is a process of doing things for many years that are not at all that exciting, and could be really boring on most days for someone who is trying to build a business or a brand.

Some of those things are as mundane as: showing up, taking a hit, coming back, getting back up, being flexible, asking questions to find common ground, listening, being present in the moment, practicing and studying.

A remarkable thing happens though, over time. You pay the price of the Process and in return become an Expert.

2. EXTRAORDINARY ENTREPRENEURS "REFLECT" ON THEIR DAY.

Many schools, colleges and universities teach their students they should have the mindset of finding weaknesses and work diligently to master them. In 24 seasons of America's Funniest Videos, there have been entire segments devoted to learning how to ride a bike. Usually there is someone off camera who is instructing the rider not to hit a mailbox. As most viewers can predict, the rider plows into whatever obstacle that was in their way.

Why does this happen if specific instructions were given? It happens because the focus of the rider is centered on the obstacles and not the desired path. Where the focus of the rider is, the bike will surely go. The mindset of an Extraordinary Person is that their focus is on maximizing their strengths and managing their weaknesses. By intentionally scheduling time to reflect on the day's realities and the gaps in where one wants to be is priceless knowledge. Those that intentionally take action on learning, living and leading in their strength zone will move to another level of experience. Scheduled reflection and journaling are the best use of time.

Alice Block expressed that we often hear, "We are just wasting time but in reality we are wasting ourselves." Experts are the ones who are intentional in building a bridge that eliminates the gap from knowing and doing.

3. EXTRAORDINARY ENTREPRENEURS KNOW THE DIFFERENCE BETWEEN GOOD INTENTIONS AND INTENTIONAL LIVING.

Going to 'The Tank' with a weak presentation is not wise. This is like blood in the water to a Shark. Then giving a lame excuse such as, "See, this is why I need you to collaborate with me and show me the ropes."… is the kiss of death.

Why? Because Sharks know there is a difference between Good Intentions and Intentional Living.

The Extraordinary Entrepreneur knows the fast lane to success is through failure and learning from it rather than making excuses. Creating excuses can really slow down a process.

I must admit for much of my life I assumed there was no difference between good intentions and intentional living. In reality however, I found that there is a good reason for the phrase: "The road to hell is paved with good intentions."

"Assuming" has caused me a lot of wasted time. For example:

- I assumed that good mentoring would help every employee.

- I assumed encouragement would bring peace of mind to everyone.

- I assumed training would bring the same value to everyone in the class.

- I assumed owning a business would be a lot like managing a business.

- I assumed a larger wage would bring more loyalty.

Sharks know the language of 'Good Intentions' and they also know that if the Entrepreneur is using words like: hope, not yet, sometime, my dream, my passion or impulsive in conversation – they are more likely

NOT going to see a return on their investment anytime soon.

If on the other hand, the Sharks sense that during their interview with the candidate a person that is driven, systematic, action-oriented, disciplined and consistent—it could be a deal maker and possible offer. Shark Investors know the risk will be a lot less with a candidate that lives intentionally than with someone who only has good intentions. It may surprise you to know that studies reveal that only 5% of the population is practicing Intentional living.

4. EXTRAORDINARY ENTREPRENEURS GET INTO THE GAME AND STAY THERE.

Investors and Entrepreneurs seldom agree. However, when there is a match you will find "they believe the same things but think different thoughts." Dr. Ivan Misner founder of BNI (Business Network International) wrote a book on gender differences in social situations and networking. He concludes along with his co-authors that the majority of men are transactional and will go straight to the destination-no distractions or detours. Women want to go to the same destination but they will bring their relationships with them on the journey. There may be some distractions along the way but no worries, I value our time together. Both Investor and Entrepreneur want the same thing but the Investor will want to know when he/she will be paid back with interest and how quickly can they move on to the next investment. The Entrepreneur wants to get the product or service out to the public. In their vision they see the admiring consumer wondering how they ever lived without this product or service.

Barbara Corcoran, Shark Investor, wants to hear a simple presentation pitch. Give her the basic concepts of the product or service, what is a _reasonable_ growth plan and what is the potential market. It might surprise you that the content of a pitch to an Investor is far less than you might imagine. If you pass the questions on content then you are now in the game! How do you stay in the game to make the winning score? The answer: It is found in Relationships. Whether it is a joint venture, power teaming, partnering and/or collaboration, relationships will bring home the win and in a big way! So what is it in a relationship that builds trust and credibility you might ask? It is to add value to the relationship by being totally present, listen without thinking of what you will say next, and ask questions that are more important than the answer. Just as sports have their seasons, so do relationships. By intentionally being grateful for the experience and possible ongoing opportunities, be sure to remember to express gratitude in unique ways. You will be laying the foundations for future collaborations.

Linda Kaplan Thayer is the marketing genius behind the AFLAC Duck, the "Toys R Us" jingle and a number of other marketing campaigns that you would know instantly if I listed them. Linda tells of the time when she had managed to land an interview with the legendary Warren Buffet and she was determined to make it the best 10-minute interview Mr. Buffet had ever given.

At the start of the interview, Linda walked with confidence and determination over to Mr. Buffet's desk and took from her purse an ice-cold Cherry Coke, poured it into a glass and offered it to Mr. Buffet right before the interview began. Shocked he exclaimed, "No one has ever offered me a Cherry Coke before an interview. Young Lady, you can have all the time you want!"

I tell you that story because your competition is "in the game". There are times when staying in the game means to know your audience better than you're your competition. Are you willing to make yourself memorable in a good way so that you will be making the winning score at the end of an exciting game?

5. EXTRAORDINARY PEOPLE INVEST IN THEMSELVES.

The key deciding factor of why the Extraordinary Person invests in personal growth and development is the desire to reach their full potential. There are all sorts of ways one can get the job done yet in the end it comes down to pay to play, and then jump in the deep end. I love the saying—"It doesn't matter how deep it is if you are in over your head." How true!

The average person looks at personal growth as just another activity to take more time and money away from other activities they could be engaged in. The Extraordinary Person strives for progress and knows that the investment of time and money is an act of paying forward to reach full potential in the future.

Mark Burnett is the award-winning executive producer of Shark Tank. His vision when he first contacted Kevin Harrington about being a Shark was to produce a show that proved that the entrepreneurial spirit was alive and well if only given a chance.

Extraordinary Entrepreneurs everywhere can reclaim their future by realizing and taking advantage of opportunities available to them. And for the lucky few who stand in the Tank and hear "I'm In." Congratulations!

About Alana

Alana McKinney is one of the Nation's foremost experts and advocates on the benefits of networking, word-of-mouth referral marketing and social capital.

Alana is an award-winning, best-selling author. She has been honored by the National Academy of Best Selling Authors with 2011 and 2012 Quilly Awards for two of her best-selling books: *The Success Secret*, which Alana co-authored alongside America's #1 Success Coach and co-creator of the legendary Chicken Soup for the Soul best-selling book series, Jack Canfield, and *Building The Ultimate Network*, which Alana wrote with world-renowned practitioner and teacher of networking, Dr. Ivan Misner.

Alana received two 2014 EXPY Awards from The National Association of Experts, Writers & Speakers in recognition for her achievements in media, communications and professional international leadership training.

With her own professional training organization, AGM Connects, Inc. Alana is a frequent presenter and a coach on networking strategies and techniques. She helps entrepreneurs, businesspeople, and not-for-profits across the globe using only the most successful strategies. She has worked with Action Coach International, The Brian Buffini Organization, Herbal Life, Mary Kay Cosmetic, SendOutCards, Shaklee Corporation, Signs By Tomorrow, State Farm Insurance Company and Allstate Insurance Company among many others.

Alana has been featured on *The Oprah Winfrey Show, The Today Show, NBC Nightly News,* CNN, ABC, NBC and CBS as well as in *Forbes* and *USA Today, The Chicago Tribune* and the *Chicago Sun-Times.*

CHAPTER 3

LEAD FOR ORGANIZATIONAL EXCELLENCE

BY CATHIE LEIMBACH

"Where's Dad?" I asked as a child.

"At the county pork producers' meeting. He's chairing the meeting since he's president this year," replied Mum.

"Where's Mum?" I asked a few days later.

"At the church ladies' meeting taking the minutes, doing her job as secretary," replied Dad.

I quickly learned that one of the things adults do is take leadership roles in community activities and organizations. My desire to be a "big girl" meant that as I was growing up, I served at church banquets, helped host bridal showers, and organized youth retreat weekends. By the age of 14, I was an officer in my 4-H club. At 16, I was an officer in our Junior Farmers' Club. I soon became editor of the high school newspaper and yearbook. At university, I spent most of my time with involved people and led various clubs and activities. Wasn't I just doing the normal thing – getting involved and offering to lead? I was learning to lead by taking initiative and making things happen.

In my mid-twenties, I had the surprising realization that there were lots of adults who didn't lead, and many who made no volunteer contributions within the community. Since many people didn't demonstrate initiative, I had opportunities to make things happen that others had been talking about for years. For example, for several years students in my university major had been complaining about a scheduling conflict with two valuable elective courses. Since a number of my classmates were frustrated with being unable to take both courses, I reviewed the university course schedule for a timeslot that offered no final year agriculture courses. Since I didn't have any connections with senior university administration, I approached the program faculty advisor to request that one of these courses be moved to the open timeslot. He passed the request up the ladder. On the first day of class the next semester, two professors were surprised at the sudden increase in student enrollment in these courses. I was learning that leaders could accomplish more when they engaged others to help get things done.

Upon entering the working world, I continued to identify ways that the desired results could be achieved more effectively. National policies for a lending agency were changed due to my suggestions. Creative program adjustments allowed a professional development organization to offer more relevant, affordable, and accessible workshops to thousands of business managers. Diverse companies and associations have revised their bylaws and policies with my input, adopting more effective structures and practices. The leadership practice of aligning my efforts with organizational goals was instrumental to my requests being fulfilled and clients expressing satisfaction with my work.

Several months into my first job as the senior staff person of an organization, I remember sitting at my desk pondering how I could get more work done. So much of my time was being spent organizing work, supporting others, and being an administrator that my list of accomplishments with clients was disappointingly short. That's when I had an eye-opening insight—I wasn't supposed to be the highest producer of bottom line results in the organization. My job was to delegate most of the client service work to other staff, ensure they had the resources to complete the work, and acknowledge their achievements. I learned that leaders whose organizations accomplish a lot, delegate well.

My understanding of effective leadership has developed over many years of diverse experiences. I have led change initiatives, engaged the support and involvement of others, aligned my suggestions for change with the organization's purpose and goals, and delegated many projects and tasks. I have influenced change that has enabled individuals and groups to turn their back on the pain and frustration of organizational dysfunction and experience the joy of healthy cohesive teams achieving group goals.

I have experienced that "lead" is both a verb and an acronym. People who choose to get in the game of building a better world for themselves and others are proactive in leading, engaging, aligning, and delegating so that change for the better is an ongoing reality in their organizations and communities.

LEAD

Let's take a look at each of the four aspects of LEAD as an acronym. The 'L' in LEAD stands for lead. When leaders see opportunities for improvement, they define the desired results, communicate the goals, and cultivate teamwork. They take the initiative to define goals and develop action plans that will move the organization toward the desired ends. They record the goals and plans for ongoing reference and maintain operational focus on desired outcomes. As the late Stephen Covey said, "[They] begin with the end in mind."

Once leaders are clear on where they are going, they communicate clearly with others. They share the desired end-results and strategies for achieving these results. They communicate frequently and in various ways. Communication research indicates that only fifteen percent of people take action on new ideas before hearing them at least seven times. The most effective leaders repeat messages several times, increasing the chances that their followers and potential followers will buy into the plan and work towards achieving the goals. The message might be communicated in person, by telephone, electronically, or on paper. It might be presented to people individually, in small groups, or in large groups. When individuals receive a message in ways that click for them, they can truly hear the message. Intentional communication is the first step to their buy-in.

A third element of leading effectively is cultivating teamwork. Goals will be achieved most effectively when people work together. Not only does this require that they understand the task ahead of them. It also requires that they trust each other and communicate comfortably with each other. Leading well involves cultivating a cohesive team in which people work together to achieve common goals. Leading well involves defining, communicating, and cultivating.

ENGAGE

The second letter in the LEAD acronym is 'E' for engage. Leadership requires that you have followers, and you will only have willing followers if you proactively involve them, appreciate them in a way that makes them feel valued, and utilize their strengths. Great leaders involve people by asking questions and encouraging group discussion about diverse issues. They involve them in the decision-making process on matters that impact their work. Simple, effective facilitation techniques create an environment in which almost everyone is comfortable sharing their ideas.

Another aspect of engaging people is to express appreciation so they feel valued. For individuals to feel appreciated, they need to receive heart-felt appreciation frequently – in their preferred style of appreciation. Some people feel most appreciated when they are verbally thanked, others when they receive gifts, and yet others when someone spends time with them. Dr. Gary Chapman and Dr. Paul White have identified five languages of appreciation in the workplace. When leaders take the time to understand their colleagues' preferences and express appreciation accordingly, the staff and the organization benefit from enhanced job satisfaction, morale, and productivity.

A third element of engaging people is to utilize their strengths. During planning meetings, a work assignment matrix can be developed. All projects or tasks that need to be completed are listed in separate rows in the first column of a table. Each team member's name is written as the heading for one of the subsequent columns. Whether the individual has strong, average, or weak skills in each area is noted. As much as possible, people are assigned work that uses their strengths. Remaining work is assigned to individuals who have at least average skills in these areas. If there are still unassigned tasks, the organization may provide training to equip team members to complete this work or recruit individuals who already have the necessary strengths. Engaging people within an organization includes involving them, appreciating team members, and utilizing their strengths.

ALIGN

The third letter in the LEAD acronym is 'A' for align. This includes enrolling, planning, and redirecting. Enrolling people means getting their buy-in. This requires involving them in discussions and then using many of their suggestions. It's not necessary that you implement all of their ideas but it is important that you listen to their input, frequently modify organizational procedures and practices to incorporate their ideas, and explain to them the reasons for not implementing suggestions that may not enhance the organization's results.

A second element of aligning is planning. What are the team's responsibilities regarding each of the organization's goals? What are the team goals that have to be met for the organization's goals to be achieved? In turn, what are the goals for each member of the team? What tasks will each team member be responsible for? Who is leading each goal and task; who is assisting? Everything that each team member does at work or in their volunteer role with an organization should contribute to achieving an organizational goal. Planning for such alignment increases the organization's efficiency because it sets the stage for all payroll dollars, volunteer hours, and other resources to be spent on organizational priorities.

Another element of aligning is redirecting when people are off track. Human beings all have personal preferences. They prefer doing work they enjoy and doing it their way. Some approaches are efficient and effective while others don't make wise use of available resources. When individuals are off track — not focused on achieving team and organizational goals — it is important that leaders take action to redirect the individual's efforts. A sensitive way to do this is to ask the team member what goal he is working towards and what progress has been achieved so far. This reminds him of the group goal and whether he has been focusing on it. Ask what his strategy is for completing his work towards this goal. Ask how you can help him move through any bottlenecks. Work across various departments within an organization can be aligned if leaders define, plan, and redirect when appropriate.

DELEGATE

The fourth letter in the LEAD acronym is 'D' for delegate. When leaders delegate it is important to clarify the goal, assign responsibilities, and monitor progress. Clarifying the goal requires being very specific and using common vocabulary. What is it that you wish to achieve? When do you want it done? Saying "increase sales next month" is quite vague, but "close $25,000 of sales during May" is clear. Clarity requires two-way communication. Check that team members know what is expected by asking them to restate what they are to accomplish. If they haven't grasped the full message, more dialogue is required.

Another element of delegating is assigning responsibilities. Is John responsible to lead the work towards a specific result, assigning tasks to other team members? Or are you the project coordinator who determines the work assignments? Who has authority to approve spending and to buy necessary supplies? What is the project budget? To whom is the project coordinator accountable?

A third element in delegating is to monitor progress. Great leaders stay in touch with those to whom they have delegated work. They establish milestones, indicate when progress reports are due, and state what they should include. They remind the delegatees when reports are coming due and follow up promptly if a deadline is missed. When milestones are not met, the leader asks the project coordinator and/or team members to outline how they will get back on track to achieve the goal. The fourth aspect of leading is delegating which includes clarifying desired results, assigning responsibilities, and monitoring progress.

SUMMARY

Leading for organizational effectiveness includes leading, engaging, aligning, and delegating. Three elements of each aspect of leadership have been outlined. All twelve elements are intertwined. Great leaders have willing and competent followers who focus on achieving the organization's and the team's goals.

How could embracing The LEAD Wheel model enhance your leadership effectiveness? Which elements do you already implement well? How can you become even more effective in the weaker areas or partner with someone who has strengths in these areas?

LEAD for organizational excellence. Lead by taking the initiative to act. Engage the people around you. Align your and your team members' work with organizational goals. Delegate to leverage the available human potential. Experience the joy of a healthy and effective organization!

About Cathie

Cathie Leimbach, President and Senior Consultant at Agon Leadership, is dedicated to moving organizations from dysfunction and frustration to effectiveness and success. She is a governance, teambuilding, and engagement expert who provides organizational leaders with access to simple and effective leadership best practices and personalized strategies. After working several years in financial management and business management training, Cathie moved full-time into the leadership development field. She shares leadership best practices to create healthy and productive organizations where people can experience the joy of aligned, cohesive teams. Cathie's enthusiasm is contagious as she customizes and delivers programs to enhance business and leadership practices.

She has been a business loans officer and credit advisor, a financial management instructor at the college level, and the senior staff person of a non-profit offering professional development programs. Cathie has managed a workplace team of full-time staff, part-time contractors, and volunteer contributors totaling several hundred individuals, delivering five hundred programs to ten thousand clients annually.

Cathie has been walking-the-talk of effective "direct and protect" board leadership practices for over thirty-five years. She has served on a diversity of boards, and has held the position of Board Chair in professional, educational, cooperative, for-profit, and non-profit organizations. Her knowledge and experience give her the perspective to guide clients along the route to a healthy productive board.

Cathie is an accomplished meeting and retreat facilitator. With an extensive toolkit of interactive discussion and training techniques, she engages all attendees. Full participation enables organizations and teams to tap into the diversity of human expertise and skills within the group. This provides the foundation for developing synergistic strategies that greatly enhance organizational results.

Cathie holds a B.Sc. with a major in agriculture and a minor in adult education, as well as a Masters in business administration. She is a graduate of both Leadership Lorain County and the Ontario Advanced Agricultural Leadership Program. The Agricultural Institute of Canada recognized her as an Outstanding Young Agrologist.

As a founding partner and current affiliate of STRIVE!, Cathie makes extensive use of its bestselling governance book, *The Imperfect Board Member*, and its board self-assessment tool, *The GEM Assessment™*. Cathie is also a Premier Partner and Certified Facilitator with Appreciation at Work, the developer of T*he 5 Languages of*

Appreciation in the Workplace. As a Certified MERIT™ Profile Advisor, Trainer, Coach, and Consultant, she supports individuals who are enhancing their self-leadership and group leadership behaviors. Cathie has received team development training on the *Five Dysfunctions of a Team* and is certified in the Myers-Briggs Type Indicator®. She is a member of the Cleveland Chapter of the International Coaching Federation.

As Cathie engages with her clients, she expands their leadership knowledge and behaviors, encourages them to adopt best practices that will overcome their organization's current challenges, and coaches them for successful implementation.

Cathie hails from Ontario, Canada, and now lives in Ohio, USA, with her husband and two teenage daughters. She enjoys travelling, reading, and walking.

CHAPTER 4

WAKE UP TO WHAT'S POSSIBLE – AND BE EXCITED AGAIN!

BY DEBBY MCKINNEY

You really can be pursued by customers and stop chasing after them.

Imagine creating a personal marketing machine so strong that it *attracts* customers rather than chasing them…one so powerful that even when turned off it would continue to produce results. You can. I've done it, and I'll show you how. It's a transformative, empowering process that's truly life-defining.

Years ago, my husband and I built a fabulously successful brick-and-mortar business. We created that marketing machine using what I call the **5 Keys**. Potential customers sought us out and continued to do so for 16 years after turning it off.

The Great Recession of 2008 and the years that followed changed everything. What didn't change was our understanding of how we'd built that marketing machine and would again.

My Dad was an entrepreneur in the truest sense. A business consultant always on the very vanguard of marketing innovation, so I'm proud to say I come by it naturally. And showed it early: my first business was a neighborhood newsletter. I was ten.

We'd grown our brick and mortar business from scratch by sheer determination, hard work, and our decision to invest in our future the right way at the very beginning. For years I'd watched my father create marketing machines for his clients, so we brought in Dad to help us with ours.

Dad sat us down and explained the **5 Keys**, much like I'm going to outline for you here.

We followed the steps and did the work – was it worth it? Totally. He reminded us that business is relationship-based, and there is marketplace advantage realizing that. I look back as that transformation in my thinking, understanding customer development is much like a courtship.

If you chase, they often back-off, and you get the opposite results of what you wanted. But become alluring, interesting – and interested in *them* – and amazing things happen. The right one *pursues you!*

Here are a few rules of the road:

I. BEING PURSUED IS THE FIRST OF MANY REWARDS ... THERE ARE MANY MORE.

You'll be excited about life, with the rich possibilities before you, rather than scattered and pulled in different directions. Feel sexy and delicious and confident, not overwhelmed. Strut your stuff, walk differently and when you talk to people they'll see the change in you.

When you're pursued you have more time to do what you want to do, because you feel more in control.

You'll find yourself attracting your ideal clients, concentrating on serving a particular tribe or group of people. You actually *increase margin* with less price resistance and *increase* profit when you lay out the marketing machine correctly.

II. YOU ALREADY KNOW THE STAKES ARE HIGH AND THE CONSEQUENCES ARE REAL.

Are you feeling like the hamster running at full-speed on the wheel, but getting nowhere, sprinting at high speed yet not creating the revenue you need to live the life you deserve? To say nothing of worrying about cash flow 24/7/365...and feeling like a prisoner in your own business, trapped, overworked and with only darkness at the end of the tunnel. Get ready to change that.

III. PREPARE FOR THE JOURNEY WITH A CLEAR PICTURE OF WHERE YOU'RE GOING.

You'll know what you have to do to create your marketing machine driving an endless stream of highly-qualified prospects pursuing you rather than chasing them.
- Dedicate yourself to integrating them into your life.
- Commit to working smarter, not just harder.

IV. CALIBRATE CHANGE TO ATTRACT YOUR IDEAL CLIENT.

It starts with your business attitude. Simple adjustments make great things possible.

Power positioning strategies can incorporate untrusting prospects today, to not only understand your power, but how to turn it into new opportunity for your business.

- *How do I find customers?* …is the wrong question.

- *How can I get highly qualified prospects who are ready to buy to seek me out?* …is the right one.

You'll reject a commonly-held belief about *getting the sale* and be glad you did.

THE 5 KEYS TO BEING PURSUED AND TO STOP CHASING PROSPECTS

1. Your Mindset & Attitude
Everything starts with attitude. Your approach to life and your approach to business are influenced by your attitude. Warning! You may be required to think differently; just a little for some, maybe a lot for others, but you must embrace it.

The wrong approach. Same-old, same-old.
No more excuses like it's not a priority, just another thing on my To-Do list. I just don't have the time, I'm too busy. I don't know how, I don't have money for marketing … so what's the point???

The right approach. A new mindset.

Change the way you view your customers and prospects – it's not randomly selling, but selling to your most valuable asset to build, maintain and develop a strong community of customers that can stand the test of time.

Positioning not prospecting.

This is the opportunity to stop prospecting forever. Positioning is about how you want your customers and prospective customers to think and feel about your business compared to other similar businesses that are competing for their attention.

Start at the beginning.

If you're just starting, go for the most easily obtainable customers first, the low-hanging fruit. Then come back and review the **5 Keys**, but remember it's about mindset and attitude, first.

2. Identify Problems and Find Solutions

People buy things they need to feel good or that they believe will relieve pain of some sort. We can debate why, but the pain point is the more consistent motivator. But what causes pain? You can't solve your customer's problems until you identify them.

Have an idea before you start talking.

What do you need to know? Compile a list of questions potential clients are asking and problems they face. You want to get to the real problems, not the surface ones...the problems that keep them up at night...the ones they ask their spouse about when their head hits the pillow...the *what-will-we-do?* questions.

Learn what's important to them.

To understand problems they are experiencing, go where they are, do your homework and learn. If your target market has a professional association, go to a meeting and read their publication. If they have a LinkedIn group, join it. Browse comments and read a variety of topics. Attend an event and volunteer to do a job that requires you to talk to a lot of people.

Providing solutions to problems are really about creating important opportunities for your business. Use your list of questions. Simply answering those questions will lay a solid foundation for finding solutions. Then consider what do you offer (or could offer) that provides a solution to their problems.

3. Build Rapport, Responsiveness and a Relationship
People buy from people. Business is relationship based, it's about people. We've all heard we have to develop the Know-Like-Trust, and while I agree it's an integral part, it's not the driving force. After all, don't you know people in business that you know, like and trust, yet don't buy from?

So what's the secret sauce?
Rapport. *You create rapport by giving value*, which creates *responsiveness*. Responsiveness, which means they buy from you. They feel that you know who they are, and offer solutions to *their* problems and because they do, they respond to what you offer. Showing their trust in you with their wallet or purse.

So what exactly is rapport?
It's the trust built by delivering real value, created by providing real solutions that build trust. Meet clients where they are and join the conversation already in their head. You want them to feel like you are reading their mail, speaking directly to them – do that by offering solutions to their problems – that's your message.

Master these principles, put them into practice, and you'll gain customers who believe in you, promote you and will buy what you have to offer. But there's more to it than the relationship before the sale – that's only the beginning.

4. Target the Client You Want
You've already targeted primary customer targets and identified their problems matched with the solutions you offer. But out of the universe of potential customers, who are the ones you really want? The best of the best, the ones worth working even harder to keep.

Just who is your favorite client or customer?
Who comes to mind? Was it the one you worked longest and hardest for? Is it your biggest or oldest client? Ask yourself what it is about that customer that you like best, because in a perfect world, wouldn't you like more of them?

Identify and Profile Them.
Who do you like doing business with? And why is that? Do they give you less hassles, but buy more? Do you put up with more, and go above beyond because it's worth it? What would you change about them if you could? This is your opportunity to design your ideal client and then go after them.

As you do, remember the opposite is true. Avoid the ones that make you cringe when you think of them. If you can imagine and strive for a world of perfect clients, you can imagine and strive for a world without nightmare clients. Profile both.

5. Build Your Marketing Machine
You want to be discovered, so the customers you want most will find you. To do it, create a simple but targeted and laser-focused marketing machine that brings them to you rather than chasing them. You will be attracting your ideal client, the customers you've profiled, rather than a shotgun approach.

Make a sale to get a customer.
Target your ideal customers, to make a sale and build a relationship. You create an easy entry point into your sales process. After the sale, then the relationship is changed from prospect to customer. This changes everything. They've already bought from you, you aren't chasing, you're optimizing. It's easier to sell or upsell a customer than a prospect.

Marketing Machine is an asset you build once.
Deliver value, build loyalty and they stick around a long time. Create it once and it keeps working for you, and you tweak it, refine it and maximize results. Like any machine, human minds included, you get out what you put into it – which is why you revisit the **5 Keys**.

It's not just a website, it's your online marketing machine.
An online presence is essential for every business today, so embrace technology and make it work for you. Don't be overwhelmed, you don't have to know it all, it's an invaluable tool and it's nothing to fear.

Summing up the 5 Keys:
The machine processes prospects that have sought information, perhaps receiving a free gift in exchange for permission to communicate with

them. Guide them in making a buying decision which solves their problem – your product or service.

Remember, in a perfect world, everyone would buy the first time. But the world isn't perfect and not everyone does. Stay in touch, follow-up, build rapport and sell.

Ready to start but don't know how? That's where I come in!

DEBBY MCKINNEY'S LIFELONG MARKETING JOURNEY

I told you my Dad was an entrepreneur all his life and that newsletter of mine at the age of ten leaves little doubt I was destined to follow in his footsteps. It's been an amazing journey. High-highs and low-lows, but I wouldn't change any of it. I'm stronger, smarter, and tougher because of it and life lessons come from both success and failure.

I had businesses during my college years, learning from all of them. Then I married a great guy, we had three wonderful kids, and built a fantastic business. For a number of years the business we built together was incredibly successful. We were more than a little proud of a multi-million dollar brick-and-mortar business that employed hundreds of good people. We thought we had it all and were truly some of the fortunate ones.

But the Great Recession had other plans for us. So, I've seen boom times and bust times. It didn't care about what we'd built and sacrificed for over more than twenty-five years. The economy tanked taking our real estate construction-dependent business down with it.

I needed to re-invent myself. Again. This time I was determined it would be on my terms with a focus on helping others and sharing what I've learned. I consult, teach and provide services to help market people, products and businesses. I know my Dad would be proud.

My approach combines fresh and innovative ideas with common-sense best practices. I share what I've learned every day and learn something new every day. That will never end.

…Practical strategies to empower clients to succeed in diverse marketing arenas and in life.

To me, succeeding in business is a *process, not a science*, so I come at it with a uniquely client-focused mindset. It starts and stops with my clients' dreams, and the mission is to help clients achieve their dreams by taking action. Best of all, the emphasis is on successful entrepreneurship that can build a sustainable business. A business focused on more than merely the next sale, supported by ongoing mentoring, and a support-network that really sets it apart...Consulting, business and life coaching empowering clients to succeed on their terms...Working with clients to develop marketing machines built upon personal brands, to succeed without compromise, and live the life they dream of – to really, truly, have it all.

Today I'm building what I think of as personal marketing machines for clients. I realize that today true wealth is built through equity, and by systems and processes that consistently perform – any time and from anywhere.

Now I can travel and go see my kids and have a life. I'm living the life I've dreamed of. You can, too. I'm proof of that and the future is brighter every day. Will it work for you? Absolutely. Will it work without you working at it? ...Of course not, nothing will.

Stop settling, reinvent yourself and redefine your future as I have. Wake up to what's possible and be excited again. You really can. It starts with a little conversation, so reach out and let's get it started.

I can't wait to hear from you!

About Debby (with a 'Y'!)

How Debby McKinney spells her name is only the beginning of what sets her apart. An entrepreneur since 10 – folks still remember that neighborhood newsletter – she combines a fresh and innovative approach with common-sense best practices. Practical strategies to empower clients to succeed in today's diverse marketing arenas and in life. She calls it *a process, not a science*, coming at it with a uniquely client-focused mindset. It starts and stops with her clients' dreams, and her mission is to help clients achieve them by taking action.

Deep marketing expertise comes from lessons learned in the most competitive and highly- challenging marketing trenches. In an entrepreneurial career that included building a multi-million dollar brick-and-mortar business with hundreds of employees, she's seen boom times and bust times. Insights were enriched by raising a family, and putting continued personal development at the core of everything she does. The journey, and the lessons ultimately learned on it, pointed her to ask herself the biggest questions of all:

"What do I really want out of life and how will I get it on my terms?"

"When I talk about perspective," Debby said, "I've got it, because I've lived it. The ups and the downs. I've made all the mistakes and lived the dream, but also know the fears first-hand. The high-highs, the lowest lows, and about rising up, reinventing myself and battling back to reach higher than ever. Each of us has the capacity to live the life we want. It's real, I'm proof of it. But wishing and hoping isn't enough. Big companies have the resources to get the help they need, but what about the rest of us? It's easy to get lost in the backwash of the digital world, but that's where I come in:

With:

(1) Consulting, business and life coaching empowering clients to succeed on their terms, and

(2) Working with clients to develop marketing machines built upon personal brands, succeed without compromise, and live the life they dream of – to really have it all."

Contact Debby
850-598-0200
hello@berealmedia.com
http://www.BeRealMarketing.com

CHAPTER 5

SUCCESS BY DESIGN

BY DIONNE GORDON

Starting a business is easy but it takes more than vision to make dreams become reality. Building a successful business requires hard work, ethics, focused planning, financial organization, and a dedicated team. This chapter outlines how to create a plan to achieve success.

WHY START A BUSINESS?

People start businesses for many reasons:

- Jenna was tired of working for others. She started Anderson Landscaping and soon had more clients than she could handle. Today she employs eight people in the summer and is able to spend four days a week skiing in the slow winter season.

- Terry worked nights developing a B2B software product that he wanted to market independently. He put together a business plan that netted him $1,000,000 in venture capital. Today his product is considered a must have in marketing circles.

- Kate wanted to take control of her life and knew the best way to do that was by working independently. She turned her hobby into a custom furniture business. Today her rare wood tables and chairs are in boutiques in major cities and she is expanding her production facility.

It is often said you should follow your passion. I'm not convinced this is sound advice; don't JUST follow your passion, develop a plan for success. In order to build a successful business, you need to do more than something you love. You need to find something you can succeed at. Being great at something takes time and energy. The writer Malcolm Gladwell says it takes 10,000 hours to achieve mastery in a field. If you take the time to analyze your activities; you might be surprised where you are spending your time. It's not always where your passions are. Once you find something you are good at, oftentimes it becomes a passion.

Even if you don't have a terrific original idea you can still start your own business. Do you think the area you want to go into is flooded? Maybe not: the data indicates that the fastest-growing sectors for small businesses included auto repair shops, beauty salons and dry cleaners.

Owning a business is, bar none, the best way to take control of your personal finances. The tax code has been designed to raise revenue, not save money. A basic citizen, earning their income from a payroll source, has a limited ability to shelter their income from taxes. Business owners, however, are able to get the greatest benefit out of the tax code. The tax advantages are so beneficial that even if you don't have a burning desire to be an entrepreneur, you should start you own part-time business. Network marketing companies are a great way for employees to take advantage of the tax code while incurring minimal risk, and potentially earning extra income.

It does, however, take a great deal of work and energy to build the momentum required to get a startup off the ground. You aren't necessarily going to see the payoff immediately. Start with a plan and then put your nose to the grindstone and get it done!

CREATE YOUR PLAN!

Before you do anything else you need a roadmap for success: a business plan. There are lots of resources for creating one. They can be fairly simple or highly complex. In all cases you need to address the following steps.

Step One: Decide Your Business Structure
Once you decide what sort of business you are creating you need to

make some decisions. The structure of your business is chosen for both legal reasons and tax purposes. Possible options include Sole Proprietorship, Partnership, Limited Liability Corporation (LLC) and the "S" or "C" Corporation. A good accountant can help you decide the best entity structure for your situation. Your accountant can also help you get the most out of the tax code. This includes explaining how the right strategies and documentation can keep you from fearing an IRS audit.

Once you know your business structure you can get an Employer Identification Number (EIN) from the IRS. You need to figure out what sort of federal, state, and local licenses your business needs, what sort of taxes you must pay, and what sort of financing options are available. You need to register your business with state agencies and establish a business identity. This includes trademarking your business name, getting a domain name, and creating a website. And please, get a branded business email address. Does this make you money? No, but a branded email gives you credibility, and credibility makes you money.

Step Two: Know Your Numbers
Building a successful business requires you to review your business data weekly and know your numbers. Let me repeat that because it's really important – KNOW YOUR NUMBERS!

Are you saying to yourself "What is she talking about? What numbers?" If you are, find a good accountant and get them on your team. Your accountant can help you with everything from creating a budget to tax planning to packaging your business for eventual sale.

The numbers I'm speaking about are a detailed snapshot of your income and expenses. You need to understand where your money is coming from (income) and where it's going (expenses). This is called your Profit and Loss Statement. You also need to understand your Balance Sheet. A Balance Sheet is a list of your assets and liabilities. It gives you an understanding of how your business is doing and helps you understand what your projected cash flow is.

If you are not a numbers person, your accountant will be your most important resource. Never, ever, do your own taxes and, unless you are an accountant, outsource your bookkeeping as well. You can't grow your business, do your own bookkeeping, and keep all your records up to date. You need to hire help. This ensures your reports have integrity and you don't make mistakes the IRS won't easily forgive.

Hard as it might be to stay current on this task, you need to be aware of your numbers because you need to be able to change direction when necessary. If a product, a program or marketing campaign isn't working, change it. If a vendor is costing you money, renegotiate the contract. If a job lost money, you need to know exactly why and then make necessary changes so it doesn't happen again. You can only do these things if you know your numbers.

If you structure your business well, you should be able to, ethically and legally, save thousands of dollars in tax liability every single year. Your tax accountant can set you up with a system and an understanding of what deductions you can and should be taking. Even if you are an independent salesperson for a network marketing company, your tax accountant can help you avoid the dreaded "hobby" status and put more money in your bank account.

Step Three: Plan To Succeed
Successful businesses are designed to succeed and succeed by design. Your business plan should include a detailed list of your product and service offerings, how your operations function, who your customers are, and why they choose you over your competitors. It should also define how you measure success.

Be sure you thoroughly understand your product and service offerings. Know how much each item or service is going to cost, who your suppliers are, how much you need to charge, and what your loss-leaders might be. Loss leaders are inexpensive "deals" you can offer that bring in clients.

Make it a point to learn how these relationships and the time value of money impact your bottom line, because it's important to protect your cash flow. One way to do this is to set up terms with your vendors. Don't pay off bills too early but always take advantage of any early payment discounts. To be succinct: use other people's money as often as you can, don't pay interest if you can avoid it, and always take advantage of discounts and rebates.

Get a Customer Relationship Management system. This is really important, a CRM system is critical to managing your marketing campaigns and your relationships with customers. It's how you know who to market to, who your best clients are, and how you can take a little business that is barely profitable and turn it into the biggest game in town.

Create 90 day and 12 month milestones in your Business Plan. These should be robust and include detailed revenue models. Find other companies like yours and see how they do things. Modeling other successful companies can save you time, money and heartache. Good business owners learn from their own mistakes, but the best businesses learn from the mistakes, and successes, of others.

Pre-tax planning is an important part of your business plan. It has been said that when you go into business for yourself, you enter a partnership with the government. The partnership agreement is called the tax code and it controls how you split the money you earn between yourself and the government.

When choosing a tax accountant, find one that helps you ethically and morally be aggressive with the tax code. Remember, by the time you are completing your taxes, you are reconciling a year that WAS. There is only so much your accountant can do at that point to minimize your taxes. Pre-tax planning is what's required. Too many businesses pay too much in taxes because they either have an insufficient accounting system in place, or they haven't captured the data they need to make the most of their deductible expenses. If your accounting system doesn't capture every reasonable deduction, you're missing out on the easiest way of making money.

There are some tax deductions that most small businesses miss. These include purchased equipment, HSA medical expenses, and retirement plans. According to The Tax Foundation, over your lifetime, taxes will cost you more than any other single expense. That's a lot of money; it warrants making an extra appointment once a year with your accountant to do serious pre-tax planning.

This might seem like a lot of research and detail work; and it is. But don't make the mistake of waiting until you finish your business plan before you start marketing your business. Make it a goal to talk about your business to new people every day. Join BNI groups, a Rotary club, your local chamber of commerce, and any other network available to you. Every interaction is a selling opportunity.

Step Four: Build a Great Team

One of your most valuable assets is your staff. There are significant guidelines for employment taxes so it's usually best, for liability purposes, to hire a payroll processing company. Make sure you have systems in place to reward your talented people and weed out those who don't move your company forward. Excellent employees aren't the only team members you need. You also need to rely on the expertise of outside professionals to make your business successful and then take it to the next level.

Besides your accountant and bookkeeper, another outside resource to consider is a good attorney. This is especially true if you're forming a partnership. Partnerships can go sour for any number of reasons, and most of them aren't nefarious or unscrupulous. Having a solid contract in place that covers as many eventualities as possible is just good planning. You also need to have a good dissolution strategy in place before you begin. Your attorney can help you with all sorts of issues including patents, trademarks and lease negotiations, to name just a few.

You should round out your team with a Mastermind Group and Accountability Partners. A Mastermind group is made up of other successful business owners, ideally ones that are a step or two ahead of you. Be prepared to bring value to the group. Accountability Partners help you accomplish the goals you set for yourself each week. A good accountability partner won't let you slack off.

It's easy to fall into the trap of doing it all yourself. However, when you do things you aren't great at, you're costing your business more money than you're saving. The opportunity cost of what you could have achieved if you were putting your efforts into the areas you're best at, just might be the difference between success and failure.

GET STARTED!

If you want to start your own business, don't hesitate. Even if you're considering starting a business just to get the most out of the tax code. Maintaining a successful business is simple, but the momentum and hard work it takes to get you from an idea to profitability isn't easy. Don't let that keep you from doing it. Start now, follow your dreams, and include these elements in your plan:

1. Decide your business structure.

2. Know your numbers.

3. Plan to succeed.

4. Build a great team.

Ultimately you need to have a crystal-clear goal. The skill is understanding what your numbers are telling you. Businesses that achieve crazy success are driven by people who diligently monitor their numbers, are laser-focused on their goals and ruthlessly prioritize their activities.

About Dionne

Dionne Gordon helps her clients realize their full potential as entrepreneurs. After working for multi-national corporations such as NEC, Thomson and Microsoft in quality and audits, she left the corporate world and began her career as an independent tax accountant.

Dionne is a graduate of the University of the Pacific. She is the founder and Senior Partner at Ember Financial Services, Inc. specializing in small business, start-up and tax accounting, as well as mergers and acquisitions. Dionne has also been a guest expert in the fields of individual and business taxation.

Dionne is a national speaker on the topics of, and teaches, Small Business 101, Business Bookkeeping, as well as Basic and Advanced Taxation Classes.

You can connect with Dionne at:
Dionne@ember-accounting.com
www.linkedin.com/in/dionnegordon/
www.Ember-Accounting.com

CHAPTER 6

FOLLOW THE LEADER: THE IDEAL INVESTMENT STRATEGY

BY CHRISTIAN G. KOCH, CFP®, CPWA®, CDFA™

This true story begins in 1997, the year my wife and I were married. It was a traditional wedding that took place in a Methodist church. My great uncle gave us a $1,000 investment gift in a large well known mutual fund company. At the time, the typical conventional wisdom was to diversify. *My uncle chose a diversified asset mix of five different mutual funds.*

Here's where the Lost in Space, a science fiction TV series, comes into the story line. The TV series was centered on the Robinson family, which set out on a space mission to visit another planet with hopes of colonizing it. However, their mission is immediately sabotaged by a crew member who reprograms the robot. The ship is ultimately saved but consequent damage leaves them lost in space. Eventually, the Robinson family spaceship crashes on an alien world where they must survive.

Our family is like the Robinson family, as we had a Lost in Space experience with our wedding gift. Ten years and five children later, our $1,000 investment, in a reputable mutual fund, was only worth $970.00. Unfortunately, my story appears to be like millions of other individuals who have put their retirement savings in defined contribution plans. In the real world we lost precious time to make our money grow.

How could this happen? Mutual Funds are flawed investment vehicles. There are a number of reasons why the individual investor has a poor experience and appears to be in a disadvantaged position. One of the primary reasons is lack of tax efficiency. Individuals can't incorporate tax loss harvesting on mutual funds like they can on individual stocks. Furthermore, high expense ratios and load fees tend to eat away at the original investment. Finally, in general, the typical US equity mutual fund has around 300 stock positions in the portfolio. So, if 100 stocks go up and 100 stocks decline in value and 100 stocks are flat, you really have not moved from your beginning investment point. Too much diversification can hurt long-term wealth creation.

A TRUE ALTERNATIVE: LEGAL INSIDER TRADING

Let me provide some context. The Securities and Exchange Commission on their website (www.sec.gov) defines the term "insider trading" as having a dual definition. The first definition has a negative context and is connected or identified with illegal behavior. This is done by individuals trading on non-public information for their own benefit. We are not suggesting this approach. However, the second definition of insider trading is what I am focused on in this chapter and would like to emphasize. Legal insider trading is when corporate insiders (corporate officers, directors, and employees) acquire a stake or interest in their own companies. Legal insider trading can also be the sale of the company stock. Both directions, entry and exit, are part of the second definition. When Insiders make purchases or sales of their own company stock, they MUST report the transaction to the SEC. This is all public information.

The Chief Executive Officer, Chief Financial Officer and all Directors of publically traded companies are required to file a FORM 4, which is public information, for every purchase and sale transaction they make. From experience, I have found legal insider trading information to be extremely timely and a great starting point to build a portfolio.

What is a Form 4 and what key information does it provide? Form 4 is an SEC filing that relates to legal insider trading. It must be filed with the SEC before the end of the second business day following a change in ownership of securities. The data on the form itself provides details such as name of the insider, their relationship to the company, date of the transaction, securities acquired, number of shares, price acquired and if it was a direct or indirect purchase.

I believe this is the best complete and opportune information an individual investor can have to build an educated investment framework. Who else in the world should have more understanding and knowledge about the growth prospects of their specific company than corporate insiders. Let me show you how I use this data to construct portfolios.

The unique 4-step investment process:

- Step 1: review the <u>Form 4</u> data to see what purchases company insiders are making. I have found that they usually come in groups or a bunch of trades. For example, it's not unusual to find a pattern of buying that the CEO, CFO and Directors are all purchasing their stock during the same time frame. To me this would indicate the insiders feel the stock price is undervalued relative to the long-term prospects of the company.

- Step 2: research the fundamental business prospects of the company and the market they serve. For example, understanding the competitive dynamics and primary competitive drivers for the company and its industry. Asking questions like, "Who has the dominant market share position? "Are there any significant barriers to entry?" "How susceptible are the company's products to switching?" In this step, I am trying to determine if the company has a sustainable competitive advantage in the market place.

- Step 3: review the company's earnings track record. Review the past five to ten year trends (growth rates and degree of cyclicality) of company and industry. Understand the risks and issues that may influence the forward growth rate. Determine if the earnings per share growth rate is accelerating or decelerating. Over time, an improving earnings track record dictates stock price performance. I believe that a portfolio of stocks, with improving earnings characteristics, purchased at a discount to fair market value, should provide above average returns.

- Step 4: review the valuation structure of the company. Understand historic approaches and past take-over prices within the industry, if appropriate. The two valuation model metrics I use are: (1) price relative to sales and (2) price relative to book asset value. On an absolute basis, both ratios need to be below one to build in a risk safety margin. With valuation structures, there is always a range of outcomes that can be used to determine a fair value for any company. Also, corporate management, in terms of their skill set, track record and strategic vision, is worth adding additional valuation points if management acts for the long-term benefit of shareholders.

THE CATALYST: A POSITIVE EFFECT FOR CHANGES IN PRICE ACTION

On a weekly basis, I review the largest individual purchases by dollar amount and size from the Form 4 data. My goal is to narrow a list to a few manageable names to start my investment research process. As a value investor and student of the Graham and Dodd's school of security analysis, I have read most of the academic work. From my experience, the missing ingredient from the traditional value investing body of knowledge is a catalyst or an element that creates change and action in a company's stock. I have found that Insider transactions, specifically open market purchases, can be that catalyst. As a value investor one tends to be looking at out-of-favor and unloved securities. The word contrarian often is used. By definition, a low valuation on a security usually means that some element of the company is in flux, misunderstood, cyclically out of favor or is a risk to investors. From my perspective, the catalyst or insider purchase helps to build a bridge for a clearer picture of the long-term prospects of the company. After all, why would corporate insiders purchase their own stock if they did not see an opportunity to profit. Building an investment portfolio brick-by-brick or stock-by-stock should improve an individual's financial resources in real terms, just like the corporate insiders.

PATIENCE: WAIT FOR YOUR PITCH

As I look back on my 20-year career in the investment business, there have been several defining moments that shaped my perspective. The first concept that most individual investors don't realize is that there are always going to be good investment ideas from which to choose. Take the long-view as that will be where the largest gains should be. Most of Wall Street is too focused on near-term results. Be patient and wait for the right pitch. Having played baseball as a younger man, I realized not every pitch is right for you. Most batters have a sweet spot where they have the most hitting impact. Investing is very much like a baseball game in that you are always looking and waiting for the next pitch to be a strike so you can get on base.

The second concept that I learned from my work experience is that it is extremely hard to manage large amounts of money. In my second job, I worked for a large commercial bank in their Trust and Investment department. In general, our weekly investment policy meetings were like reviewing history. They were always backward looking, reactive and focused on benchmark investing. There were really no out-of-the-box superior thinkers in that group. This is what the average individual gets when he or she puts their money in a mutual fund.

Having been a securities analyst during the technology stock bubble and crash it's important to remember that trends in motion stay in motion much longer than expected. During the period from 1999-2001, I worked in the equity research department for one of the largest institutional money managers in Atlanta. At the time, I remember trying to make 'sell recommendations' to our investment committee. The more pushback that I received, the more I knew I was right on the money with my unwelcomed sell recommendation. Eventually, all those technology darlings fell from grace and wiped out a decade of investors' capital.

I have enclosed five principles that may help in the journey to be a successful long-term investor:

1. Don't pay too much! The starting price determines your rate of return.

2. Your beginning holding period should be no less than 1-year.

3. You are usually right when the herd or crowd hates the stock idea.

4. Solid and skillful management teams are worth a higher valuation.

5. It's OK to leave some money on the table.

THE SECOND ACT: IT'S NOT WHAT YOU EARN, IT'S WHAT YOU KEEP

After you have implemented my four step investment process and have built a solid nest egg from buying and selling with corporate insiders, the question becomes, "what's next?" Well, the real truth is: It's not what you earn, it's what you keep! That line of distinction is important to understand. The winds of change appear to be blowing for higher tax rates in the next decade. Retirement investment accounts will be affected by future changes to individual tax rates. The best term to define this impact is government policy risk. This means individuals have to have a clear focus on taxes, changes in tax rates and how to position their assets after-tax in retirement. All 401K, SEPs, Traditional IRAs and other defined contribution plans are infested with taxes. It's like having a joint bank account with the IRS. Over time, you will want to move some of your retirement savings into a ROTH IRA account. The ROTH account is unique in that it provides individuals a tax-free growth bucket.

As an instructor for a retirement planning education class, I have focused on educating pre-retirees on the main financial issues that they should address in their golden years. What I enjoy the most about the classes is the open dialog and new perspectives these attendees bring up for discussion. One of the big take-away moments is when the attendees realize that their retirement is not a point in time but a process to move through in which financial decisions tend to be interrelated. During the retirement journey trade-offs between different financial decisions should be made not all at one point in time but step-by-step to get the optimal result. For example, a client of mine who lives in Newnan, Georgia has his own military electronics company. His wife is also employed by one of the branches of our government. They are both 56 years old and have done quite well in terms of saving a nice nest egg for their retirement. In 2013, because of budget sequestration and automatic spending cuts to the U.S. federal government his electronic business saw a large decline in both sales and profits. In fact, the profits from the business that year were actually losses. This situation presented an opportunity to do some retirement tax planning. Before the end of that year, we did a large ROTH IRA conversion, which helped him in two ways. First, he was able to move a large sum of money from an asset that was infested with taxes to a ROTH IRA account that is after-tax. Furthermore, we were able to do this with zero tax effect as business losses can be used dollar for dollar to offset any ordinary income tax from a ROTH conversion. Secondly, now all the future capital appreciation or growth in the ROTH account is tax free.

In summary, avoid mutual fund investing at all costs. It's really a loser's game where too much diversification and poor tax efficiency hurts real returns over time. Just remember my Lost In Space story. Follow the "smart money" or legal corporate insider (Form 4) transactions where they are eating their own cooking. Finally, avoid the tax man by using the ROTH IRA conversion strategy to protect yourself from government policy risk.

About Christian

When it comes to the investment consulting process and creating portfolios for retirement, you need an experienced wealth management professional. Christian Koch's expert knowledge and approach to traditional investments, individual security selection, retirement income distribution planning and more, can help you face the future and the intricacies of your investment portfolio with a fresh new outlook. "My mission," explains Christian "is to provide wise counsel and a strategic framework for retirement planning."

Christian has a unique investment perspective and a four-step retirement planning process system that has served clients for years: develop the vision, build the optimal portfolio, focus on distribution strategies and then evaluate wealth and estate transfer planning. He says asset location is extremely critical to maximizing efficiencies, especially during a slow-growth economy, and that minimizing taxes are a significant component of success.

Christian is a Harvard Business School AMP graduate and former investment research analyst. He also holds the prestigious Certified Financial Planner ™, Certified Divorce Financial Analyst ™ and Certified Private Wealth Advisor® certifications, placing him in a select group of financial professionals. He focuses on retirement portfolio construction but says real success is defined by helping people make informed decisions and by client satisfaction. In 2013 and 2014, Christian's credentials and work were rigorously examined and he was honored with a coveted Five Star Wealth Manager Award!

When not assisting clients, Christian enjoys his involvement with the Rotary Club of Buckhead and is heavily involved in the Harvard Business School Club of Atlanta.

You can connect with Christian at:
www.kamsouth.com
Christian@kamsouth.com

CHAPTER 7

REMOVING THE PAIN FROM THE STORY

BY DR. DIANE BRYAN

10:00 p.m. the call came in, the call that no parent is ever prepared to receive! It meant the end to two lives and one of them was mine.

A little earlier in the evening I was having dinner with some friends who were celebrating their graduation the next day. A very happy evening with thoughts of finally receiving their hard-earned Master's Degree. On the other side of the country, my daughter and her boyfriend were preparing for a moonlight snowmobile drive with some friends. At the end of the trail they, too, would end up sharing a dinner and a dip in a spa with friends. I, then, made my way home through the streets of El Paso, Texas and when I arrived home, I was tired.

I was changing into my nightclothes when "that call" came. The caller ID read that it was 10:30 p.m. and that the call was coming from a cell phone that was unknown to me.

"Grandma!" my granddaughter Hayden started. "Mommy is hurt and it is more serious than a broken arm."

My heart skipped a beat. "What honey? What is going on?"

"A neighbor is taking us to the hospital." Hayden seemed a little unfocused and frantic.

"Hayden, honey, is there someone I can speak to there?" I asked.

There was a shuffling of the phone.

He said, "I am taking the kids to the hospital in Boise, something has happened to Dawn. They are taking her to Saint Alphonsus Regional Medical Center."

"What happened? What is going on?" I was now getting a little frantic.

"There was an accident." He was talking cryptically, he did not want to give me straight answers. He said, "It is hard to talk right now" and then I realized he was shielding the children from the information. "Can you at least tell me if it is serious?"

"Yes, I am afraid it is very serious." And, I asked, "Like death?" He answered, "Yes." I had heard that awful word, that one word that no parent is ever prepared to hear.

When I hung up the phone I found the number to St. Al's Regional Medical Center, and called the emergency department. No one seemed to know what was going on or the condition of my daughter. They suggested I call the coroner, which I did immediately. And, she, too, could not tell me anything at that point in time.

Three hours later I was informed that the coroner from Boise had pronounced Dawn dead. This time, I felt my heart had stopped beating. My daughter and her friends had been on a snow mobile drive that ended in the thick trees on the mountain. There would be no dinner.

It seems Dawn and her date had joined some friends on a planned snowmobile ride. They met in a parking lot, the designated area to pick up the snowmobile. They all climbed aboard their snowmobiles and headed for the trail, through the woods to the forest road. Their adventure through the woods ended on the forest road, a very snowy and snaky road. There were huge berms of snow on either side of the road from snowdrifts, and where snow trucks had attempted to push ice and snow from the road.

My daughter and her boyfriend were on the last snowmobile in the caravan with several other snowmobiles preceding them. She was sitting in the back holding on while her date made it through the first snake in the road, but he drove too fast to clear the next curve and he lost control and he ran into a berm, the impact of which threw my daughter from the vehicle. She was fine but her driver was not as lucky – he went out over the berm broke his ankle on a pine tree as he and the snowmobile tumbled down a hill into a freezing cold creek below.

My daughter got up, crawled over the berm, and went down the hill to the river to try to save him. Somehow, through adrenaline-infused strength, she dragged him up the hill and back over the berm onto the road. At this point their friends realized that Dawn and Dan were no longer following them, and they turned their snowmobiles back around.

My daughter was assessing her friend that lay in pain, and at the same time becoming frostbitten numb on the road. There was not much time before shock or hyperthermia would claim him. The first snowmobile arrived and her friend saw what had happened and told her, "Hang tight, I'm going back to my car, it has *OnStar*, and I can contact emergency services." He left quickly, and my daughter was consoling her friend on the dark road telling him that he was going to be fine, just to stay alert until help came.

The next snowmobile arrived but was traveling too fast to stop on the slippery snow. She rolled over my daughter's date and broke his hip and pelvic bone, and in the process hit my daughter head on and in an instant, she was dead.

The autopsy report confirmed that she had died instantly, which was a small relief that she did not suffer long. There was a three-month investigation into the accident and it was concluded that there was no one at fault, that it was just a tragic accident. My heart stopped again. How could it not be someone's fault? It was simply unfathomable that no one owned this outrageous behavior. Nobody would stand accused?

I was distraught and like many people that experience this level of extreme trauma, I wanted to inflict pain on those that caused it. I wanted retribution. I wanted someone to be accountable for killing my daughter, but in this case, it was determined that no one was to blame. How could this be?

There was no retribution. No payback. No pound of flesh. My grief over the loss had no outlet, no balancing, and so I died all over again, and stayed in that state for a whole year. I was stunned. Too numb to move. I just couldn't put any day together. I didn't want to see people and I certainly didn't want to show up.

I am a psychologist, and had already worked with people and modalities related to trauma, substance abuse and now I was stuck in my own grief. This forced me to find my answers. If I could learn to save others, maybe I could save myself from my self-imposed purgatory.

THE TREATMENT- BILATERAL STIMULATION

I believe everything happens for a reason and there are no real accidents. It is just difficult sometimes to make sense of tragedy and pull something positive from it, but for my daughter Dawn, that is exactly what I have done.

I developed a non-talking therapy, because I learned from some of the veterans I worked with that if they talked about being in Baghdad and hellfire raining down, they make the story brighter in their mind. I have found that the way to detox the ugliness from traumatic memories is to trigger the mind by stimulating both hemispheres. During this stimulation process, the brain takes the memory from a state of being irrationally stored to being rationally stored and stripping it of its negativity.

Your brain knows everything that happened to you, in every detail, perfectly. It stores all of that information, and so working directly with the brain, you get positive, excellent results.

Spider Monkeys

I have worked in emergency rooms, and with crash teams, and worked in the prison with men who killed people and distributed their parts all over town. I've worked in Mexico, I've worked in the United States, and always it has been trauma, trauma, trauma. I began realizing that trauma works on the brain the same way, no matter the source of that trauma.

I have been on the National Response Team and provided first response assistance in Oklahoma and at Ground Zero. One of my first assignments was Hurricane Andrew. I remember being on one of the teams that arrived first and Washington called us and asked us, "What do you need? What do you need?"

Hurricane Andrew cleared everything away; there was nothing left. Out in the field were three small spider monkeys, sitting there looking at each other. I responded, "Send bananas." That is a type of traumatic event that stays with those it touched long after the TV cameras have been packed away and shipped to the next horrific event.

A TRAGEDY OF THE WRONG LANGUAGE

Long before my daughter's tragedy, I was in college in Long Island, when one night I saw blue lights of emergency vehicles speeding toward the shore. I was a volunteer and followed them to a plane wreck that occurred at the edge of the water. It was an Avianca Airlines plane that had run out of fuel on its way from Brazil, and there were 16 children and 11 babies on board that had been bound for New York.

The trauma of the Avianca Flight 52 was nobody in the emergency response team spoke Portuguese. We couldn't communicate with the children, we could only hold, and hug, and love them. It was at that time I began becoming interested in what trauma was, and how response teams could help in these types of emergencies. Sometimes it is not the trauma we think it is, it can be something relating to an event, but not the event itself.

Hurricane Katrina is another example of that. For many it was not the storm that was traumatic, it was the fact that they had run out of water. The people could not stay alive or sustain themselves without simple drinking water. It's the trauma within the trauma that you are really dealing with. During Hurricane Andrew, it was the fact there were no diapers and no formula that was the real trauma. I learned never to assume what was traumatic for people, because I could end up talking about and treating the wrong thing, and in the process, I could create a new trauma that had not existed.

The Bilateral Stimulation of a Snake

I work with war veterans, and the bilateral brain stimulation can be very effective in treating PTSD. I worked with a soldier who had been stationed in Vietnam. He told me a story of his troop lying in wait to ambush the enemy in the dark of night. He and his thirty comrades were lying quietly in the rice fields near a small village until they were given the word to move. They had to be very quiet so that they would not give their position away. They were spread about 15 feet apart from one another waiting for the signal, but before the signal came my client heard noises coming from his buddy next to him. He had to watch in silence and horror as his buddy was swallowed by a python. Afterward, they cut the python open and got the body out, but he was long dead.

He lived with the horror in his brain for years, and so I asked him, "What's the ugly part of it that makes the trauma so bad?"

He said, "It was Charlie's sounds."

"Can you get that sound in your head?" I asked

"Yeah." He cringed.

"Hold it in your memory." I told him. As he held that thought in his head, I bilaterally stimulated his brain. This sent a signal to the brain and his mind sheds all of the ugly voice off of it, and it puts it over in long-term memory completely neutral. You don't want to forget that there are pythons in rice paddies, but you don't want to be paralyzed in your life because the soundtrack keeps playing in your head over and over.

THE PROCESS

The bilateral stimulation of the brain can be done a number of ways. I have lights that go off, right side, left side. This stimulates the optic nerves in both hemispheres.

For little boys, I will used a drum. I'll drum with them, right, left, right, left, right, while he's telling me about the green ghouls in his closet. If I am working with a girl I might use castanets.

Teenagers love lights, or music that plays different sounds in each ear. I can make the lights go off in different modalities, different colors, and different speeds. I also use what I call thumpers. They are paddles that you can hold in your hand and they thump alternatively. This stimulation helps your brain walk through the trauma and make it neutral.

TRAUMA BEGINS IN CHILDHOOD

I have found in my experience that in 99% of my cases, every single trauma a person is suffering from is connected to something that happened in their youth. In the case of the man and the python, when the fear was detoxed from that memory, it also cleared the fear that stemmed back to when he three years old – when his father whomped him harder than the little boy thought he should, and he was frightened of his dad.

That fear and trauma exists in a node inside your brain and through the process of bilateral stimulation, you begin to unravel that whole node. As I helped the veteran get rid of his python story, we also got rid of 50 years behind all the fear he had in his life, because it was all connected.

People's response to this type of therapy varies, from the simple dissolution of trauma to the occasional rape victim that will wind up under my desk in the fetal position. We just keep going, and next thing you know, she'll just stand up and say, "Whew, I'm glad that's over."

Moreover, I will respond, "I am too, and I bet your husband will as well."

The great thing about this type of therapy is that the client does not have to talk to me. They just have to trust me and be willing to go to that dark place one last time and blast it with light or motion. I've had soldiers from Vietnam come to me and say, "I can't tell you my story because if I told you my story you would hate me forever."

"Do you know your story?" I will ask.

They will say, "Yeah."

"Well, sit down in this chair and hold on; we'll figure this out together."

And we do. I don't need to know anything that happened. It is your gig. It is you and your brain, and you are trying to figure it out. I am just an outsider helping communicate with your brain to let it go.

About Diane

Dr. Diane Bryan has served the therapeutic community for 30 years as a crisis intervention therapist. She has worked in direct care, day treatment, residential treatment, in the forensic system, the de-institutionalization of the mentally ill and the population with intellectual disabilities for the states of New Mexico and New York, helped design and implement the Ombudsmen Program for northern New Mexico, and as a lead member of the Crisis Intervention Team at several hospitals.

Dr. Bryan is state licensed in New Mexico and Texas and runs her own private practice, On-Site Crisis Intervention. In addition, she holds several national certifications in bilateral stimulation and addiction counseling, with a PhD in clinical Psychology from Walden University, a MS in Behavioral Psychology from the University of Long Island, and a BS in Family Studies from Arizona State University.

Dr. Bryan is an ordained minister and offers spiritual counseling and guidance. She has also served as an adjunct professor for the U. S. Army Sergeants Major Academy teaching eight-week courses: *Understanding Families From a Global Perspective, Theories of Personality, Sociology, Understanding the Learning of Behavior, Abnormal Psychology and Military Psychology,* and has taught various courses in psychology and counseling at several universities.

Her life opened up to horses in 1972 when she moved from Connecticut to New Mexico, and two of her children had horses and one had a donkey. From then on, it was a matter of adding more and more to her herd, which now consists of thirteen horses, 12 donkeys and 3 colts born this spring. Her life centers around her equine activities: therapy and equine assistance is like peanut butter and jelly for her; they just go together.

After a long career, Dr. Bryan has established an impressive record of working and successfully treating people who have experienced life-debilitating trauma. She has developed her own theoretical construct for a Non-talking Bilateral Stimulation therapy to help free people from their nightmares, flashbacks, and general demobilization due to issues related to trauma they have experienced.

Her treatment center offers programs that foster holistic and spiritual healing as well encouraging personal growth by using various alternative modalities. Dr. Bryan loves to combine her Non-talking Bilateral Stimulation Therapy for trauma patients with Equine Therapy. She allows the "magic of horses" to lead her clients to relief from pain and sorrow. The Bi-lateral part removes the irrationally stored memory to a rational neutral memory.

Dr. Bryan is a member of the American Psychological Association, the Society for Personality Assessment, the National Association for Drug and Alcohol Counselors, the Eye Movement Desensitization Reprocessing International Association and the American Psychotherapy Association.

Dr. Diane Bryan can be reached by email at: drdhbryan@gmail.com.

CHAPTER 8

THE 4 KEYS TO ACHIEVING MASSIVE SUCCESS IN REAL ESTATE & FAST TRACK YOUR RESULTS WHILE HAVING FUN

BY DJ THIELEN

1. Believe what you desire to have is already yours.

2. Take action and don't become an educated poor person.

3. Learn to handle stress for success.

4. Leverage your time and resources and evolve.

KEY #1 – BELIEVE WHAT YOU DESIRE TO HAVE IS ALREADY YOURS

On April 1st 2010, my mom, who raised my brother and I on her own – working multiple jobs – finally retired. Then on April 30th 2010, she unexpectedly had a major heart attack and died instantly. What a shock! Have you ever had something happen in your life like this, a tragic or eye-opening event that really shook you up?

Well, after she passed I was going through some old drawings and memorabilia she had of mine from when I was growing up. To my complete amazement I found something that was so incredible I had it framed. So what was it you may ask? It was an assignment from when I was in the 3rd grade on "What I want to be when I grow up." Funny thing is, I remember that after reading when I actually wrote it, something I hadn't seen in decades, which would shed some light. I said in the article, "When I grow up, I want to be a professional baseball player and play in Pittsburgh for the Pittsburgh Pirates." After reading this and looking at the drawing, I had chills. You may be asking what is so unique about that...it seems like nothing special. Fast forward many years later in my life, I was fortunate enough to get drafted in 1991 in the 6th round by the San Francisco Giants and after my professional baseball career, I have owned a thriving business out of the Pittsburgh area for many years.

You see, this was something I had thought about growing up with such passion and conviction, that it actually came-to-be in a roundabout way. Not exactly as I had written, but close enough for me to be in awe. If you have ever had a dream and seen it come to pass – such as being a doctor, firefighter, or whatever it may be – then you understand what I am saying. As kids we all have dreams like this, and are constantly being asked what we want to be when we grow up, for me it was always a professional baseball player. You can call it a coincidence but I believe in the "Law of Attraction" and what you constantly think about with emotion and belief has a high likelihood of coming to pass in your life. Maybe not in the time frame we all would like, but it will. I say this to encourage you, whether you are successful in many areas of your life and want to improve, or you feel defeated, it doesn't have to be that way anymore. When I started investing in Real Estate, I had an unusual draw inside me to speak to large crowds one day – even though I was not very comfortable talking to groups or crowds. Now I speak to large groups, including some of over 400 people, and I love it and feel right at home.

You see, after working with many wealthy investors over the years, I saw a common thread. They thought differently and expected things to work out unlike people that didn't have the money to invest or had very little. As adults, we forget sometimes to dream, set goals, and have continuing vision for our lives, but I'm here to tell you it's never too late. Create a vision board of everything in your life you desire, from a relationship, to religion, to a new house, a new car...whatever you want, put it on a board and look at it everyday and truly believe you already have it. You see, I know this works 100% and a big part of it working for you is YOU believing it will work in your life. Have faith it will come to pass. You might surprise yourself with what happens!

KEY #2 – TAKE ACTION AND DON'T BECOME AN EDUCATED POOR PERSON

If I received a nickel, (well maybe a dollar), for every person that went through Real Estate courses, spent thousands and thousands of dollars, and never took action, I'd be RICH just from that! I have talked to dozens and dozens of people over the years that went through extensive training and coaching only to never purchase a Property or piece of Real Estate at all. I recently had a lady in July of 2012 that came to us to finally start buying foreclosures. She had been taking coaching courses for five years and had spent over $100,000 for coaching, yet she had never taken action and bought her first property. If you're not saying "WOW – that's ridiculous," then you can give me a call to buy some coaching courses (…just kidding). She now has over 13 properties and has had great success; she said to me one day "WOW DJ, you know I never had to even go through all that coaching to do this, I just needed to be with the right people and believe I could do it," and she was right. Why? Because she simply began to believe she could achieve what she wanted to do, and then jumped on the coattails of a successful team that had already done what she wanted to do.

You see the problem with this is that it isn't getting educated, it's getting over-educated which can lead to being over-analytical and then not taking action by getting sucked into the "shiny new object syndrome" of the next great way to make money with Real Estate. Maybe you can even relate to this yourself. I'm sure you would agree that the Real Estate market is in a constant shifting pattern, right? Well by the time you learn one technique and or strategy the so-called "GURUS" sell you, by then it's outdated already and useless, because the market changed and that strategy doesn't work anymore. So what do they do??? They have a coach call you and sell you again on the newest, latest and greatest way to make money and this cycle continues until you either run out of money or stop taking courses. We are all emotional people and I have bought into this and went through a course myself in 2002 and you know what, I honestly never looked at that enormously confusing book again after that weekend. How many of you can relate to me?

Now I want you to know I am all for Real Estate education, and truly believe it can be extremely helpful if done correctly – especially the mental aspect of being an investor and with ongoing market knowledge. The right coach and mentor group can lead to huge success. However, I am not for taking advantage of people – which can sometimes happen with coaching programs, that's all I'm saying. We all learn differently but I would bet you would learn more from doing rather than reading and studying. I mean think about it, would you or did you learn how to hit a baseball or softball by reading a book on how to have the perfect swing and studying the perfect technique for months on end, or did you learn by having someone throw a ball to you and you hitting it. So what am I saying?

"GET IN THE GAME!"

Jump in and take action and if you make a mistake or two that's ok, that's how we learn and evolve and get better. And if you're in the game keep on playing and align yourself with the right people who can expedite your goals faster than you can do on your own. Either way, take action, go make some money, and have fun along the way – embracing the learning process. By mixing this Key of Taking Action with Key #1 of *Believing What You Desire Is Already Yours* you will already be on your way to big things!

KEY #3 – LEARN TO HANDLE STRESS FOR SUCCESS

I hear people say all the time...that's too stressful OR I can't take the stress OR I don't need that stress in my life. I'm sure those are all valid points and I've said those things before myself. However, an investor and a good friend of mine, Dr. James said to me one day, "DJ, listen, we will always have stress in our lives and it will never go away, so the key is learning how to deal with the stress differently - to where it's healthy rather than unhealthy." How profound. And that one comment has dramatically changed how I handle stress now myself. It's amazing how I can now handle the same things with even more grace and calmness than before.

I've found that the most successful real estate investors have an ability to push the stresses aside and handle business anyways.

Let me ask you a question. Do you want to have your Real Estate Investing experience be an enjoyable one? I would assume your answer is yes, and if so, this is a major key and piece to the puzzle. In baseball, the best players in the Major Leagues have learned how to not let the highs be too high and the lows too low. In other words, they don't get too excited when things go great or too down when things go bad. Yes, sometimes you'll see a guy yell at an umpire or smash a Gatorade Container, (yes, I'm guilty of doing that before), but this is because they play the game with such high intensity and even this is very rare to see. Derek Jeter the ALL-STAR future hall of famer shortstop for the New York Yankees has played in the major leagues for 20 years and can you believe he's never been ejected from a game! Now that's a perfect example how approaching a career with a positive attitude and dealing with challenges without flipping out can be of huge benefit.

This is the same for you with your investing. Learn to be positive even when things don't go your way, and in the end you'll enjoy the ride a lot more and be an ALL-STAR in your own right with your Real Estate venture, does that make sense? This keeping your cool is a big KEY when becoming a successful Real Estate Investor. No risk means no reward, and high returns in Real Estate can come with some challenges, but being able to work through them and staying positive will always benefit you. This mindset and behavior will also make the venture much more enjoyable which is extremely important to alleviate any burn out, frustration, or unneeded stress. When you now love what you are doing and have a vision you are working towards, then any small speed bumps or challenges are really no big deal.

I had a time in my life when I allowed stress and anxiety to get the best of me, so I know about this from firsthand experience. Overcoming the ups and downs emotionally, this can be a serious breakthrough like it was for me. When we learn to not live in panic mode and realize that no matter the situation, everything will all work out and it's no big deal… its incredible the relief this gives us. Less stress, I'm talking about a life-altering attitude and shift in thinking, and when this is realized its amazing how the things that use to worry us or keep us up at night will no longer have that vice grip on us anymore – and life is more enjoyable as a whole. Remember the famous song Bobby McFerrin sings…*Don't worry, Be happy*. Sprinkling this Key of Learning To Handle Stress with Keys 1 and 2 you are now way ahead of those that don't know this information. But don't just know this, you must put this into action and I think you'll be glad you did.

KEY #4 – LEVERAGE YOUR TIME AND RESOURCES AND EVOLVE

When I first started my Company many years ago, I use to do virtually everything myself…how many of you can relate to that? It actually took me many years to understand a very powerful and important principle of having a successful business. Leveraging other people's time and resources.

Now this was a difficult thing to do and very uncomfortable, however, it is a must in any business – especially when building a real estate portfolio or simply investing in real estate in any way. So get uncomfortable and leverage your time and resources, you can thank me later.

Also keep evolving. Businesses that don't evolve usually go out of business. Just look at Companies like Blockbuster video. They didn't evolve and went from being a huge thriving company to non-existent almost overnight as live-streaming videos, *On Demand*, and *Redbox* have taken over now. I can only imagine how many businesses this has happened to. Don't allow that to be you. Be open to keep evolving, and if you haven't evolved or are a new business, make sure and adapt this principle into your business now.

If you're Joe's corner mart or a small store, you can open the doors, stock the shelves, take inventory, answer the phone, do your own books and accounting…etc. However, once you become a Wal-Mart or a large store, you cannot possibly do all those things yourself. It is physically impossible and you would be insane to even try it. However many people do this in their Real Estate Investing. Let me ask you a question. If you can do all the work and make less money or none (very little) of the work and make more money, which would you do? Obviously the answer is the latter, so here's how it's done. Find someone to find your investment properties, find someone to fix them up, find someone to rent them out, find someone to manage them. This is how you leverage your time and resources so you still make good money with Real Estate, but do so in an enjoyable and stress free manner. Even if you were able to do all the work yourself, most people would be so stressed out after one deal they wouldn't want to do it all themselves anymore. This is the OLD way (the Blockbuster example) of doing things, when people maybe had to do all this themselves and the technology we have access to today wasn't available, however, *this isn't the NEW way.*

So, go find a Realtor to get you properties, a construction company or crew to renovate them, and a management company to rent them and manage them. Or better yet, find a Company that can do all these things for you ALL in one place. By leveraging your time and resources you'll achieve more in a shorter amount of time while enjoying the journey at the same time…now, doesn't that sound good?

Warm Regards,
DJ Thielen

ACKNOWLEDGEMENTS

First and foremost I want to thank God as without him none of this would be possible.

Secondly, I want to say Thank You to my amazing and beautiful wife, Sharon, for all your love and support. I am so blessed to have you as my wife, friend, and partner. I appreciate all your love and guidance more than words can say. Also a special thank you to my son Deaven and my step-kids Presli and Cade, you guys inspire me and light up my life!

To my amazing ALL-STAR Team and some of my superb business associates, Tony Adair, Liz Folweiler, Rebecca Reichenbach, Colleen Daniels, Tammy Cox, Thomas Will, Kathy Fetke, Andy Przybylek and ALL the rest of you. You are why what we do is all possible.

Last but not least, Thank You to ALL our Investors around the world for entrusting us with your investments, your time, and your futures.

About DJ

DJ Thielen is a Real Estate Investor and Leading Expert in Real Estate Investing and he has assisted hundreds of people from around the world with their investing success. As the current Founder of Fortune Foreclosures LLC, DJ's articles and essays have appeared in *Personal Real Estate Investor Magazine, The News Tribune*, and *National Real Estate Alliance*. He has also been recognized nationally and internationally as an industry expert, and he has been featured on the cover of the national magazine *Personal Real Estate Investor* as a "Master Investor".

DJ lives with his family in the Seattle, Washington Region. He is a former professional baseball player with the San Francisco Giants Organization. He speaks regularly to local, national, and international audiences on various real estate topics: from being a landlord to analyzing investments to cash flowing properties to building real estate portfolios. His Portfolio Partnership Alliance which was formed for those that wish to "FAST TRACK" their success and achieve extreme results in a very short amount of time has received notoriety and rave reviews from his investors, and as a result he has built a thriving business while helping others. DJ is also a heavily sought-after motivational speaker for schools, businesses and social events, due to his unique style and ability to connect with his audience.

CHAPTER 9

DISRUPTIVE SALES

BY ELLIOT GROSSBARD

GDS Management is a family-owned business that manages commercial property in Detroit, Michigan. The founder George, is a well-respected leader of the community and recognized as an expert in the real estate industry. With an eye for opportunities for his clients, he built a nice portfolio for himself as well. Unfortunately, George became ill, and after several years he passed. His son Dan was now responsible and assumed control of the family's real estate portfolio and management company.

It was a learning curve for the 30-year-old, however, most clients were loyal to the company and Dan. Taking what he learned from Dad, there was stability for a few years. However, over time Dan felt **"stuck."**

This is how we began our discussion at the Starbucks café where I met him. The sales team was from his father's tenure; growth and increased revenue was not on their radar. They were content with what they had, and counted down the days to retirement. Dan however, was in his mid-30s, and saw the market ripen with potential to make his own name. Replacing the salespeople with years of contacts, and with a history of the company built on old school relationships, wasn't going to happen. An attempt to install a mentoring program, bringing in young brokers in the hopes of staff "buying in" as a way to continue receiving a percentage of commissions even after they retired, fell on deaf ears. Morale was now an issue as well.

After identifying what Dan wanted (increased revenue), who the POI (people of influence) in his industry were, and what he *really* wanted, (to grow revenue *without* turnover of staff who by now were considered family), we set a plan in place.

I told him, "What you need Dan, is to align yourself with another business targeting the same prospects that you do, and offer a different service or product." Introducing him to the A-SAP Property and Casualty Agency was a "Win-Win" situation for both companies. Dan now is getting referrals that increase revenue, and with morale up, the re-energized sales staff has brought in new deals, and A-SAP is writing the policies of Dan's and his client's properties. Joint Ventures are a great way to do business. However, the hard part is identifying who the right partner is. The only way to really know that is to understand the person's business and their needs. (...And a diverse network helps.)

At Disruptive Sales Consulting we don't just learn about a client's product or service, we sell with the sales team, we manage with management, market with the marketing department and have lunch together with employees. In essence, we *"become the company."*

"WHAT IS DISRUPTIVE SALES?"

The term "disruptive" has been widely used as a synonym for "innovation." Disruptive Sales is about creating new strategies to sell the same product or service to existing customers – which results in disrupting stagnant or declining sales. We go on sales calls as trainees, get trained as a new hire, sit with the sales staff one-on-one, collect data including morale, brand and culture, and most importantly, the mindset of the salespeople and the customers. By matching our 20 years of first hand sales experience in multiple industries, we are able to disrupt and implement innovative ways to increase current sales, and in the process, identify new streams of revenue from never-before-thought-of clientele.

Why are you, or even more importantly, why is your staff in sales? Sure the commissions can be extremely lucrative, and don't get me wrong I wouldn't do what I do if I were not able to provide for my family from it; however, the reason I personally have made a career in sales is the satisfaction of *helping others.* When someone needs something and you fulfill that need, it makes themselves, their job, and their company better. What's more satisfying than walking into a customer and to be welcomed with smiles and appreciation? The following are some of the ways we do things at **Disruptive Sales** Consulting.

1. "Stop Selling and Start Helping"

These words by the legendary Zig Ziglar are on my wall so I and everyone else who visits me, sees it. Best-selling author Harvey Mackay, one of the early influences in my career, tweaks that a little, "You don't sell anyone, you *help* people get what they want and need."

If you are trying to *sell* something to someone, in essence you are trying to *convince them* they need something – regardless if they currently need it or not – and it is a waste of time for both of you. Another master salesman with a huge impact on my life, Jeffrey Gitomer, hits a home run with: "People love to buy, but they hate to be sold."

The harder you try to sell yourself to others, the more you push them away. NO ONE LIKES TO BE SOLD. Find the people who are *in need of your product or service*, and half your job is done. Now *educate* them how you can **help them**. Jeb Blount of SalesGravy.com in his book, **People Buy You**, explains: "Sales is pretty simple really: solve your customer's problem and they will buy your solution." I'm going to ONE UP Jeb (a pretty tall order) by telling you, "DISCOVER an *unknown* problem of your customer and give them a solution and you have gained a **relationship** *forever*."

2. POI (People of Interest or Influence)

These are your celebrity contacts you meet in any part of business. They have the ability to make this year be your best. The key is determining who the proper POI are for you or your company.

a. Allan, a recently-graduated CPA, joins a growing accounting firm. Business development is a team-wide effort and he is encouraged to bring in new clients. Aside from family and friends, where is Allan, fresh out of college, going to find these clients? Allen needs to decide upon which area of accounting he wants to focus; let's say it's restaurants and bars. A good POI would be a beverage company sales rep. If he specialized in dentists, network with dental supply salespeople. **Here is the thing** – by working together with a POI who is already interacting with your target market, albeit a different angle, it is as if you have a personal representative promoting your services.

b. **"Go-To" People** - You know them. They are the people within your community, company, or family to whom everyone goes to for advice on almost anything. These POI are well-connected, reliable, and have nothing but your best interests in mind. These are the all-stars of referral bases. If one of these wizards sends you a referral, it is gift-wrapped with a bow on top. Their recommendation alone can get you the business, just don't mess it up. The question remains though, "How do you become one of the musicians in this Conductor's Symphony of Business?" Involve them. Ask them to lunch, tell them a scenario in your business and ask how they would advise you to handle it. Show them you value them. If you show genuine interest in them, they will reciprocate. If you truly believe in who you are and what you do, your enthusiasm will naturally spill over. Get them excited. This is bigger than presenting to a potential client; this is a shot at a multiple distribution channel. And it doesn't happen overnight. It will take time, however, if you are genuine and sincere, and he or she is in fact a "Go-To Person," then they will value what you have to give, and more importantly for you, recommend you to everyone they know.

3. Enthusiasm

Vince Lombardi once famously said, "If you aren't fired with enthusiasm, you will **be fired** with enthusiasm." Lombardi also said, "The only place where work comes after success is in the dictionary."

It is much easier to work at something about which you are naturally passionate about. If you are happy with what you are providing to your customers you will naturally...SMILE. Even the top salespeople have down days, it doesn't matter, SMILE. The saying goes, "Frown and you frown alone, smile and the whole world smiles with you." From the instant we are born, we begin to learn a smile brings people inwards, while a frown repels them. Dale Carnegie put it best, "When you greet people with a smile, you'll have a good time meeting them and they'll have a good time meeting you." Even though you should be self-enthusiastic, keep in mind these encouraging ABC's of yet again Harvey Mackay — Any-Body-Can.

Stephen King's first novel was rejected 30 times and he tossed it in the trash. His wife Tabitha retrieved it and encouraged him to complete it.

The rest of the "story" is history as the book *Carrie* became a huge success.

Master P recalls how "We had a house full of people and an empty refrigerator." With divorced parents, Percy Miller and his four siblings were raised by their father in New Orleans' Calliope Projects, a neighborhood infamous for its high crime rate. Using a $10,000 malpractice settlement from his grandfather's death, he opened a record store No Limit Records and eventually a label. Master P promoted the albums via word-of-mouth to independent music stores, managing to sell some 250,000 copies. With Priority Records in 1996, he released his next album, Ice Cream Man, which peaked at No. 3 on the Billboard album charts. For the next several years, **No Limit Records** dominated the hip-hop industry, churning out a slew of hit records.

Oprah Winfrey was a victim of abuse by family members and eventually ran away from home. At age 14, she gave birth to a baby boy who died shortly after. "O" was fired from her first anchor job where she faced harassment. Today, she is worth a cool $2.9 billion and has more clout than the Queen of England. All of these successful stories include enthusiasm and desire to succeed. (...and a supporting spouse doesn't hurt.)

4. Momentum Selling

"Selling On A High Brings You More Sales. Momentum Selling Is the Most Successful Kind."

What did it feel like when you got that order you had been working on for months with your "Whale"? What a sensation! What a rush! Now imagine using that feeling, that rush with confidence-oozing-*enthusiasm* (there's that word again) and channeling it into more sales? What if at that exact moment you'd call those top 10 "hard to reach contacts" you've been trying forever to convert into clients? I'd bet more easily on you getting an appointment with 20% of those hard-to-get-to prospects, than the NY Jets not only not getting back to the Super Bowl in my lifetime, let alone winning it! (Unless Gary Vaynerchuk actually owns them, then all bets are off! Hope it happens for you, GV!)

Use that momentum from just closing the sale, where you feel *unstoppable*, **feed off** that adrenaline and **make-those-calls** – let those people hear the **REAL** you, let them feel that "musical charisma." "Momentum Selling" is riding that pinnacle moment and funneling it right into more sales.

5. Ask!

Asking questions is the most powerful tool in a salesperson's toolbox. By asking the right questions in the correct sequence, you are getting the other person to talk about the things that will allow you to *help* them. Daniel Pink, in his best selling book, *To Sell is Human* writes, "In the past the best salespeople were skilled at *answering* questions (in part because they had information that their customers lacked). Today, they must be good at *asking* questions - uncovering possibilities, discovering solutions." Recently, a great tagline we came up with for a client was:

"What is important to you? Time? Quality? Service? Cost? -

What is important to us...? YOU!"

6. Be Observant

Look around your customer's office; listen to what they are saying. One of my biggest relationships in a previous job and industry I worked in had an adopted daughter. I observed on her desk a *high school musical* graduation card. I asked her about the card and she explained about her daughter's obsession with Disney's cult-like hit. Two months later I was offered tickets to High School Musical on Ice by a friend. Who do you think I gave it to? I can't begin to describe how much it meant to her. However, I can tell you I received a thank you card from her *and* her daughter, and to top it off I was really happy to do it too. And the client is still a friend of mine today. (Melodie, you rock.)

7. Be Memorable

One of the challenges in sales is standing out. You need to be unique to be memorable. Contestants on SharkTank and America's Got Talent are no different than a school applying for a grant, an applicant for an interview, or you on a sales call. There has to be that special thing that makes you memorable. At one point in my career, I was known as The Krispy Kreme guy as I would bring fresh, hot doughnuts as I visited my customers. (There was not one person that wasn't smiles when Elliot stopped by!)

Here is a tip about me. I love cufflinks, specifically thematic ones. One of my clients SupplyMart, in which I have ownership in, is an office supply company operating on old school values, one relationship at a time. Its logo is a paperclip around the name. As I was helping build the company, I would gift paperclip cufflinks to clients and important connections. Just ask Kevin Harrington, he has received two pairs over the years! Again… **Be Memorable!**

I leave you with some of the Core Values Of Disruptive Sales:

- "The customer IS our business" – SupplyMart's tagline. Without the customer, we HAVE no business. Anyone who does not understand this will eventually fail in any business venture. I've seen it over and over.

- Know What Your Purpose Is (Personal and Professional) - As a salesperson, why are you or your sales staff in sales? Was it just because the job was available? Are you good at it? Do you believe in what you are selling and the company you are selling for?

- OLD SCHOOL - Have Respect. Stand up when someone walks into the room. Shake hands and make eye contact. **Ask** if you should take a seat, don't walk on the grass, hold open the door, say please and even more importantly, say "thank you" verbally and show it in the way you conduct yourself.

- BE authentic, be genuine, BE REAL! Beyond all else, be you! People can smell a phony a mile away.

- Know your numbers - Always be able to answer where your sales are YTD, MTD, and quarterly. If it was your own business, you would know...exactly. Treat the company you work for like your own.

About Elliot

Elliot Grossbard is the CEO of Disruptive Sales Consulting and an author who helps businesses disrupt stagnant sales, clarify their brand, and improve company morale.

Disruptive Sales Consulting is Elliot's way of implementing his experience including the roll out in Florida of the largest computer training company when Windows 95 launched in the 90's, managing a portfolio in excess of $200 million in assets at Smith Barney during the height of the technology bubble and the aftermath, building a salesforce for a national company that provides educational and commercial furniture, and most recently, leading SupplyMart—an office supply company that focuses on small and mid-size companies with customers across the U.S.

Through his 20 years in sales – including everything from the intangible (computer training, stocks, bonds, mutual funds, healthcare, senior living) to the tangible (furniture, office supplies, equipment), Elliot has established core values that have been shared with his sales teams, companies, and clients, which have implemented the same values and strategic methods. As a result of doing so, they have experienced increased sales, brand expansion, happier and more dedicated employees, and a new and passionate culture. You won't find a more dedicated advocate to help you and your company reach your goals.

The largest reward for any salesperson, whether an account executive or CEO of a Fortune 500 company, is: "When you deliver on a promise, execute a service, or simply give your customer a solution – that satisfaction alone is what should be the inner drive of every true salesperson."

Elliot has gained a following of sales *aficionados* and followers online through published articles on social media, Medium.com, his blog DisruptiveSalesBlog.com, and through the LinkedIn Influencer program.

Once you meet Elliot, you get a jolt of enthusiasm in whatever it is you are passionate about. He is infectiously passionate about the things he loves. It starts with his family down to his loyalty to his hometown Detroit Red Wings, Tigers, and Lions sports teams (yes, in that order). But more than anything else, Elliot is passionate about sales.

Much of his character and values come from his father who passed away when he was just 20 years old. A strong upbringing in a tight community of family and friends led him to call Miami his home for 20+ years. Adopting the Miami Heat back in the Glen Rice days as his local sports team of choice, he has aligned himself with many essential people in the South Florida business community that has enabled him to be a resource (POI) for people in his network. His family consists of his wife of 19 years, and 3 children. His love for music is well known within his circle; formerly a drummer, he has a desire to learn to play the piano and has been known to burst into song at any moment.

For more information on Elliot and Disruptive Sales Consulting:
Email: info@disruptivesalesconsulting.com

Phone: (305) 306-SELL

Websites: www.disruptivesalesconsulting.com and www.disruptivesalesblog.com

Become a part of our network: www.thedisruptivenetwork.com

LinkedIn Profile And Articles: www.linkedin.com/in/elliotgrossbard/

Twitter Profiles: @ElliotOneT, @disruptsales, @salesdisrupter

Facebook: www.facebook.com/egrossbard,
　　　　　www.facebook.com/disruptivesalesconsulting,

Articles on Medium: https://medium.com/@disruptivesales

CHAPTER 10

CREATING INDESTRUCTIBLE WEALTH

BY PAUL MATA

I didn't grow up with a silver spoon in my mouth. I was an undernourished kid in a low-income Mexican-American family. We had government food stamps and government medical care. I've heard it said 'a poor person doesn't know when he's poor,' but I knew it. We were *poor,* and we didn't have anything.

However, because of Santa Clause Incorporated I was gifted a bicycle as a child. While I was out riding one day, I fell, and hit my face on a rock. The accident didn't do damage to my face, but it chipped my tooth badly. Because we were poor and on government-provided medical insurance, I had to wait three years to get the tooth fixed.

Before the accident, if you were to look at our family pictures, you'd see me sporting a big toothy grin, but in all the photos after my tooth chipped, my smile disappeared. The same year I chipped my tooth, I started to wear glasses, and my parents divorced. Prior to that time, I'd been a normal little boy, playing outside, and having fun, but the events of that year weighed on me like nothing else. I'd lost a lot that year, including my smile.

It was at this time in my life when I swore no child of mine would ever be humiliated in the same way because of the lack of resources. I resolved that I would learn everything there was to know about money and wealth. If I had a child with a broken tooth, I'd have the financial capacity to fix it. Naturally, this resolution lead me to pursue a financial education.

In college, I made a commitment to excel in business education. I ultimately graduated with a Bachelor of Science degree in Finance as the highest-ranked student in my class.

While many of my classmates went on to be stockbrokers, I knew I had something different to offer. I was young and new in the industry; therefore, it took me a while to find my focus. But the ultimate goal always remained: succeed as a financial planner. Help people who do not understand finance and educate them. Make sure these individuals aren't victims of manipulation. Champion integrity.

I started to learn everything I could about money, voraciously consuming market information. I studied commerce, taxes, estate planning, insurance, and entrepreneurship—anything related to finances. Every few years, I'd concentrate on a new area, and ultimately, became an expert in each.

The company I was working for used Modern Portfolio Theory, but it did not work when the market collapsed in the early 2000s. As I watched the rollercoaster ride of our economy, I started to consider the fact that the kind of wealth I was working with was largely subject to the state of the market. Most financial advisors are myopic in their assessments—they're all fixated on a single topic—but my own studies had provided access to many of the areas that other advisors didn't take into account. I realized that focusing on a single area was a recipe for financial disaster. Such tunnel vision played a great role in the country's economic downturn. Much of America's wealth was destructible, and we all needed something that wouldn't be destroyed.

Then, in 2008, I watched as about nine different industries were decimated in the market crash. By looking at the indicators from all over the economy, I sensed that the "depression" would be severe, and began to systematically put client money into cash. I outraged my company—they demanded to know "What are you doing? Why are you pulling money out of the market?" The company had a selfish practice of keeping clients fully invested, since they made no money if it sat in cash, despite economic indicators.

Something just didn't seem right, and that is why I began to rescue my clients' resources and put them into cash. It turned out that the market would suffer for another 14 months. And—going back to my original thoughts about helping people—I felt that my job should have been more about the client's need rather than the company's greed. At that moment, I decided to carve a different path in the financial planning world and I would concentrate on how to make wealth indestructible.

I had done very well with the company. However, I was stressed and unhappy. Furthermore, I was miserably overweight and disappointed because despite all my "training," I wasn't able to predict and safeguard my clients from the disaster of 2008. So I had to trust my own philosophies and start over. I attended hundreds of seminars, trying to find new approaches and ideas. However, nothing seemed to work. They were singularly directed, like so many advisors in the industry.

Finally, I began my own firm, with my own formula for success. I started taking into consideration real estate, stocks, insurance, and then including a larger amount of bonds, and commodities. My biggest *"Aha!"* moment was when I realized that people who have amassed significant wealth do not do so by simply saving money. I looked at those who actually create wealth, and saw that it was not the stockholders, but the business owners.

The way to begin building indestructible wealth was not solely to try to save, but to create and manage businesses that would generate steady wealth over time. I began to piece things together for my system. I also worked on my own physical issues—I lost weight, began to eat right, kept exercising, and I got everyone at my company in tune as well. Our productivity skyrocketed and so did our profits. Suddenly, there it was: my 12-step system for Creating Indestructible Wealth.

I discovered that the first step to creating indestructible wealth was to understand your high governing values. This is a vital foundational step, because your high governing values are what every decision in your life should be based on. If people don't understand their high governing values, they have no way of making value-based decisions. The best way to determine your high governing values is to ask yourself, "What is most important to me in my life?" and come up with a list of ten items. Next, you should narrow the list down by comparing the values to each other and choosing your top three.

The second step is to strengthen your mindset. Henry Ford said it correctly when he stated, "Whether you think you can or you think you can't, you're right." Most people have a "scarcity mindset" when it comes to money. They believe that there is not enough money, and then constantly see proof of that in their lives. There are many ways to develop an abundance mindset, but one of my favorite methods is to give money away. There are many universal truths that have to do with money, but one of the simplest ones is that you must give before you can receive, and the same holds true about money.

The third step is to get your financial house in order. Money flows to where it is treated best. If your money and finances are neglected and disorganized, it's not a surprise that it's not flowing to you. The first thing you do to get your financial house in order is to know your "lifestyle number"- that is, the amount of money you need every month to maintain your *desired* lifestyle. Next, determine the amount of income being generated from each asset you own. Then determine your income shortage by subtracting your lifestyle number from the total amount of income being generated by your assets, to determine your income shortage or surplus. Finally, you need to create discretionary income by making more, spending less, or doing a combination of both. Direct that additional income into an Indestructible Wealth Account. This is not an investment account that you will consume. It is an account that you will never consume, but allocate to an Indestructible Wealth Portfolio of assets.

The fourth step for Creating Indestructible Wealth is to allocate your indestructible wealth account into income generators – that is, you must put money in places where it will grow exponentially. Rather than diversifying your assets the way a traditional advisor would suggest, I recommend seven specific categories that people should invest and diversify their portfolio with. These seven asset categories include bonds, dividend paying stocks, insurance, commodities, real estate, small business and cash.

The fifth step is to turn your passion into profits. Whether you decide to become a full-blown entrepreneur, or simply increase your income by a small amount, there are personal, monetary, and tax benefits to monetizing your passion.

The sixth step is all about equanimity. All the wealth in the world is worthless unless you are stress-free, happy, and fulfilled. In order to enjoy what you have, it's important to do everything with intention and make sure all your decisions are in alignment with your foundational values. You should also express gratitude daily for what you have – this can easily be done with a gratitude journal that you write in everyday before you go to bed.

The seventh step is to create indestructible health. For your wealth to truly be indestructible, it has to be safe from the major disasters that can threaten your wealth. Health care costs can easily destroy wealth, but the best way to avoid them is to simply not get sick. Simple ways to make your immune system bulletproof include getting proper nutrition, being physically active, getting plenty of sleep, laughter, getting air moving around you, sunshine, and drinking eight glasses of Alkaline water a day.

The eighth step is to strengthen your brain. The mind is a powerful tool, and a much more valuable asset than any amount of money. However, without proper care, mental abilities can fade away, and lead to the destruction of a person's wealth. To strengthen the mind, I recommend that all of my clients get proper amounts of exercise; fill their mind with positive thoughts, words, and affirmations; eliminate negative and limiting beliefs, and build up their mind with "brain games" through things like neuro-feedback and the computer application, *Lumosity.*

The ninth step is to optimize your taxes. There are a myriad of ways to reduce taxes, but the best way is to have a business. If you started a business as we mentioned in step five, then you can take advantage of 1,100 more deductions than an individual can. As long as you have a legitimate business, a profit motive, and you keep good records, then you can legally write off necessary business expenses like your cell phone, home office, travel, a percentage of your car, and so on.

The tenth step is to protect yourself. Wealth can be easily destroyed if it is not properly protected. Consider a Rockefeller strategy, which includes having a lawsuit-proof trust, and working with a lawyer to set up entities that allow you to control everything but own nothing.

The eleventh step is to plan your legacy with an estate plan. To make wealth indestructible and to avoid probate and additional confiscatory estate taxes, everybody should have an estate plan, including a will and trust.

The twelfth step is to start codifying your experience. Another valuable asset that every person has, yet few capitalize on, is their life experience. Whether you monetize your expertise with a published book or not, it is vital that you write your life lessons down in order to pass the knowledge and expertise you've acquired down to future generations. This way, even when you expire, your knowledge and experience can be passed down.

Indestructible wealth is possible, but it requires a holistic approach that goes beyond just a person's finances, it must include optimizing all assets including financial assets, physical assets, mental assets, and what I like to call "exceptional" assets—the unique talents and abilities that you are passionate and exceptional at. You can revamp your life simply by following all the instincts you have and making yourself into the best version of you. As you create your indestructible wealth, ensure that you are enjoying what you're doing in your life. The door is open to you; all you need to do is step through it.

About Paul

Paul R. Mata is the Founder of the financial education company, **Logos Lifetime Enterprises**, and author of the book, *Create Indestructible Wealth*. In his proprietary system, *Create Indestructible Wealth: Make, Sustain, and Protect your Wealth in any Economy*, Paul teaches people how to have an abundant and prosperous life without taking excessive risks.

Paul's background includes working for a Wall Street firm for over two decades as a senior financial advisor, certified financial planner, and managing principal, working with thousands of clients and personally managing over $50 million worth of assets.

In his presentations, Paul shares numerous stories of his days at the Wall Street firm, and how he spent those years becoming an expert in asset allocation, investment planning, retirement strategies, estate planning, insurance, tax optimization and minimization strategies, and asset protection.

Paul has combined his backgrounds in both financial advising and business establishment, and is now a professional speaker and author promoting his indestructible wealth system all over the country, teaching individuals, retirees, entrepreneurs, small businesses, and the self employed how to create indestructible wealth—a wealth that they can never lose. He does this by exposing what traditional financial planners would never tell their clients.

Because money and finances are such an integral part of our lives (we think about it all the time), Paul believes that everyone should become financial experts, and his educational system is designed to help people master their money.

You can connect with Paul at:
Paul@CreateIWealth.com
www.twitter.com/CreateIWealth
www.facebook.com/CreateIndestructibleWealth
www.CreateIndestructibleWealth.com

CHAPTER 11

THE POWER OF GETTING OUTSIDE OF YOUR COMFORT ZONE

BY FREDA CORNELIUS

You have to be prepared to stand up for what you want and to do what it takes to get it, especially if it is not in your comfort zone. These have been very powerful lessons that I have learned because, for a proper southern lady, I had to step outside of my comfort zone to play hardball and win the company I had been running and always dreamed of owning.

THE STORM CLOUDS ON THE HORIZON

If you live in a flat part of the country, with nothing obstructing your view, you can see storm clouds on the horizon for miles and hours before they arrive. At the end of the storm is a rainbow, but you have to weather the tough times to get to the pot of gold.

I started with a company in August of 2001, just before the tragedy of 9/11. I had been in sales for years and had been hired on/laid off/ hired on and laid off more times than I can count. I had resigned myself to attending massage therapy school while I earned my certification. I decided to work in customer service in order to make enough to pay my bills. When I started with this company, I found fertile ground, and so my perceptions changed a bit. I saw clearly how I could go in, make a difference, put up a new website, and automate everything. I was so motivated that I basically took charge of the company; the owner let me do it because he was getting burned out and he saw my enthusiasm and drive. Yes, we butted heads frequently, but he knew and trusted my intentions. After I had worked with the company for six years, the owner's wife convinced her husband to move across country to live where she preferred to raise their children and they did.

LIGHTNING FLASHES WARN OF APPROACHING STORM

Soon after moving, the owners got into a financial crisis and took a lot of money out of the company to cover their debts. I was frightened when I saw the company begin to nose dive. I had put a lot of sweat equity and passion into the company, and I did not want to lose it. In fact, I wanted to buy it.

I had some money, but not nearly enough to buy the company. It was 2009, and I tried everything – as I was attempting to get funding for the purchase of the company. I could not get any SBA loans or any kind of capital to buy the company. There was no money. So I started negotiating with the owner and his representative as if I had all the money lined up. They were bullies. I had worked for this man for eight years, but when it came to negotiating to buy the company he became absolutely vicious.

The lightening was getting closer, and the business was on the verge of going under because the debts were becoming greater than the income, but I knew, in my heart, that this was a successful business. I just needed some way to come up with the money, not only to buy the company, but to make sure the doors stayed open. The storm was approaching fast, and I knew that I had to stay centered and keep my focus on the outcome.

A BREAK IN THE CLOUDS

I reached out to my dad for financial help. My dad believed in me and agreed to help me out as much as he could with the investment. This was a big decision for dad and tears of gratitude came to my eyes. I knew it was a big step out of his comfort zone, too. Dad was a chemist and he worked with the Federal Food and Drug Administration his entire life, starting after he graduated from college. A big reason he stayed with the FDA until he retired, was fear. He came from the Great Depression era. Dad needed security. This caused him to be fearful of taking chances. I fought against this mindset, because I wanted, and still want, to make a difference in the world. I knew that being an owner came with a lot of risk, and I could hear echoes of my father's fears in my mind. I kept shutting out the fears by shifting my focus onto my vision. Often times, I would reach out to my Mastermind Group and friends to help me shift my focus. I just knew there had to be a way to do this! I had to release all doubts, and yes, I was uncomfortable but I was determined.

I told a select few people about my situation. I was reaching out for help. This shifted the winds, as people started connecting me to people that could help advise me and keep me strong and level-headed. I call them my Mastermind Group. It was their support and wisdom that helped me work it out. I cannot overstate the importance of my having the mentor and peer group that not only were supportive, but offered very solid advice. I was, and still am, very grateful to have this mastermind team in my life. Two of the people in the group were my attorney and a financial advisor. The group, as a whole, was honest with me and encouraging. They strongly advised me to walk away from the deal; however, they continued to support me in my belief and vision.

Throughout every day, I would pray the Serenity Prayer:

> God grant me the serenity
> to accept the things I cannot change;
> Courage to change the things I can;
> and wisdom to know the difference.

As everything was slowly coming together, I had the confidence within myself that I was doing the right thing and this helped me persevere. I continued negotiating a price and a plan for purchasing the company, even though I had no money. I just had the confidence and trust that when I needed the money, it would appear…. and it did!

THE STORM SHIFTS

Sometimes a storm, for unknown reasons, will shift direction. Many people watch hurricanes build in the ocean, and are prepared for the worst, then, at the last moment, the storm shifts and misses them entirely. Is it the hand of God?

I presented my plan to private investors, banks, loan companies, etc., but no one was interested in a company that was bleeding money. I was sitting in my office late one night and when I began to think that I was being blocked because I needed the "serenity to accept the things that I cannot change," and the phone rang.

"Freda," said the voice on the other end. "I am glad I caught you in your office. I was just calling to check to see if you needed anything." It was one of the vendors that our company worked with.

I paused and looked within myself to see what I really needed at that moment. Well I need money to purchase the company and so I said, "Yes, do know of anyone who has half a million dollars?" The words that came through phone next gave me the sign that I needed!

"Maybe," he responded. He was not kidding- his wife's family were millionaires. We set up an appointment to see if they were willing to front the money. I met with the family and negotiated terms. They agreed to help me buy the company, but we hit a snag.

THE RAINBOW APPEARS

I was raised to be a southern woman, always respectful, quiet and never to be contrary. I am always respectful in all that I do, but I have learned that remaining silent and not standing for what you want, will assure you never achieve your dreams. You have to get out of your comfort zone.

The investor wanted 51% of the business in exchange for providing all the necessary money to purchase the company and get it back on its feet. I did not have 51% of the money, heck I didn't have 10% of the money, but they were at least offering me 49% of the company.

"No, I cannot accept that," were the words that left my lips. I had worked hard to build up the company. I was the business; and I knew it better than they ever could. I had gone from being an employee to seeing my vision of being the employer and now I risked being an employee again by accepting only 49% of the company. I was growing a backbone, along with a business sense that has grown and served me well. Again, I had to get out of my comfort zone and persevere.

You never know what people are going to say, unless you ask. The worst they could say was no, and then I would have the choice to either accept their terms, try to find a different investor, or to quit the whole thing. By asking, I at least opened up another option – I could be the controlling partner in a company that I loved.

"The controlling member of the family NEVER takes less than 51%, however, she has agreed to make the deal with you at 49%," was what they said at the end of our negotiations.

A DOUBLE RAINBOW APPEARS

The negotiations were coming to an end. It was time for me to complete the deal with the owner, but at least now I had a backer. Again, my gratitude for my Mastermind Group was immeasurable as they had given me advice throughout the entire process. I now had the money to buy the company, but it had to be at the right price.

I can't remember exactly the verbiage of the last day of negotiations, however, I told him that the price was just too high, we can't give you any more money. I had given him a final spread sheet for the negotiation and it had come down to the last few details. Many times, he would say to me, "I thought we had a deal, and then you came back and said it was too much." I told him that I was doing my due diligence research and conferring with my Mastermind Group.

"I explained to you that your valuation of the company was too high. There is just too much debt, and I cannot pay the kind of money you are talking about, because the company is not worth that currently." I responded.

"Ok, I'm just going to stay here and I'm going to take over the business myself. I guess I will do whatever it takes. This is all your fault anyway." The owner retorted.

I went back to my office and sat there for a few minutes contemplating his words and visualizing the future under those circumstances. My gut told me to run! But I had come so far and knew that I was unwilling to go backwards.

"I really can't do this," I replied. "I'm just not going to do this. I'll just start my own business or whatever." In my mind, I thought, you can have this company and all the debt that goes with it. You have no idea how to run this company. You have not been here for years.

It was ultimatum time. I started taking all my pictures off the wall, and I packed up my office. He helped me take everything in boxes down to my car. This was the end of a relationship that had spanned almost a decade, and he knew enough to know that I was not bluffing. I walked back to my office one last time, and I believe that reality set in for him. We finalized the deal.

How un-lady like it was of me to act like that, I had never done anything like that before but there was a lot on the line. I did what I had to. I had to get out of my comfort zone. The rainbow was, not only did he agree to my price, he agreed to let me make payments on part of the purchase of the business. He owner-financed for one year.

Double rainbow, pot of gold, and the keys to the company were in my hand. I had done it all with the help of Mastermind Group, investors, friends, and people that believed in me as much as I believed in myself.

THE SUN IS SHINING ONCE AGAIN

It was a snowy day in February, and I had driven the former owner to the attorney's office to sign the documents. As we got back into the parking lot, I turned to him and said with passion and love in my voice, "I want to thank you for being an ass to me all these years because you've really helped me grow."

He turned around to me and he said, "Are you complimenting me?"

I said, "Yes, absolutely!"

After all, he was a catalyst in helping me to learn and grow. He set me on my path to becoming a strong owner and leader...a true entrepreneur. He was the kind of person who pushed me out of my comfort zone and he continued to push me out of my comfort zone. This experience was instrumental in my growth as a person, leader and entrepreneur.

I have learned that there are easier and gentler ways to push yourself out of your comfort zone, however, the harder the lesson, the more it becomes engrained into your being. Be grateful, honor and love them. It's from these challenges, and the support of a select few people, that we gain the courage to break from the safety and comfort that bind us, and rise to the exhilarating new perspective that we desire and deserve.

About Freda

Freda Cornelius is currently the president and CEO of the Professional Framing Company located in Kennesaw, Georgia. She attributes her growth as a person, leader and entrepreneur to coaching through books and CDs, such as Michael Gerber, Zig Ziglar and John Maxwell, just to name a few. She has an extensive library and she devotes an hour daily to study. She has been personally coached by Howard Partridge with Phenomenal Products and the Ziglar Corporation.

Although Freda was raised in Georgia, she worked in several states. She moved from administrative work into sales back in 1985 because she knew that is where freedom and money could be found. She traveled throughout five states by car selling two-way radios, in the days prior to cell phones. As she drove, she always listened to self-help tapes, especially Zig Ziglar. She went on to recruit for a school that trained electronic technicians and then she was transferred to Texas where she worked as their placement director. She has sold cell phones, staffing services, alarm systems, and software. She worked for small companies and large corporations. Through this extensively diverse background, she experienced diverse people, success, great leaders, poor leaders, joy, drama, hardships and many challenges.

In her story, Freda demonstrates not only the Power of getting outside of her comfort zone, but also the courage it took to change. Freda is writing a book that will expand on her experience and the lessons she learned. Look for it to be published in 2015. Freda truly desires to help people learn from her experience as she moved from an extremely shy and insecure person into a confident business woman. In her writing, she encourages people to step outside of their comfort zone and go for it.

CHAPTER 12

RIGHT FROM THE START: SAFELY NAVIGATING THE TREACHEROUS WATERS OF ENTREPRENEURSHIP WITH LEGAL COUNSEL

BY NATHAN MCCOY, ESQ. & GARY WILSON, ESQ.

If representing entrepreneurs and startups in legal matters has taught us nothing else, it is that most of them suffer from the same thing: tunnel vision. They focus on their business ideas or products with such passion and intensity that, unbeknownst to them, they have sailed a course into waters filled with legal and operational treachery. Once they finally recognize the unfriendly waters to which they have navigated, it is too late...their ships have sunk and what remains of their once promising ideas has been devoured by industry sharks.

Not surprisingly, we have learned that the success and failure of most startups is determined not a year or even months down the road but, instead, at their inception. Indeed, problems originate when entrepreneurs or founders fail to properly chart a course for their businesses or, by way of example, fail to choose the right legal entity for their businesses. Inevitably, such failing startups will try to "right the ship" when they have gone too far off course. Conversely, successful startups do things "right from the start."

For example, one of our most successful clients is a multi-media startup which goes toe-to-toe with media giants such as ABC and ESPN. Four years ago, this company started as a web-based passion project among friends, but it soon showed promising signs of a money-making venture and began to grow – almost uncontrollably. The Chief Executive Officer ("CEO"), while youthful in both appearance and age, was wise beyond his years and determined he needed assistance so his ship did not take on too much water. He was relentless about his brand and business concept; however, he did not allow tunnel vision to lead his company astray. Instead, as the true captain of his ship, he gave an honest assessment of his knowledge and skills and determined what he *could* do and what others *should* do.

The CEO humbly identified his lack of legal knowledge as a likely limitation to the ultimate success of his business. Accordingly, this young entrepreneur assembled a legal team to cure this deficiency and help advance his company's goals. By doing so, his chaos quickly turned into order: he locked up his intellectual property; he transcribed his company's culture into policy; and he recruited and retained talented people through tailored compensation and employment agreements. With his ship's leaks now plugged, the CEO was able to singularly focus on his brand and sail a course of controlled growth and success at an exponentially quicker pace. As a result, his brand has taken off like wildfire, and he can now walk into meetings with CEOs of some of the nation's largest media companies exuding confidence, and knowing that he and his company can navigate safely in what were once dangerous waters filled with sharks in suits.

Like this successful startup, you too can "get in the game." As you go out in the world and navigate the treacherous waters of entrepreneurship, we implore you to implement these three key foundational principles:

1. DON'T SET SAIL WITHOUT MAPPING OUT A COURSE

All too often, entrepreneurs think of a business idea – whether it is a product or service – and do whatever they can to get it to market without thinking about the long-term. Among other casualties of this short-sided approach is the lack of a sound business plan, discussion of fundamental organizational status, and agreements among founders.

a) Create a Solid Business Plan

When entrepreneurs first start a business, they generally jot down a business idea on the first paper they see – a napkin, a notebook, or a computer – and list a few tasks they need to accomplish. By doing so, they have, in essence, written a basic business plan. A business plan, in its simplest terms, is a plan for how and why your business is going to work. Creating a solid business plan is the first step toward successfully mapping out a course for your new business.

A business plan, if properly prepared, can assist entrepreneurs and fledgling small businesses with keeping business on track through budgeting and strategic planning, reminding owners of key founding principles, and in obtaining loans or attracting investors. Sample business plans are available everywhere for download. Do yourself a favor and find one, it will serve as your map during your entrepreneurial adventure.

b) Draft a Founders' Agreement

The second step toward successfully mapping out a course for your new business is to draft a founders' agreement. A founders' agreement allows people to discuss prospective, pre-business ideas on fair and equitable terms and encourages open and honest discussions of the goals and financial arrangements of the individuals involved with a startup. A clear and well-defined founders' agreement will address ownership, contribution of capital, responsibility, decision-making, operating procedures, and founders' departures. Bear in mind though, flexibility is a must when preparing these types of agreements as the roles of founders may change early and often during the startup phase and until everyone has settled in to their niche role.

If you are testing the entrepreneurship waters alone, you have little need for a founders' agreement. However, if or when you take on a partner, you will want to document your arrangement, whatever it may be, in writing. Lastly, the founders' agreement should be replaced with other agreements (i.e., a buy-sell), if the company incorporates or files for other formal corporate status.

c) Determine the Correct Legal Entity

The third step toward successfully mapping out a course for your new business is to determine the correct legal entity type for your business. In most jurisdictions, unincorporated, for-profit ventures are deemed general partnerships for purposes of contractual liability and taxed as partnerships. A general partnership is flexible and easy to set up; however, it is also riskier to its members. Each founder will have joint and several liability for the obligations of the new business. In other words, your personal assets will be at risk.

There are many reasons founders of a new company may choose to maintain the general partnership structure. For instance, if the company has no products, customers, investors, or revenue, then it may make sense to postpone the expense and administrative headache of corporate filings until a later date.

In most cases though, founders will want to limit their liability. Accordingly, they will need to determine under which legal entity type, other than a general partnership, they will want to operate their new business. Such a decision should not be taken lightly. It is important to choose the right entity for a number of reasons, including the application of employment laws, liability, and tax consequences.

When determining whether your new venture needs to limit its liability, consider the activities for which your business will be engaged and the risks involved in each. For instance:

- Will customers or clients be walking into your store?

- Is your brand similar to others in name or likeness?

- Will you be doing work on someone else's property?

- Are you doing business in a highly competitive industry?

- Will you have employees or independent contractors?

Now, imagine what could possibly go wrong in each of the above scenarios – ultimately, you could get sued. If this is a concern to you, *which it should be*, you and your fellow founders should form an entity that can protect your personal assets.

The most commonly filed legal entities which provide for personal asset protection are limited liability companies ("LLCs") and corporations. As an LLC or a corporation (or sub-S), you must do things such as: file correct papers with state and local governments, maintain separate bank accounts and financial records, contract in the entity's name, avoid mixing personal assets with company assets, and provide adequate funding for the business to operate. Although such activities may seem like an administrative nuisance, they are essential to your new legal venture and, as with many things, can be delegated to an attorney.

2. "CAPTAIN" YOUR SHIP BY DELEGATING DUTIES

a) Delegate Duties

Without question, one of things we have observed from our entrepreneur and small business clients is that most could do a better job with delegating duties and responsibilities. While it is certainly acceptable to wear multiple hats within your business, you simply cannot (nor should you) handle administrative duties, finances, marketing strategies, human resources issues, IT problems, and legal issues all by yourself. Inevitably, something will slip through the cracks, and those cracks could ultimately sink your ship.

When it comes to legal issues, this warning cannot be emphasized enough. Indeed, Abraham Lincoln famously said, "He who represents himself has a fool for a client." Accordingly, entrepreneurs and small business owners should regularly consult with an attorney to proactively address any potential legal issues before they grow into larger and more costly ones. As they say, "An ounce of prevention is worth a pound of cure." Many of our clients often come to us after they have been sued. Usually, the lawsuits stem from a simple, but costly, ill-advised decision by the client who believed he or she knew the law. The law, however, is not always logical nor is it fair, so don't view it that way.

b) Hire an Attorney

When hiring an attorney, you should find one (or several) that specializes or is experienced in your business' industry, or, at a minimum, someone who possesses common knowledge of contract law, employment law, intellectual property, and business organizations. In short, all attorneys are not created equal. Conduct your research and find the best fit for your business before entering into an attorney-client relationship. This means you must leave the confines of your entrepreneurial laboratory and go meet with an attorney in-person to determine whether he or she "gets it," "gets you," and "gets your business" concept. Absent such an understanding or fit, your attorney-client relationship will be a frustrating one.

In addition, be certain about how your attorney handles billing. Will he or she charge by the hour or bill you on a flat-fee basis? Paying for an attorney's time on an hourly basis can be pricey, so we have found that flat-fee pricing is beneficial to most clients allowing for easy budgeting and giving our clients access to regular advice without the fear of mounting monthly bills

3. PROTECT YOUR GREATEST ASSETS.

a) Intellectual Property

One of the greatest benefits of hiring an attorney is that he or she can help you protect your greatest assets: intellectual property and employees. Naturally, your business should consult with an attorney to trademark, copyright, or patent its intellectual property. At a minimum, your business should lock up domain names, social media, and file trademarks to protect its brand. Attorneys can perform requisite searches to ensure that your brand is best protected and that neither you nor someone else is infringing upon intellectual property rights.

b) Human Capital

The importance of human capital is often overlooked by entrepreneurs and small businesses. No company can truly attain its goals without the support of its employees, including those who help formulate some of the initial ideas of the company. Although employees are essential to the growth and development of businesses, they can also be your worst nightmare if they are not handled with care. Inevitably, employees will leave your business due to disagreements with you, greener pastures, or to work for a competitor.

The risk of such change can have significant impact on startups and small businesses, but those risks can be mitigated or controlled by attorneys with well-crafted agreements, policies, and procedures. Each company and culture is unique, but we have found that employee handbooks, bonus or incentive plans, stock-option agreements, work-for-hire agreements, as well as non-competition and non-disclosure agreements, are generally beneficial to entrepreneurs and small businesses, as they clearly set forth the rights and expectations for both the employer and the employee throughout their relationship. Having such documents in place generally ensures "smoother sailing" for all.

CONCLUSION

With an attorney on board, your ship's course can be properly charted before you set sail, and you can focus on what you do well – your business. So, as you set sail into the entrepreneurial waters, hire good counsel. He or she may just protect you from yourself and save your business at the same time.

NOW, GO GET AN ATTORNEY, RIGHT YOUR SHIP, AND "GET IN THE GAME!"

About Nathan

Few attorneys can say they have done it all in their area of practice. Nathan McCoy can. From defending Fortune 500 companies at one of the nation's largest and most distinguished management defense firms to practicing with one of Florida's most well known "Plaintiffs Firms," Nathan has gained invaluable experience from every angle of the courtroom and bargaining table. His diverse experience has given him keen insight into the minds of corporations (both large and small), individuals, and their counsel as they position themselves in legal battles and negotiations. Because he has been behind enemy lines and back again, he has developed a breadth of legal and business knowledge, as well as a true balanced perspective.

Nathan has parlayed such experience into co-founding and managing Wilson McCoy, P.A., a law firm dedicated to coaching, counseling, and representing businesses and individuals in business and employment related matters. Since its inception in 2012, Wilson McCoy, P.A. has been named by and featured as a "Best Law Firm" by U.S. News & World Report from 2013 – 2015. As a true "lawpreneur," Nathan enjoys working with entrepreneurs, startups, and small businesses to ensure complying with the law does not interfere with the creativity needed to succeed in today's legalistic business environment.

Nathan graduated with a Bachelor of Science degree in General Business Administration, *magna cum laude*, from the University of Central Florida and obtained his law degree from the University of Tennessee, where he served as Managing Editor of *Transactions: The Tennessee Journal of Business Law* and was a member of the Board of Editors for the *Tennessee Law Review*.

Nathan is a published author, has served as a guest professor on contracts, and often lectures at legal seminars. He is married to his wife of 14 years, a proud father of two, and an endurance obstacle race enthusiast.

About Gary

Some lawyers' reputations precede them for the wrong reason. Gary Wilson's reputation precedes him for all the right reasons. Gary is a skilled litigator who has the intangibles, social skills, and desire to "do good," which make him a well-rounded individual and well-respected attorney. Some might even say that Gary has never met a stranger.

With more than 20 years of employment law experience, Gary's work as an employment and labor law attorney has been recognized by publications and his peers, consistently naming him as one of the "Best Lawyers in America," a Florida "Super Lawyer," and one of Orlando's "Best Attorneys." He is admitted to practice before the United States Supreme Court, the U.S. Court of Appeals for the Eleventh Circuit, the U.S. District Courts for the Northern and Middle Districts of Florida, and all State courts in Florida. In addition to being a practicing attorney and co-founding and managing Wilson McCoy, P.A. with Nathan McCoy, Gary is also a Circuit Civil mediator certified by the Florida Supreme Court, and also a Florida Supreme Court qualified arbitrator.

Gary graduated with a Bachelor of Science degree in Real Estate from Florida State University, and earned his Juris Doctor degree from the University of Mississippi School of Law, where he received the Julius Owen Memorial Scholarship in Law, the Dean's Distinguished Service Award, was a student body senator, served on the Moot Court Board, and was named to "Who's Who Among American Law Students."

In addition to his legal work, Gary regularly volunteers his time to non-profit organizations, serves as an officer in his church, has engaged in missions, and has served his University on several boards. In fact, because of his distinguished career and dedication to his alma mater, the Florida State University awarded him with entry into the University's "Circle of Gold," one of the University's highest honors. Gary has been happily married for 23 years and he and his wife have two children.

CHAPTER 13

NUTRITION FOR YOUR BODY AND MIND: ARE YOU KILLING YOUR FOOD?

BY GRACE TOGUN OLUGBODI

Food is supposed to be **natural medicine** to the body.

Let food be thy medicine and medicine be thy food. ~ Hippocrates.

Last year, I did a nutrition cooking workshop for a health-conscious client who was pretty much doing all the right things. She tried to do exercises as much as she could, always tried to eat the right foods, vegetables, fruits and so on. She even bought organic foods.

Still there seemed to be something missing; a part that left the mystery unsolved. She had always sought out how she could feel better and look it, prevent health problems and their complications, lose some weight and have more energy. She had initially complained that she still had low energy, a weight problem, metals in her body, and other health issues.

By the end of a couple of sessions, she was feeling much better. She understood exactly what she needed to do and why it had been so difficult to keep her weight down (because her body kept craving food), and how lack of nutrition could affect long-term health.

After putting what she learnt into action, she said to me: "people are eating dead food, but expecting to live."

Today's lifestyle diseases include High Cholesterol, Obesity, Diabetes, high blood pressure, Stroke, Cancer, Heart Disease, Digestive Problems, IBS and other related ones.

In the UK:

- **Every two minutes a person is diagnosed with cancer (Cancer Research UK)**

- **Every three minutes one person is diagnosed with diabetes (Diabetes UK).**

- **And every 5 minutes someone has a heart attack (British Heart Foundation).**

In America:

- **Heart disease is the leading cause of death for both men and women, followed by cancer (www.theheartfoundation.org and www.cancer.org); and every 33 seconds, someone in the U.S. dies from heart disease.**

- **A new cancer is diagnosed every 30 seconds; 1 in 3 women will have cancer. (National Cancer Institute – www.cancer.gov)**

- **2,200 people are diagnosed with diabetes each day (http://www.grantregional.com)**

All of these diseases are diet related and World Health Authorities say the main reason they ensue is the lack of proper nutrition in our diets.

A lot of us know the right foods to buy and tend to do that. The problem is that the ways we prepare the food can prevent its nutrition from getting into our bodies. You **can** lose a lot of the nutrition in your food just because of how it is prepared and cooked. This chapter will show you how you can combat nutrition losses and how to **maximise, retain and get to eat** (and not kill) those all-important nutrients in your food.

This is not about dieting (diets don't work long-term and some may be dangerous). It's about understanding how to combat eating dead food and methods that can help reduce the risk of today's lifestyle diseases.

Tell me, how important is good health to you? How high a priority is it in your life? Do you want it enough to take practical steps to ensure you have it? Or do you take your health for granted?

Indeed, for a lot of people, looking after their health is usually not a major priority until there's a problem. As long as there is no health problem, many people take their health for granted—**until something goes wrong.**

But life doesn't work that way, it catches up sooner or later.

YOU ARE WHAT YOU EAT!

Killers of Nutrition

Doctors and dieticians say that **what** you eat and **how** you prepare your food play a huge, significant, vital role in your health and wellbeing, and that of your family. They play a central role to whether your body is in balance and whether it's acidic or in an alkaline state.

These are six main ways you can avoid losing nutrition in your meals.

1. Peeling

Do not peel foods that grow under the ground before cooking. For foods like potatoes, carrots and yams, a lot of the vitamins are found just under the skin.

Just by peeling such foods, you peel past the thin layer under the skin and lose a lot of the nutrients. Wash very well instead.

2. Cooking with Water

When you cook vegetables with water, many of the minerals and vitamins end up in the water, and water leaches them out of our foods.

When you cook carrots with water, the water turns orange. This is because the water takes on the colour of the vegetables. Another example is cooking peas or spinach with water. The colour of the water turns to green, and this usually ends up down the drain.

Nutritional experts say, when you lose colour, you lose vitamins; and when you lose taste or flavour, you've lost minerals.

This nutrition being thrown away is exactly what our bodies need to fight diseases, to perform its functions properly, and for good

subsistence.

Now you may ask: "How about using the water used in cooking vegetables to make sauce or gravy?" I will mention the slight caveat with this in the next section.

Keep in mind that, most foods have natural juices in them and you do not need to add water to cook them. The key is to cook vegetables and any foods that have natural juices with **<u>NO</u>** water at all. Otherwise the nutrients end up in the water instead of in your body and those of your family members.

It may not be possible to use ordinary pots and pans to cook without water, but waterless cookware, and certain brands of healthy cookware achieve this easily. They help you retain and protect the nutrition in your cooking and in your meals.

3. High Heat
Many heating methods destroy nutrients. Excessive heat can be split into a few common methods of cooking. It's important to cook only with methods that use medium heat or low heat.

3.1 - Boiling
This is where the vegetable water I mentioned in the previous point comes in. The problem is that in most cases, food being cooked is heated to boiling temperature and above (100 °C or 212 F).

The amount of nutrition you lose from cooking will depend on how much heat has been applied **and** for how long.

You should be cooking your foods at temperatures just high enough to kill the potentially harmful bacteria and germs, but not high enough to kill nutrition. In other words, keep the food LIVE and maximise nutrition. In my eight years experience, I have seen that the optimal temperature is under 90°C (around 85 °C is best).

Do away with the temperatures that kill the nutrition in your meals.

Each time you recognize the killers of nutrition and act to combat them and teach others, **you're saving health, you're saving nutrition, and you're saving and changing lives.**

3.2 - Steaming

Steaming is better than boiling, but can be even higher temperatures. It occurs at over 100 °C, because the water has to boil first. This is why the water at the bottom of a steamer *still changes colour* when you steam. Remember that when you lose colour, you lose vitamins. You can see in the small print of many steamers, that you are advised to only steam for a few minutes.

The trouble is that most people can't realistically do that always, unless of course you want to eat your vegetables half-cooked. So we end up steaming for a little bit longer, until the vegetables are cooked and soaked and water changes colour.

3.3 - Microwave

Microwaves also heat at 100 °C and higher.

3.4 - Grilling and Roasting

Typically occurring at around 150 to 200°C and higher, we need to avoid grilling and roasting on high temperatures as you lose a lot of the moisture and nutritional content in the food. It's the reason that fish comes out dry.

Summarily, many vegetables and healthy foods are packed with anti-oxidants, vitamins, minerals, phytonutrients, phytochemicals, and help towards neutralising free radicals, therefore help in fighting and preventing cancer, diabetes and protecting our heart, and have other things that the body needs to function properly. So it is important to be able get these nutrients out of our vegetables and essential foods, and not lose them while preparing and cooking.

4. Oxidation

Use airtight saucepans that stop air and light from getting into food. Oxidation is the effect of air and light on our foods. A good example of this occurs while eating an apple. Put it onto the table after a bite or two, it starts to turn brown right? That's the effect of air and light attacking the nutrients.

5. Fats and Oils are a Big Culprit

Cut out fats and oils from your diet, or greatly minimise their use in your cooking. Fats and oils make our food so much harder to digest, and they give us those extra pounds we spend so much time, money and effort trying to lose.

A common misconception is that frying is ok as long as you're using olive oil. **Wrong.**

Many oils being sold have been destroyed during processing and heating by producers/manufacturers, and many are bad for you. The good news about cold-pressed oils (such as cold-pressed virgin olive oil) is that they should still be nutrition-intact. So they are excellent when raw and also on salads. The bad news is that frying or cooking with even cold-pressed oils above their smoking points turns them into dangerous fats - the types of fats that clog up arteries and produce free radicals that make it more conducive for cancer cells to live. Most people don't have a way of regulating the temperature of oils they are heating.

Frying a piece of chicken or cooking some food with oil is like wrapping it with a bag of oil. After eating, the body tries so hard to get through the bag of oil to get to its nutrients. But it finds it hard to get through, because it's been wrapped with oil. And so in no time we are hungry again.

Simply put, learn to cut back on dietary fats, and you will reduce your risk of obesity by 100%.

6. Your Cookware, Pots and Pans

In many ways, your pots and pans determine the nutritional content of your food. Why? Because **it is the last thing your food touches before going into your body.** So it makes perfect sense that it should be a major appliance and a major step in the health of your family, and not just the last thing to pay any attention to. Your saucepans can either be a foe to your nutrition or a friend.

Many pots and pans leach toxins or heavy metals into food. That can't be good for health, can it? I have had many people in the over 2,000 nutrition workshops we have conducted over the last eight years (including 80/90% raw eaters whose only food they cook/boil is pretty much only ginger tea), who, after doing research for years into one problem or the other they were experiencing, found that heavy metals were responsible! Studies and news have shown some types of pots and pans to contain carcinogenic and other dangerous substances that can leach into food. Some have been linked to diseases like Alzheimer's. It's like putting contaminated fuel in your car.

Many other saucepans, apart from reacting with food enzymes and acids, are also corrosive (they rust) and **porous** (make you lose vitamins and minerals from nutrients from food). Many saucepans also scratch and chip and become unsafe for you and your family. Think about where all the metal that have come off the scratches have gone?

There is a common phrase that "modernisation is killing us!" Even clay pots and earthenware pots that previous generations used (and were safe as they didn't leach metals) have now been "modernised" to have **glazed coatings and other dangerous substances** in an attempt to stop them being too heavy and breaking easily.

Pay more attention to your cookware types. You may need to throw some out and get healthier ones. It is usually better to purchase good quality ones that will last you a long time, rather than throwing out sets and buying new ones over and over, when they chip, scratch or rust. The type of material your cookware is made of and where it's from matters a lot. The best material for cookware are high grades and austenitic implant-grades of stainless or surgical steel that most importantly don't rust, do not react with food, can cook food in its natural juices and natural oils (no water and no oils), are air tight, and non-porous.

IN CONCLUSION

The body **needs** the nutrients in food to live; how you prepare and cook your food determines how much nutrition you get from it. Good nutrition in turn fortifies and builds up your immune system. Your body always tries to fight everything from common colds to diabetes to cancer. **Proper nutrition** is what makes that immune system strong enough to fight effectively and keep fighting, without weakening or giving in.

Lack of nutrition in a person's diet could eventually lead to health problems. This can also lead to behavioural problems, not only in children, but also in adults. The conventional ways of cooking steal the nutrients out of your foods and rob you of the much-needed vitamins and minerals you need for your body, all of which are meant to keep you and your family healthy, strong and prevent disease.

The secret of healthy cooking and getting proper nutrition is to cook your foods without adding excess water or fats, on low heat. Your food will taste so much better, even with little or no spice. Guaranteed. It is important to be able to regulate the heat; otherwise cooking on low heat will eventually get the temperature high sooner or later. Your saucepans should also be good quality pans.

I once heard someone say, "We eat a little bit of non-stick in the morning, a bit of crappy stainless steel in the afternoon, top it up with aluminium at night and then we wonder why we don't feel good."

The subject of health and nutrition is a very profound one. Do you think a billionaire will give back all of their money, in order to have another year of life to live? Of course they would. All the wealth in the world can be pretty much pointless without your health. Nothing tastes as good as good health feels.

So, take responsibility for your health. Learn your way to wellness and act on it. Get proper nutrition. Be nutritionally balanced. You cannot underestimate the POWER of MAXIMIZING THE NUTRITION IN YOUR MEALS.

In fact, **without health, you wouldn't have time to make money or spend money**. Health is Wealth. Take charge of your health today!

Copyright © 2014 Grace Togun Olugbodi

About Grace

Grace Togun Olugbodi helps her clients and their families to get proper nutrition for their body and mind. Over the last eight years, she has helped over 2,000 families find solutions for their nutrition, to enable them look better, feel better, live better and be more energised; with practical tools that last a lifetime. Her company also runs healthy cooking workshops internationally – teaching families, companies and government officials how to retain nutrition and turn their food into natural medicine for a lifetime.

Before then, she worked as a programmer in five different investment banks in the City in London for eight years, then resigned to set up a firm to help people with nutrition seven years ago.

Grace has since developed further mind nutrition for children and adults who are either struggling with numbers/math or simply want to become better or whizzes at it, and has invented two special fun games to help children fall in love with Math and do more calculations effortlessly, as if by magic. These games have greatly impressed adults, children, School Head teachers, Head of maths co-ordinators and the Head of a Top reputable international Educational Tuition company branch.

Grace believes by helping people find ways to love maths and know their numbers, people will easily develop to know their numbers, and therefore be self-confident as children and successful as adults both in business, as entrepreneurs, or in whatever chosen field of career they choose, in turn changing more lives for the better.

Her forthcoming book is on that subject, how to create lifelong success and confidence for children through math, and how to bring out the math genius in your child.

Grace has won two awards back-to-back in the last two years – Women Inspiring Women National Awards June 2013 and July 2014. She was also selected as one of America's PremierExperts® and has been quoted in NBC, FOX, ABC and CBS News. Grace enjoys working hard and says: "It's not about you, it's about helping as many people as you can to change their lives for the better, and your life will be changed for the better too."

She is a first-class honours graduate of London Guildhall University and holds an M.Sc. from the same University.

Grace strongly believes that a wholesome approach to health is key; and that body, mind, memory, nutrition and health are closely linked. Everyone deserves to live a healthy life, so that they can protect what's really most important and be successful.

Grace is also a qualified PCRM instructor and sponsor, part of a Not-for-Profit organisation, helping people to prevent and reverse diabetes and increase cancer survival (Physicians for Responsible Medicine). She also sets up successful Franchise Dealerships for serious entrepreneurs.

You can connect with Grace at:
grace@nutritionforbodyandmind.com

www.nutritionforbodyandmind.com
www.begeniocity.com

uk.linkedin.com/in/gracetogunolugbodi/
https://www.facebook.com/graceetogun

www.twitter.com/graceetogun

CHAPTER 14

THE X FACTOR™: HOW BRANDING YOURSELF AS THE EXPERT IN YOUR FIELD BOOSTS YOUR PROFILE, PRESTIGE AND PROFITS

BY NICK NANTON AND JW DICKS

You wouldn't expect an astrophysicist to approach rock star status – especially one whose record as a scientist is described by academic colleagues as "sound, but not extraordinary."[1]

You wouldn't expect an astrophysicist to author huge best-selling books, host a multi-million dollar TV series or be named one of the 100 most influential people in the world by *Time Magazine*.[2]

And you definitely wouldn't expect *People Magazine* to create a special category, "Sexiest Astrophysicist Alive" for this individual.[3]

But then again, you wouldn't expect an astrophysicist, in preparation for his first appearance on *The Daily Show with Jon Stewart*, to study

---

1 Mead, Rebecca. "Starman," The New Yorker. February 17, 2014.
2 Lemonick, Michael D. Lemonick. "Neil deGrasse Tyson," Time Magazine. May 3, 2007.
3 "Neil De Grasse Tyson: Sexiest Astrophysicist." People Magazine. November 13, 2000.

interview segments methodically to see how many sentences a guest usually was able to say before Stewart interrupted one with a joke [4] - so he could plan the length of his answers in advance.

Dr. Neil DeGrasse Tyson has become a household name, as well as the most famous person in his field since Carl Sagan, not because he necessarily knows more about his specialty than anyone else, and not because he's accomplished any sort of incredible breakthroughs in his field.

No, he became a huge pop culture celebrity simply because he focused on *communicating his expertise in the most accessible way possible.* And that is the essence of "The X Factor," an intangible asset that any professional or entrepreneur should seriously consider acquiring.

THE X FACTOR

There are roughly 23,000 physicists and astronomers in the U.S. alone[5] - and it can be assumed that the vast majority of them possess a knowledge level roughly equivalent to Dr. Tyson's. Yet, the media spotlight shines brightly on him, while the others toil in relative obscurity. Yes, the others may publish books and do media interviews from time to time, but Dr. Tyson is in constant demand by all major media outlets and can even cause a minor public uproar when he releases a series of tweets detailing scientific errors in the hit film, *Gravity*[6].

The secret to Dr. Tyson's success is a simple one: It's not enough to simply be an expert – that expert must also demonstrate his or her knowledge in a public forum that directly connects to a receptive audience. It all goes back to the old philosophical question, "If a tree falls in a forest and no one is around to hear it, does it make a sound?" Similarly, even if one does become an authority in one's field, what good does it do that person if potential clients are never made aware of that expertise?

That's why, to truly be a superstar in one's profession, one must attain "The X Factor" – by finding a way to deeply connect with one's

4 Mead, Rebecca, "Starman."

5 U.S. Department of Labor, Bureau of Labor Statistics http://www.bls.gov/ooh/life-physical-and-social-science/physicists-and-astronomers.htm

6 Nordyke, Kimberly. "Famed Astrophysicist Neil deGrasse Tyson Criticizes 'Gravity' on Twitter," The Hollywood Reporter. October 7, 2013

audience in order to demonstrate a mastery of whatever one's specialty happens to be. And *The X Factor* works with any number of specialties, demonstrated by the fact that even an astrophysicist can become a media superstar.

Why should, say, a doctor, lawyer or even a CPA want to attain *The X Factor*? Well, it isn't just about going on an ego trip. To quote a Forbes article, "There are many powerful aspects to positioning yourself as an authority for your brand. Remember, by raising your own profile, you will, in turn, raise the profile of your company. You'll also significantly widen your reach…The bottom line is, people buy products from brands that they know and trust. And they'll trust you—once they know where to find you."[7]

In other words, working to develop *The X Factor* is just an excellent business move.

INFLUENCE AND "THE OZ EFFECT"

When an entrepreneur or professional is successful in establishing an expert persona, that person's influence grows exponentially along with his or her fame. Because the person is seen as someone who is accepted as a master in a specific field, the public is willing to not only accept whatever the person says as gospel – but is also motivated to act on that person's advice in a quick and decisive manner.

Nothing illustrates this phenomenon better than "The Oz Effect." Dr. Mehmet Oz first became known to television viewers through his frequent appearances as a health expert on *The Oprah Winfrey Show* beginning in 2004. Winfrey herself, because of her deep connection with her viewers, became, in the words of ABC News, "one of the most influential figures in media"[8] and created several household names, such as Dr. Phil, Rachael Ray and Suze Orman, simply by conferring expert status on them on her program. In Oz's case, she dubbed him, "America's Doctor" – and Oz took that ball and ran with it.

---

7 Honeysutt, Alex. "4 Easy Ways to Become an Expert in Your Field," Forbes.com. October 16, 2012
8 Effron, Lauren. "Oprah-Made: 8 Stars Who Shot to Fame Thanks to Winfrey," ABCNews.com. October 15, 2012. http://abcnews.go.com/Entertainment/oprah-made-stars-shot-fame-winfrey/story?id=17236783#

Dr. Oz went on to star in his own popular syndicated series that began in 2009, but became only the base of his efforts to add *The X Factor* to his expert status. Oz's best-selling books, magazine articles, radio shows as well as his TV show all cemented his image in the public's eye as THE health expert to listen to.

The result? "The Oz Effect." Whenever Dr. Oz mentions a product on his show, sales shoot up dramatically. For example, after the Neti Pot, a relatively obscure device used to ease nasal dryness, was showcased on Oz's show, Internet searches for it rose by 42,000% - and sales rose by an unbelievable 12,000%.[9]

Oz's influence grew to a point where he simply had to mention a supplement or herb and sales skyrocketed. Unfortunately, many marketers took advantage of Oz's influence and used his on-air mentions to aggressively sell their merchandise – which culminated in Oz having to testify before Congress about his influence being used to sell all types of health products. Missouri Senator Claire McCaskill defined his massive influence when she said to Oz, "When you feature a product on your show, it creates what has become known as the 'Dr. Oz Effect' — dramatically boosting sales..." [10]

It's obvious that very few can take **The X Factor** to the heights of a Dr. Oz – but it's also true that it's not necessary to become an international superstar to reap its benefits. *The X Factor* can work just as effectively for a dentist in his or her community as it can for a national figure seeking to bond with an audience of millions.

CONNECTION AND COMMUNICATION

The real key to achieving *The X Factor* is *effective communication that connects you to your intended audience.* When you find meaningful ways to bond with your intended target group, you don't need the power of an Oprah Winfrey to become a success.

---

9 Walton, Alice G. "The Oz Effect: Medicine or Marketing?," Forbes.com. 6/6/2011. http://www.forbes.com/sites/alicegwalton/2011/06/06/the-oz-effect-medicine-or-marketing

10 Briggs, Bill. "How 'The Dr. Oz Effect' Has Hooked American Consumers," NBCNews.com. June 18, 2014. http://www.nbcnews.com/health/health-news/how-dr-oz-effect-has-hooked-american-consumers-n134801

John Green is a writer who, back in 2007, was critically-acclaimed and had written an award-winning young adult novel, *Alaska*. However, sales were relatively modest. In other words, he did not have *The X Factor* working for him.

That same year, he and his brother Hank decided to communicate solely through YouTube videos. Hank lived in Montana, John lived in New York City, so they barely saw each other and thought this would be a great social media gimmick, as well as a fun thing to do. Billing themselves as the Vlogbrothers, they posted several videos a week – and quickly built up a huge following from young fans who loved their in-jokes, their philosophic musings and their goofy humor. Viewers of the Vlogbrothers described themselves as "Nerdfighters," in honor of one of John's videos where he talked about the concept of being a warrior for Internet subcultures and things that were considered "geeky."

With this massive prebuilt audience in place, what happened with John's next book was nothing short of phenomenal. From a New Yorker article about Green: *"Publishing executives talk about successful books as if they were lightning strikes, but the popularity of 'The Fault in Our Stars" was no accident. Nerdfighters, who by then numbered in the millions, were evangelical about it, tucking notes into copies of the book and encouraging readers to join their movement. In fact, "The Fault in Our Stars" reached the No. 1 position on Amazon six months before it was published, when Green announced its title online."*[11]

That phenomenal success continued with the movie adaptation of the book. The movie opened in the number one position at the box office after the online trailer for the film had twenty million views.[12]

What's interesting about the John Green case study is that the expertise he demonstrated in his online videos had little or nothing to do with his actual novelist skills – and everything to do with bonding with his audience. By keying into their feelings and entering into authentic discussions with them, he built a base of trust and credibility that translated into massive sales of his book. He showed himself to be an expert at understanding his readership – which may have, in turn, been

---

11 Talbot, Margaret. "The Teen Whisperer," The New Yorker. June 9, 2014.
12 Ibid

more important than his actual writing ability.

In other words, although his literary prize did not translate into success; his reaching out to his base did – to such an extent that, through the first half of 2014, The Fault in Our Stars was the best-selling book in 49 out of 50 of the states in the USA.[13]

ATTAINING THE X FACTOR

The X Factor can be an invaluable asset to real estate agents, attorneys, medical practitioners, small business owners, entrepreneurs and professionals of all types and stripes. As seen, <u>it ultimately elevates one's profile above the competition, empowers higher product and service sales and transforms one into a major influencer of those in one's niche.</u>

Here are a few proven strategies for making *The X Factor* a major aspect of one's business, based both on the preceding case studies and other similar ones.

• EXHIBIT

Sometimes all that's necessary to be recognized as a notable authority in a field is by simply *exhibiting* expertise when the opportunity arises – even if one has yet to attain a higher level of experience and knowledge.

A doctor, who, when he was still only a medical student, appeared as an expert on a local Sunday night radio call-in show entitled, "Ask a Surgeon." After he graduated, he became a regular co-host on a relationship advice program that aired every weeknight on the same radio station. The program became so popular that it went national after a few years, and then made the jump to TV.

Three years later, Dr. Drew Pinsky was ready to start his own media operation. Based on his "celebrity brand" alone, investors put 7.5 million dollars into the pot in October of 1999 when he was ready to start DrDrew.com, an online community designed to give health advice to young adults.

Heidi Roizen, managing director of the Softbank Venture Capital Fund,

---

13 "Top Purchased Books (Jan.- June 2014)," Mashable.com. http://mashable.com/2014/07/10/top-purchased-books-amazon/#:eyJzIjoiZiIsImkiOiJfOWRkbDA0MHJ3bnN6dW50NSJ9

said at the time, "Dr. Drew has the ear of a large and important audience. He's earned their trust and respect. We hope to build on this great franchise with ever-expanding content, community, and commerce opportunities."

Clearly, Dr. Drew from the start understood the power of *The X Factor* and made it an essential part of his highly-successful career path.

• EXPLAIN

Because effective communication is all-important to *The X Factor*, professional jargon and overly-technical phrasing should be avoided at all costs when interacting with one's niche (unless that niche understands such terminology). Instead, <u>one must *explain* key concepts in clear and easy-to-understand language.</u>

As previously discussed, *X Factor* master Dr. Neil DeGrasse Tyson works hard to make difficult scientific concepts comprehensible to the average person – even going so far as to use a reference to such network comedies as *Family Guy* or *The Simpsons* to make a point.

Similarly, former president Bill Clinton has often been called "The Explainer-In-Chief" during Barack Obama's residency in the White House. When Obama had difficulty making a policy clear to the American public in a way that resonated, Clinton would be called upon to do it in his stead - which is exactly what he did when he spoke at the 2012 Democratic Convention. Here's how Time Magazine defined Clinton's "X Factor" at that event: *"There have been a lot of analyses of Clinton's political style — empathy, people skills, wonkiness — but one that may be underestimated is the fact that the man can explain the hell out of a thing. Clinton didn't deliver poetry; he gave a talk and told a narrative."* [14]

• EXPAND

Most professionals and entrepreneurs are content to market themselves through normal advertising venues and techniques. *The X Factor* requires <u>a different approach that expands beyond those conventional methods – by generating useful and credible content in one's field through these platforms, which distinguishes the provider of that content from those</u>

---

14 Poniewozik, James. "The Morning After: Obama Turns to Bill Clinton, Explainer-in-Chief," Time Magazine. September 6, 2012.

that merely trumpet their greatness through paid advertisements.

For example, a fitness expert who authors a book has a verifiable, tangible item that both promotes expertise as well delivers added prestige. A real estate agent who contributes a home buying and selling advice column in the local newspaper or a call-in show on a radio station accomplishes the same feat. In all of the above examples, the professionals are (a) the featured attraction, (b) demonstrating mastery of their industry's specialty and (c) immediately raising the value of their names by providing content in a legitimate media forum. How much more effective is that than buying a commercial or print ad that any competitor could easily duplicate?

This is why generating content is of primary concern to *X Factor* adherents such as Dr. Oz. Here, a *New York Times* article describes the incredible amount of information Oz and his staff delivered outside of his TV show at the beginning of its run:

"Oz is also on the radio every day...Oz is in bookstores, where you can find half a dozen titles in the ongoing "You" series — including "You: The Smart Patient," "You: On a Diet" and "You: Having a Baby" — that he has written with Dr. Michael F. Roizen, the unofficial co-chairman of what might be called Oz Industries. There are about nine million of their books in print so far. Oz is in magazines and newspapers. In February, he wrote what will be the first of six Prescription columns a year for Time magazine...In the fall he will start writing one column every other month for the AARP magazine. He reaches out to men with a monthly column for Esquire, to women with regular contributions to Winfrey's magazine. All of this comes on top of the newspaper writing that he and Roizen, under the "You Docs" banner, produce for King Features Syndicate."[15]

It's hard to conceive of one man putting out that much content. But presumably, that's a large part of how he earned his title of "America's Doctor."

• EXCEED

The X Factor also demands that one *exceed* the profile and exposure of the competition in meaningful and innovative ways. The aforementioned

---

15 Bruni, Frank. "Dr. Does It All," The New York Times. April 16th, 2010.

focus on generating content is one of those ways; another is simply finding new venues for exposure and new paths to influence that competitors aren't exploiting.

In the early 1990's, David Letterman and Jay Leno were both up for the job of replacing Johnny Carson on NBC's *The Tonight Show*. Both had a strong case for the job; Letterman had hosted his own 12:30 am show for 10 years and enjoyed strong ratings, while Leno had filled-in for Carson on a regular basis and had also done well.

But, while Letterman relied strictly on his performance on his show to get him the job, Leno went out of his way to build relationships with NBC affiliates all across the country. He would do stand-up at their meetings, fly in to a station to help them sell their commercials or do an interview with the local press. He went beyond the normal bounds to connect with the NBC decision-makers who would influence the network's final decision in his favor.[16]

Similarly, a dentist who specializes in implants and spends two or three hours a month speaking directly to senior citizen groups and informing them about the advantages of implants stands a better chance of growing his or her business than the dentist who doesn't do any outreach.

When professionals or entrepreneurs go beyond the competition's level of exposure and find innovative ways to directly communicate to either potential clients/customers or influential leaders in the community, *The X Factor* suddenly works in their favor.

• EXCITE

In order to fully galvanize a niche audience and motivate them into buying a product or utilizing a service, one's ongoing message must excite that niche on a deep psychological level. By keying into who the audience is and what their needs are, the entrepreneur/professional builds a strong relationship that transcends the usual business transaction.

As already detailed, author John Green did exactly this with the series of YouTube videos he and his brother posted online. He connected with his readership in a vital and exciting way that bonded them to him.

---

16 Rosen, Jay. "Books of The Times; How Letterman (and CBS) Won," The New York Times. February 22, 1994.

This aspect of *The X Factor* can also be attained simply by an individual's charisma and ability to engage a crowd. Contrary to popular belief, these qualities can easily be taken on when one is willing to train and learn. To quote the Harvard Business Review, *"...charisma can be learned through deliberate practice. Bear in mind that even Winston Churchill, one of the most charismatic figures of the twentieth century, practiced his oratory style in front of a mirror."* [17]

SUMMARY

As demonstrated, *The X Factor* – i.e. being seen as a visible, engaging expert in one's field – can go a long way towards launching professionals and entrepreneurs to a new level of success. When the right effort is made to demonstrate one's expertise in innovative venues, and to use inventive communication strategies that actively engage one's niche in those venues, one's reputation and profile both improve significantly, and create substantial revenue improvement in their wake.

In the words of *Forbes Magazine, "You are an expert on your brand— and more than likely on your industry, too—and you can leverage that expertise to help your brand further its reach. When you share what you know, you'll start to gain visibility in your industry and build a community around you—and when a big product announcement comes along, that community will be ready to engage with you on your news."* [18]

By putting to work the building blocks of Exhibit, Explain, Expand, Exceed and Excite, a doctor, lawyer, financial analyst, business owner or entrepreneur can make the all-important "X Factor" a vital part of their professional portfolio. That, in turn, will become a huge factor in generating an ongoing success story that will reap rewards for years to come.

---

17 Ericsson, K. Anders, Prietula, Michael J. and Cokely, Edward T. "The Making of an Expert," Harvard Business Review. July, 2007.
18 Honeysutt, Alex. "4 Easy Ways to Become an Expert in Your Field."

About Nick

An Emmy Award-Winning Director and Producer, Nick Nanton, Esq., is known as the Top Agent to Celebrity Experts around the world for his role in developing and marketing business and professional experts, through personal branding, media, marketing and PR. Nick is recognized as the nation's leading expert on personal branding as Fast Company Magazine's Expert Blogger on the subject and lectures regularly on the topic at major universities around the world. His book *Celebrity Branding You®*, while an easy and informative read, has also been used as a text book at the University level.

The CEO and Chief StoryTeller at The Dicks + Nanton Celebrity Branding Agency, an international agency with more than 1800 clients in 33 countries, Nick is an award-winning director, producer and songwriter who has worked on everything from large scale events to television shows with the likes of Steve Forbes, Brian Tracy, Jack Canfield (*The Secret*, Creator of the *Chicken Soup for the Soul* Series), Michael E. Gerber, Tom Hopkins, Dan Kennedy and many more.

Nick is recognized as one of the top thought-leaders in the business world and has co-authored 30 best-selling books alongside Brian Tracy, Jack Canfield, Dan Kennedy, Dr. Ivan Misner (Founder of BNI), Jay Conrad Levinson (Author of the Guerilla Marketing Series), Super Agent Leigh Steinberg and many others, including the breakthrough hit *Celebrity Branding You!®*

Nick has led the marketing and PR campaigns that have driven more than 1000 authors to Best-Seller status. Nick has been seen in *USA Today, The Wall Street Journal, Newsweek, BusinessWeek, Inc. Magazine, The New York Times, Entrepreneur® Magazine, Forbes,* FastCompany.com and has appeared on ABC, NBC, CBS, and FOX television affiliates around the country, as well as CNN, FOX News, CNBC, and MSNBC from coast to coast.

Nick is a member of the Florida Bar, holds a JD from the University Of Florida Levin College Of Law, as well as a BSBA in Finance from the University of Florida's Warrington College of Business. Nick is a voting member of The National Academy of Recording Arts & Sciences (NARAS, Home to The GRAMMYs), a member of The National Academy of Television Arts & Sciences (Home to the Emmy Awards), co-founder of the National Academy of Best-Selling Authors, a 16-time Telly Award winner, and spends his spare time working with Young Life, Downtown Credo Orlando, Entrepreneurs International and rooting for the Florida Gators with his wife Kristina and their three children, Brock, Bowen and Addison.

Learn more at: www.NickNanton.com and
www.CelebrityBrandingAgency.com

About JW

JW Dicks, Esq., is America's foremost authority on using personal branding for business development. He has created some of the most successful brand and marketing campaigns for business and professional clients to make them the credible celebrity experts in their field and build multi-million dollar businesses using their recognized status.

JW Dicks has started, bought, built, and sold a large number of businesses over his 39-year career and developed a loyal international following as a business attorney, author, speaker, consultant, and business experts' coach. He not only practices what he preaches by using his strategies to build his own businesses, he also applies those same concepts to help clients grow their business or professional practice the ways he does.

JW has been extensively quoted in such national media as *USA Today,* the *Wall Street Journal, Newsweek, Inc.*, Forbes.com, CNBC.com, and *Fortune Small Business*. His television appearances include ABC, NBC, CBS and FOX affiliate stations around the country. He is the resident branding expert for *Fast Company*'s internationally syndicated blog and is the publisher of *Celebrity Expert Insider*, a monthly newsletter targeting business and brand-building strategies.

JW has written over 22 books, including numerous best-sellers, and has been inducted into the National Academy of Best-Selling Authors. JW is married to Linda, his wife of 42 years, and they have two daughters, two granddaughters and two Yorkies. JW is a 6th generation Floridian and splits his time between his home in Orlando and beach house on the Florida west coast.

CHAPTER 15

GETTING BACK IN THE GAME AFTER BEING SIDELINED BY LIFE — THREE POWERFUL PRINCIPLES TO HELP YOU OVERCOME LIFE'S SETBACKS

BY CRYSTAL TALLEY

Because of the positions I have held in business, people usually made the assumption that life was good for me and probably always had been somewhat of a proverbial bed of roses. But very honestly, life has thrown me many curves and I have come through some very dark times. However, I choose not to live in the past and I don't allow my past to dictate my future. While I have great empathy and compassion for everyone I encounter, the experiences I have encountered in life allow me to especially identify with others who struggle with similar situations and it enables me to help them in their own personal healing process.

If people knew my story they would likely say my life has been filled with tragedy. However, I would say my life has been filled with lessons on how to become a stronger and self-sufficient person. Without going into detail, I can tell you some of my past experiences have included being a victim of domestic violence, having my father murdered by my sister, losing a sister in a fire, my son being sexually assaulted, bankruptcy, foreclosure, living in a shelter, job loss, obesity, addictions and depression. I was also working at the Pentagon on September 11, 2001 when great devastation and destruction was brought upon that building and our country. I could list several other items here, but I think you get the picture. To say the least, life has not always been easy and there was a period of time when I lived with a great deal of bitterness and anger as a result of my experiences. However, I came to a point where I chose to confront that inner turmoil and allowed healing to be my path. I have been sidelined many times by life's circumstances, but I have always managed to get back in the game.

While an entire book could be written on this subject, I would like to share with you a few basic principles that you will need to get back in the game if you have been sidelined by life in any form or fashion. These principles are essential to your successful re-entrance into the game.

Forgiveness is a gift you give yourself.
~ Tony Robbins

FORGIVENESS

Forgiveness can be defined as exercising your ability to stop feelings of anger and retaliation toward someone who has inflicted upon you a wrong or an injustice. That is not to say you accept their hurtful actions or behaviors, but you have to be able to forgive them in order for your own healing to begin. Someone once said, "Forgiveness doesn't excuse their behavior. Forgiveness prevents their behavior from destroying your heart." It's not an easy decision by any means, but it is a necessary decision if you are going to move away from the pain you have experienced.

I have found that trying to better understand the person that hurt me gave me the ability to look at them with compassion rather than anger and revenge. I came to realize that everyone that hurt me had themselves been hurt at some point in their life. Unfortunately, people that are hurting will often hurt others in response to their own pain.

Forgiveness is a process that will take time, contemplation and introspection. I found that I had to begin by first forgiving myself. After being hit hard by many issues in life, I was somehow convinced that I allowed these horrible things to take place or was responsible for them in some way. I had to bring myself to understand that I was not responsible and that the pain inflicted on me was not by my choice. It was the choice of another person that was obviously struggling with a great deal of their own personal hurt and pain. This required me to change my thought process.

I lived through a horrific domestic violence situation and suffered the usual consequences. Often the abuser will constantly tell you that you are dumb, stupid, ugly, weak, etc. The victim gets to a point where they actually believe that about themselves. In my situation, I had to take myself through an entire thought transformation process in order to believe that I was not what someone else said I am. I learned that I must believe I am what I believe I am and not what someone else says I am.

Victims of domestic violence or some form of demeaning rhetoric often don't understand why they feel so negatively about themselves. In my situation, I became aware of my own negative feelings as I reached out to and became closer to God. You have to find something higher than yourself in which to believe. I also began to read and study extensively the subject of inner healing. I eventually became a New Life Story Coach and found the education I received through this program has helped me immensely on a personal basis. My personal experiences combined with my education have also enabled me to help others in their inner healing journey.

In fact, a major part of my personal healing has been related to my efforts in helping others through their own personal healing. The more I help others, the more I am helped along my own path of forgiveness and healing. Now, helping others become more whole in their life has become my life's passion. One of the many things I do is teach anger management and healing to men who have been court-ordered as a result of their role in a domestic violence situation, and I have discovered that having compassion on individuals such as this is a precursor to forgiving others.

I have seen first-hand the tragedies of domestic violence. Not only as a victim, but also living through the death of my father who was stabbed numerous times by my sister before he would succumb to his injuries. I was a member of the National Guard at the time of my father's death. Since he was a veteran of World War II, I chose to honor him by standing for hours at attention beside his casket, in full dress uniform, without movement and without shedding a single tear. To this day I don't know how I did that other than the pure motivation to honor my father. However, I never allowed myself to grieve and I held those emotions inside for many years until I had to face them, along with many other issues, at another catastrophic time in my life. That's when I went through the journey of inner healing and was able to forgive not only myself, but others that had harmed me in the past.

I encourage you to take the following steps to begin your journey of forgiveness:

- Understand that you are capable of forgiving – When painful things happen to us it is easy to lose perspective and revert into the trap of non-forgiveness and resentment. Sometimes we even feel unable to forgive. However, forgiveness is a choice and you must first realize that you are capable of forgiving no matter the depth of your pain.

- Make a deliberate choice to forgive – After you have processed the fact that you are capable of forgiveness, the next step is to actually choose to forgive. You will never experience peace within yourself if you harbor unforgiveness. Your next step to healing is making this choice.

- Say the words, "I forgive you," out loud – Verbalizing these words will make them more real. Whether it is forgiving yourself or another person, actually saying these words will help you begin to actualize forgiveness.

- View the person who hurt you with compassion. Remember, hurt people will hurt people. The person who hurt you undoubtedly is dealing with unresolved hurt. Look at them through the eyes of compassion; it will change your perspective.

- View your choice to forgive as an act of self love – The only way for you to be truly free and at peace is if you give up resentment and forgive. Forgiving others is indeed an act of self love.

Don't forget to fall in love with yourself first.
~ Carrie Bradshaw

SELF-LOVE

Self-love is simply exercising the ability and giving yourself permission to love yourself in spite of any imperfections that may exist in your life. It is also about loving yourself regardless of what has happened to you, what place you're at in life, or what material possessions you may or may not have acquired.

Very honestly, there was a time that I hated myself. I began hating myself even more when my son was sexually abused. In my mind, I believed I wasn't a good parent or a good mother because I should have been able to prevent this horrible thing from happening to him. I so desperately wanted to take from him that insidious pain. I wanted to turn back the clock so I could be there to protect him. My spouse at the time would tell me I wasn't a good parent and that only served to magnify and solidify the hatred and self-loathing I had for myself. When people would look at me they would see a successful career woman who drove a nice car. They had no clue how I felt about myself. I found that I worked hard so I could over-provide for my children, and especially for my son who I felt I was not there for when he needed me the most.

I was forced to deal with all the emotions I had contained for years on end when I lost my job and then began losing the material possessions for which I worked so hard. Facing these issues head-on was actually the beginning of my inner healing process. It was then that I eventually began to acquire a self-love that I never before experienced. I discovered that every time a tragedy or negative in life happens, it becomes my choice as to how I will respond and move forward.

Self-love requires a transformation of how you think. This transformation of mind and thought is what transforms everything else in your life. Your mind is so powerful that whatever you think is what you become. If you think you're weak, then you're weak. If you think you're strong, then you're strong. I battled with my thoughts for a very long time and it took me a tremendous amount of time to overcome certain things. My mindset of thinking I'm weak, stupid and dumb kept me trapped for years. But when I began to transform my mind and thoughts I realized

I wasn't any of those things and that allowed me to move forward to experience greater confidence and accomplishments.

Here are a few suggestions to get you started toward self-love:

- Begin thinking positively about yourself – Don't fall prey to the lies someone has told you. Don't allow yourself to think you are stupid, no good or weak because someone told you that repeatedly. You are smart, you possess goodness and you are strong. Think of yourself in those terms and watch your life change.

- Begin to focus on your physical health and wellbeing – Take care of your body because it houses something very precious – YOU. Go for walks, run, or go to the gym. Get rid of the sugary foods and fast foods. Begin eating things that are nutritious. Good nutrition and exercise will literally cause a positive chemical reaction in your body and it will help you fall in love with yourself. Always be sure to seek your doctor's advice before entering into any type of exercise program.

- Make an investment in your emotional health – Read books that will help you grow emotionally, spiritually and psychologically. Surround yourself with people that are emotionally healthy. Attend seminars that will benefit you. You can't put a price on those kinds of resources and the benefit they will bring.

Gratitude is not only the greatest of virtues, but the parent of all others. ~ Marcus Tullius Cicero

GRATITUDE

It's actually very easy to become caught up in the struggles of everyday life. You may even find yourself in complaining mode most of the time. Maybe you complain about your job, spouse, kids, co-workers, boss, or the temperature in the room. Have you ever been around a chronic complainer? It seems there are some people who can't get through a minute of their day without complaining. Often others will do whatever they can to avoid complainers because of the negative energy that surrounds them. Needless to say, these individuals are in need of some serious inner healing. They are typically people who view almost every aspect of their life from a negative perspective. They will never be successful, fulfilled or happy because they are bound by negative energy.

On the other hand, people that are filled with gratitude surround themselves with a very positive energy that actually paves the way for inner healing to be activated. They are people that will be successful, fulfilled and happy in their lives. They are people that others will want to be around. They are people that will find something good in the most negative circumstances.

Becoming a person of gratitude, much like other catalysts of inner healing, begins with a choice. You must make a conscious decision to be grateful and then act upon your decision. There are some very practical things you can do to initiate and practice this activity in your life. Here are a few simple suggestions to get you started:

- Change your mindset – There is good happening around you. Train your mind to recognize it.

- Learn to appreciate the simple pleasures of life – Watch the majesty of the sunset with appreciation, gaze at blue skies with amazement, and laugh with friends with delight. There are countless things that you will find under the category of "simple pleasures."

- Do something for someone else – This takes the attention off of you and places it on another. It enables you to see the plight of others and gives you a greater appreciation for your own situation that may not seem as bad comparatively.

The game of life is a lot like football. You have to tackle your problems, block your fears and score your points when you get the opportunity.
~ Lewis Grizzard

Where are you in life? Are you in the game or have you been sidelined by life? It may be time for you to become introspective, to forgive, to practice self love, and to be grateful. You will be amazed at how these principles will change your life and fill you with positive energy. Don't wait. Make the decision now. It's time for you to get back in the game!

About Crystal

Crystal Talley, internationally sought-after speaker, author, change agent and life coach, is the founder and CEO of the Crystal Talley International. An alumnus of Strayer University, Crystal's college education was focused on Information Technology. She is Lean Six Sigma Green Belt Certified and has also received certifications in Change Management and Organizational Leadership. Additionally, Crystal has held numerous leadership roles with Fortune 500 companies as well as smaller corporations and is a veteran of the armed services.

For years while Crystal was excelling in corporate America, behind the scenes her personal life was full of tragedy including domestic violence, the tragic murder of her father, and a host of other issues that she was able to keep hidden from her professional career. Coming from a position of anger and bitterness, Crystal heroically grappled her way back to wholeness through a journey of personal inner healing. As a result of the exasperating challenges she has overcome and her never-give-up spirit, today she is an emotionally healthy person that is reaching out to others to help them discover the power of inner healing.

For the past ten years Crystal has been bringing her message of hope and healing to thousands of hurting people helping them achieve dramatic change and inner healing. She is a licensed and certified New Life Story Coach concentrating on success, relationships, wellness and life. Additionally, she is a Center for Non-Violence Communication (CNVC) Certification candidate.

Crystal teaches extensively on the subjects of Anger Management, Non-violent Communication, Creating Personal Change, and a host of other subjects. She also has an extensive practice coaching others on creating a new life story and has been a featured guest on the Robert Reames Live radio show aired internationally on Global Voice Broadcasting.

Her upcoming book, *When There Are No Answers*, is being anticipated by thousands and is due to be released in 2015. The book has already received an overwhelming number of endorsements from leading businesses and Non-profit Organizations such as Gold's Gym International, A CALL TO MEN, Men Can Stop Rape, Women of Color Network (WOCN), The Visual Eating and Exercise Program (VEEP), Pear SPORTS LLC, Max Muscle Nutrition Store, Big Voice Pictures, 1 in 6, Girls Educational and Mentoring Services (GEMS), Purple Rein Social Services, Share Time Wisely Consulting Services, SOUL Requirements, Change for Life Wellness and Aesthetics, EcoME, and Robert Reames, head trainer for the Dr. Phil Show and spokesperson for Gold's Gym International, VEEP and Pear SPORTS LLC.

Additional information about Crystal Talley and Crystal Talley International can be obtained by calling 703-459-8326 or visiting her website at: www.crystaltalley.com

CHAPTER 16

FOUR CRITICAL MARKETING MISTAKES THAT ARE DESTROYING YOUR PROFITS

BY GREG ROLLETT

I am going to warn you in advance: This isn't going to be easy…or pretty.

What follows is bound to serve as a wakeup call for business owners— especially if you spend your time waiting, hoping and praying for the phone to ring with new orders. That is no way to run a business. If no one is calling, stopping in, emailing you, or visiting your website, then it may be your fault that business is stagnant.

> "…But Greg, *my business* is different."

I hear this all the time. When I hear a version of, "…but my business is different," I counter with, "Does your business involve working with people?"

At the end of the day, someone has to sign off on a purchase order, hand over a credit card, or sign an authorization form. The fundamental fact is that if there's a person on the other end of that transaction, then your business isn't different.

You see, people buy people. More specifically, they buy from people they know, like, and trust.

So, while you are sitting at your desk today, waiting for the phone to ring, I'm going to outline the four biggest mistakes you are making with your marketing that is both costing money to leave your pockets and may be the root reason why nothing is coming back in.

Look, I want you to be booked from the minute that you get into the office until you leave. But, I only want your schedule to be full of qualified people who know you, like you and trust you—ultimately making them ready and willing to do business with you. And these four mistakes are holding you back from the goldmine of clients eagerly waiting to do business with you.

MISTAKE #1: YOU SEE YOURSELF AS A DOER AND NOT A MARKETER...

Your first mistake is failing to see the significance of marketing your business, thinking clients will just show up.

I bet you are not providing goods or services out of the kindness of your heart. Sure, we are in business to help people, but let's be real: We're in business to make profits and provide our family and ourselves with a better life.

If you're in business for any reason that involves your financial well-being, then you must see yourself as a marketer of the services that you provide. You must get your mind off the idea that you are in a particular business and accept that you are instead, a marketer of the services you provide.

If you own a dental practice, you are not in the dental business. You are in the business of marketing your dental services to your market. Let's say you are the best technical dentist in the world, yet your chair is always empty. Does it matter how good a dentist you are if you have no patients to help?

It's the same thing if you are a financial advisor or a real estate agent. You are really in the business of marketing financial services or real estate services.

When it comes to marketing, you should think in terms of marketing systems. Systems are what make things work with purpose rather than the result of happenstance. If you're waiting, hoping and praying for your phone to ring, or someone to walk through the door, you don't have a system in place. And the best type of marketing system is a trust-based marketing system – a system that continues to develop relationships with your market, engaging them and allowing them to know you, like you and trust you.

Without a trust-based marketing system, you can't have predictable income or revenue. You won't have a client list that is constantly being attracted to your business and is bankable every month. That's what a trust-based marketing system does. It greases the gears of your business.

But, let's not put the cart before the horse. Having a system is just part of the battle. Winning the war for your prospects' attention and money is impossible if you are "just another business."

MISTAKE #2: YOU AREN'T POSITIONING YOURSELF AS IMPORTANT TO YOUR MARKET...

Mistake number two is about stature. If your prospects just throw you into a category with everyone else "in the business of whatever you do", then you have no competitive advantage. When there is no competitive advantage, price becomes your only ammunition against the other guys.

If you are competing on price—you are losing the war, one eroding sale at a time.

Who wants to compete on price? There is always someone who "will do it" for less, whatever "it" is. It is a terrible way to do business. You don't want to be the $19.99 oil change shop and suddenly you've got to do an $18.99 oil change, because the guy next door reduced his price.

Price should not be the reason for customers to come to you. You need to have a reason for people to do business with you, and it's generally deeper than just the features and benefits of your products or services. .

It starts by creating perceived importance. Money flows to those perceived as important.

Quick: Why do celebrities, athletes, and entertainers make more money than most people? *Because we perceive them to have more importance and stature.*

Whether you're a sales professional, in private practice, or in any other business, you need to be more important than the competition in your marketplace.

"Greg, how can I be seen as important?"

It's actually rather simple. Start talking about and doing things that are important to your marketplace. Start with media. People that are seen in the media are important. A columnist for a major newspaper is perceived to be more important than the guy who is just blogging for fun on the weekends.

Start being seen around important people and at important events. And show off your importance in your own media. In your monthly print newsletters and in marketing promotions sent to your prospects and clients. If you never tell anyone you were on TV or on the radio or met someone perceived as important, how are they ever going to know and thus raise your importance in their eyes?

The bottom line: If you are doing what everyone else does, you'll get lumped in with everyone else. That is going to keep your phones silent, your balance sheet out of whack, and keep you broke.

MISTAKE #3: YOU DON'T UNDERSTAND WHO YOUR IS, AND INSTEAD YOU TRY TO BE "ALL THINGS TO ALL PEOPLE"...

Mistake number three is a fundamental flaw that plagues nearly every business owner at some point. If you don't actually understand who your market is, then you can't properly attract them to your business. When you do that, you fail.

People pay more for absolutes. Money flows to business owners who have absolute opinions of authority. Media personalities like Sean Hannity, Glenn Beck, Howard Stern, Dave Ramsey and Rush Limbaugh have very specific topics for which they have very specific opinions of authority. While many of their viewpoints can be controversial, their absolute opinions raise their celebrity—and their profits.

People won't pay top dollar for wishy-washy answers or flip-flopping.

If every time someone asked me a marketing question, I gave a general answer, I'd be out of business. Though often the correct answer is something like this:

"It depends and we should test it."

That's not what people pay me for. When someone calls in with a question I need to give them an absolute answer:

- "Make this offer."
- "This strategy will work for you."
- "Run with this headline."

Think about it, if you went to a financial adviser with $500,000 to start planning for retirement, wouldn't you want him to tell you exactly what to do? If he waffles on the clear path to your retirement success, why should you trust him with your money?

Would you feel secure if your doctor started second guessing his diagnosis? You sure wouldn't. This is why you need to form strong opinions of authority and solve specific problems for specific markets. People want specialists with specific skill sets.

I just had a new baby, so I'm consistently in need of something for the little one. If I need sage advice on products for my child, what are my options?

I could go to a generalist, like Wal-Mart. Wal-Mart serves everything to everyone. Odds are the guy stocking the shelves in the baby section is the same guy stocking the groceries or electronics. If I needed milk AND potting soil AND baby clothes, then maybe I'd seek them out.

Continuing with the baby analogy, specialty stores like Babies "R" Us, or Buy Buy Baby at least have some people trained to know about babies and baby products. It's a step in the right direction for a customer, but the odds are slim of finding an expert who can tailor a specific solution for your problem when the guy stocking the shelves is probably still slightly above minimum wage.

So, what's the "next level specialist?" Can I find the guy who hosts a TV show, or is the go-to source for the media when it comes to baby safety? Maybe he wrote a Best-Selling book on baby safety. I could hire the guy that's on TV talking about babies and baby safety, bring him into my specific home and scenario, and can he actually do the work for me.

If I find that guy, he is getting paid a whole heck of a lot more that the guy at Wal-Mart. In your business, that is what you want to be, but you have to be a specialist for a certain market. You can't be a generalist. In order to be seen as a specialist, you must create marketing that positions you that way, to a very specific and targeted market.

If you've fixed the first three mistakes, you are heading towards a business boom, but there is one final pratfall to avoid on the way to the big time!

MISTAKE #4: YOU'RE NOT MAKING ENOUGH OFFERS...

The fourth and final mistake sounds simple, but you'd be surprised at how many business owners are making this mistake. You're not selling enough.

"But Greg, I'm on the phone selling all day."

That's not what I mean. I mean you're not making enough offers to the marketplace to give you an opportunity to sell. Your income is directly proportional to the number of offers you send into your marketplace. So, if you're not out there presenting your services, sending out offers, and pre-converting prospects to clients, then there is no way that people can do business with you.

It isn't magic or witchcraft, nor does it occur by happenstance. It means spending money on media, advertising, and aggressively going out and marketing your business.

It doesn't mean sitting in your room in your underwear writing blog posts. It doesn't mean that you tweet or post to Pinterest. It means that you're out there making a direct solicitation to do business with someone by saying,

"Hey, you have this problem. I can solve it. Here's how I can help you."

If you're not making offers, you're going to continue to NOT make the money that you desire from your business. You're not going to have the profits and you're not going to have the lifestyle that you wanted when you got into business for yourself.

People aren't just going to show up consistently. This isn't Field of Dreams. They don't come just because you built it. They come because they responded to an offer.

Send something to your prospects right now, I'll wait. Tell them about a new product or service. Go to all your prospects that you haven't converted and ask them to do business with you by demonstrating your expertise. Send them an email: "Hey, you want to do some business?" It might sound crazy, but someone's going to say yes.

Ok, I'm aware of everything I'm doing wrong in my marketing, how can I fix it and start making more money?

It all starts by seeing yourself as a marketer and not just a dentist or a financial advisor or a real estate agent. Position yourself as a trusted resource and advisor who solves people's problems.

If your perceived importance is lacking, then work on building your clout in the market. Address a specific market, add value to their lives and then directly solicit them. When they read a piece of mail that comes from you, or see an ad in the newspaper or your website, make sure they know you are speaking directly to them. Get them to know you, like you and trust you.

For example, let's say you are a financial advisor who does dinner seminars. Instead of inviting people to come eat a free steak, which is the same thing everyone else in your niche does, create perceived importance by saying:

"Best-Selling Author reveals his eight keys to success based on his Best-Selling Book. He's also been seen in The Wall Street Journal, as well as ABC, NBC, CBS and Fox affiliates."

Do you see how this fundamentally changes your position from one of sameness to one of authority?

We're all in the business of marketing. We're all in the business of sales. It doesn't matter what you do or what products you sell. Your business is not different. It's very important for you to understand that, if nothing else here today.

Your ability to market your business is the driving factor behind how much money you take home. That money is being able to keep the lights on, pay your employees, and take that vacation. That money is being able to create the lifestyle that you wanted from your business.

Isn't is time you started acting like a marketer?

About Greg

Greg Rollett, @gregrollett, is a Best-Selling Author and Marketing Expert who works with experts, authors and entrepreneurs all over the world. He utilizes the power of new media, direct response and personality-driven marketing to attract more clients and to create more freedom in the businesses and lives of his clients.

After creating a successful string of his own educational products and businesses, Greg began helping others in the production and marketing of their own products and services. He now helps his clients through two distinct companies, Celebrity Expert Marketing and the ProductPros.

Greg has written for *Mashable, Fast Company, Inc.com, the Huffington Post*, AOL, AMEX's Open Forum and others, and continues to share his message helping experts and entrepreneurs grow their business through marketing.

Greg's client list includes Michael Gerber, Brian Tracy, Tom Hopkins, Coca-Cola, Miller Lite and Warner Brothers, along with thousands of entrepreneurs and small-business owners across the world. Greg's work has been featured on FOX News, ABC, NBC, CBS, CNN, *USA Today, Inc. Magazine, The Wall Street Journal*, the *Daily Buzz* and more.

Greg loves to challenge the current business environment that constrains people to working 12-hour days during the best portions of their lives. By teaching them to leverage marketing and the power of information, Greg loves to help others create freedom in their businesses that allow them to generate income, make the world a better place, and live a radically-ambitious lifestyle in the process.

A former touring musician, Greg is highly sought after as a speaker, who has spoken all over the world on the subjects of marketing and business building.

If you would like to learn more about Greg and how he can help your business, please contact him directly at: greg@dnagency.com or by calling his office at 877.897.4611.

CHAPTER 17

TRANSFORMATIONAL CHANGE IN WEALTH MANAGEMENT

BY JAMES EASTMAN

We all know that in almost every aspect of our lives, change is inevitable. While many people resist change with every fiber within their being, I have found change to be a catalyst for me. Having grown up in the small New England town of Fryeburg, Maine, tucked into the foothills of the White Mountains, I didn't really fit into the typical "hands-on equipment operating and fixing" environment of that region since I was more of a math and science-oriented person. My excellent education at Fryeburg Academy, one of the great New England prep schools, enabled me (with the assistance of certain Fryeburg Academy teachers) to be accepted into Bentley University, a private business school in Boston.

After several years working for Ernst & Young in New Haven, Connecticut and then Edwin Land, the brilliant co-founder of the Polaroid Corporation, I moved my family to Florida and became one of the first CPA's in the country to earn the Personal Financial Specialist designation. I then began using my experience and analytical skills as a "wealth advisor." It was during this time I had my first experience working with significant wealth by helping a family who had built a very successful business. Upon retirement, they sold the business for $500 Million. This became my first experience with the super-affluent and the private wealth firm known as a "Family Office."

Over the course of the next twenty years, I worked to develop this "Family Office" concept and became the Director of Family Wealth Management for the Citi/Smith Barney Family Office. In 2010, I left Wall Street to fulfill my vision of improving the way successful families manage their wealth. My goal was to use my extensive experience to develop a way to lower the barrier of entry for this exclusive form of wealth management, in order to serve a much broader market. Today you need $100 million to form your own family office. Membership into Regional Family Offices is available to those with $3 million in investment assets. Our intention is to provide the same experience of care for our members as those who have their own family office.

100% of your money is the same whether you have $100 or $3million.
~ James Eastman

THE FINANCIAL SERVICES CRISIS IN AMERICA

Every day there are news headlines dealing with economic issues in our country. Much attention is given to the ongoing problems ranging from the out of control national debt to malicious Ponzi schemes which prey upon the most vulnerable of investors at the hands of those who were thought to be trusted advisors.

It is pure fallacy to ever hope the federal regulators and financial institutions that created the crisis will ever bring resolutions to these atrocities. For nearly two decades, we have been ravaged by government bailouts of over-leveraged financial institutions, banking scandals, undetected Ponzi schemes and the current allegations of market manipulation of commodities and interest rates involving many of the major banks and investment houses.

These financial indignities are related to one overriding issue; our society has concentrated its wealth in a small handful of the largest investment banks and financial institutions, resulting in too much money in one place. Add to that the concentration of political power in Washington, DC and the interaction between the two; you have a recipe for economic disaster. Our country was warned of the enormous harm resulting from such a concentration of wealth and power as far back as James Madison.

However, there is another, less talked about, contributing factor to the financial crisis at hand. While it is not discussed extensively, it may be even more significant than the imprudent concentration of wealth and the equally imprudent lack of proper regulation. The larger issue may be that the wealth management industry is still operating under business models that have not changed in any significant way in over five decades. While the current system is extremely lucrative for the industry, it is carelessly costly for the investor.

Unfortunately, the financial industry has evolved to the point where the consumer has few people in government or in the industry that have an incentive to advocate for them and their interests. That is why a significant transformational shift must take place. We can hope the industry will change itself or we can hope the government will legislate changes, but hope is not a plan.

Never ask your barber if you need a haircut. ~ Warren Buffett

WHAT IS TRANSFORMATIONAL CHANGE?

The best way to explain transformational change may be to look at specific examples. Over the past 20 years, many industries have seen significant improvement by visionary individuals re-imagining the business model from the customer's point of view. Consider the following that will serve to illustrate this point.

The retail goods industry has evolved from the local grocer and department store to Wal-Mart and then to Amazon. This resulted in quality goods being made available to the customer at a significantly lower cost and through a substantially more convenient venue.

The movie industry has also transformed from the local theater to Blockbuster and ultimately to Netflix. Now you can watch what you want and when you want – at a price that is 80% less than going to the theater.

The travel industry has experienced a metamorphosis from direct sales by airlines and hotels to travel agents and eventually to services such as Travelocity and Priceline. It's easy, simple, quick and less expensive.

These transformational changes resulted in convenience, simplicity, higher quality and significantly lower costs for the consumer. These industries became consumer-centric to become competitive in their marketplace.

Interestingly, the wealth management industry has undergone no such transformation. Perhaps this is because the interests of the largest firms are being well served by the current system with inferior quality and high prices driven largely by high sales and marketing costs. Incredibly, the consumer is by and large oblivious to the unnecessary expenses they incur while trying to build their wealth. If today's investor was aware of these costs, the industry may be forced to transform itself. However, because the industry makes their products and fee structures confusing and complicated, the investor must depend on the advice of an advisor. Warren Buffett once said, "Never ask your barber if you need a haircut." I agree! Do not ask a salesperson if you need what he is selling. His answer will inevitably be, "Yes!"

THE NATURE OF CHANGE

A number of years ago I did a presentation on the nature of change. In my discourse I concluded that "change happens slowly, then all at once." Remember the transformational changes that happened with the retail, movie, and travel industry? Well, those industries were in existence for over 100 years, but the most significant changes happened only over the past 15 years. These changes were due to the momentous improvements in technology, telecommunications and the use of new and improved business models that were consumer-centric. It is worth noting that all these changes were initiated by outsiders and resulted in improved quality, lower costs and a better consumer experience.

Transformational change requires a different method of thought and analysis. Consider Steve Jobs for example. He is best known as the founder of Apple. However, in his career, he changed not only personal computing, but also the music industry, the movie industry and mobile communications in the process. Steve is a great example of someone who thought differently and enabled change that benefited consumers in a broad array of industries. He didn't just understand technology, but he also comprehended what would become necessary in technology, design and business models to launch products and services to make them truly compelling to potential customers.

Transformational change requires a different way of thinking; a departure from the norm. Most reason by analogy. That is, they copy what others have done with slight variations. That may result in a gradual evolution of an industry, but it won't result in real change. Reasoning by analogy limits your imagination to what you already know. While real change, transformational change, requires us to conduct a different form of thinking and analysis. I call this First Principles Reasoning.

The traditional wealth management model lacks integration, collaboration and most importantly, transparency and clarity.
~ James Eastman

WEALTH MANAGEMENT AND FIRST PRINCIPLES REASONING

Wealth management is a serious and complex process involving multiple professionals, working in industries with different rules and regulations. Today the wealth management process is complex and costly. It lacks integration, collaboration and most importantly transparency and clarity. Perhaps the complexity of the industry is the very reason for its stagnation. Or, it is possible transformation has not taken place because of the immense size of the industry and its resulting profitability and ability to influence rules and regulations.

While improvements in technology have advanced the internal business processes resulting in greater productivity, it has not made any real changes to the traditional business model. So far, technology has only benefited the wealth management firms and not the consumer.

In the transformational change described above in the retail, movie and travel industries, the change happened via First Principles Reasoning. That is, someone began to examine the industry from a consumer perspective and determined how the business could better serve the customer and adapted accordingly. Using this principle, let's review the wealth management business from the consumer point of view using the First Principles perspective. In my experience I have found there are seven (7) principles consumers are seeking that are timeless and priceless:

1. <u>Integrity and Trust</u>. Integrity and trust must be earned. The financial industry today has too many conflicts of interests. The consumer must see their financial advisory team as people they can trust and who will always act with the utmost integrity.

2. <u>Independence and Objectivity</u>. For consumers to obtain advice they can trust, they must obtain it from professionals who give independent and objective advice, not a sales pitch.

3. <u>Integrated and Collaborative Teams</u>. Successful families know that, due to the complexity of our financial system, they are better served by a team of advisors from multiple disciplines who are leading local professionals including independent financial planners, CPA's and attorneys.

4. <u>Proper Due Diligence</u>. Successful families wish to access the finest advisors and products available to provide a level of assurance that their family goals are met. These advisors and products should have already gone through a professional due diligence process and they should be reviewed on a regular basis.

5. <u>Lower Cost Structure</u>. The cost to properly manage significant wealth today is staggering. Independent estimates generally place the total cost of investment management alone at 2 to 3 percent per year. That is $20,000 to $30,000 per million per year. This is a silent destroyer of wealth for investors and they desire a more cost effective approach to this process.

6. <u>Simplified Delivery System</u>. Successful families want simplicity and convenience. The advisor team should work in a collaborative manner to implement plans in a seamless manner while being reviewed on a regular basis to assure the family goals are being met.

7. <u>Flexibility.</u> We live in an ever-changing world where the only constant is change. Successful families need their team of advisors to be able to adjust to their unique needs and circumstances.

THE FAMILY OFFICE SOLUTION

A model that already possesses most of the above mentioned attributes has actually existed for decades; the family office. A family office is a private wealth firm that has served the needs of the nation's wealthiest families since the early 1900's. It has been the private wealth firm of choice because it is the business enterprise whose interests are most closely aligned with the goals and needs of the family.

The major obstacle for widespread use of this model has always been the high cost. A single family office costs $1 Million to $1.5 Million per year to operate, making it affordable only to families with investment assets in excess of $100 Million.

Another very important component to the family office is the preservation of wealth for future generations. It is estimated that only 8% of wealthy families are successful at maintaining wealth beyond the third generation. While families assume they are protecting their wealth with some planning, industry statistics prove otherwise. The creation of appropriate legal entities such as trusts is only the first step. Unfortunately, families often fail to put in place processes and procedures to guide future generations in the prudent management of wealth. The family office model can guide families through this complicated procedure to assure the continuation of their wealth.

This presents an opportunity. Imagine a new, unique and affordable family office business model using the latest in technology and telecommunications as well as the best business practices in wealth management.

There is nothing more powerful than an idea whose time has come.
~ Victor Hugo

TRANSFORMATIONAL THINKING MEETS THE FAMILY OFFICE

My firm, Regional Family Offices (RFO), is the nation's first member's only family office and is dedicated to the process of thinking like a client and establishing our business model accordingly. *Over the past ten years we have invested significant financial and intellectual resources to develop a service model so transformational that we use a new term to describe it; Wealth Care. The Wealth Care process brings all the essential resources required to professionally manage significant wealth across multiple generations through a single office, thus simplifying family wealth management.*

The RFO business paradigm is modeled after the successful family offices of the past, however, with one important difference. Instead of employing a staff of wealth management professionals that results in high payroll, exorbitant rent costs and a lack of flexibility, we created a membership model where we enroll a broad diverse team of local, professional advisors and world class financial product providers in the RFO Wealth Care Network thereby making the model available to a much wider market.

Traditionally, the professionals involved in a family's wealth management have been fragmented and splintered. In the Wealth Care Network model we eliminate the fragmentation and replace it with collaboration. This business model cohesively unites financial planning, tax and accounting, legal and estate planning, investment management, trust services, and insurance/risk management. While all of these services are necessary, they have never before been integrated into a comprehensive wealth management delivery system until now.

The time for wealth management transformation has arrived. The RFO business model is the transformation needed. By making the Family Office available to more people through a membership-based service, we are returning to this business the necessary values of integrity, honesty and accountability as well as helping our clients achieve their goals of wealth continuation for many generations to come.

*The goal of Regional Family Offices is to **"minimize the amount of time and money spent on family wealth management"***
~James Eastman

About James

James C. Eastman is the Founder and Managing Director of Regional Family Offices.

Mr. Eastman has over 35 years of experience as a Certified Public Accountant and was one of the first CPAs in the country to be recognized by the American Institute of CPAs as a Personal Financial Specialist. His biography was listed in the 1996 edition of Who's Who in Finance and Industry.

Mr. Eastman is a long-time member of the AICPA, the Professional Financial Planning Division and the FICPA. He previously served as an officer and director of the Estate Planning Council of Naples.

In 2012, James was nominated by *Gulfshore Life* magazine as one of the Top Financial Advisors in Southwest Florida for a third year. In 2014, Mr. Eastman was nominated for the Ernst & Young Entrepreneur of the Year Award for innovations developed by his firm, Regional Family Offices. Mr. Eastman currently serves on the Board of Trustees of the American Bible Society and is a member of its Investment Committee.

Prior to founding Regional Family Offices, Mr. Eastman was the Director of Family Wealth Management for the Citi/Smith Barney Family Office in Naples, Florida.

Mr. Eastman has been serving the wealth management needs of affluent families in the Naples area since 1987.

CHAPTER 18

HOW MARKETERS WILL SAVE THE PLANET

BY JOSEPH RANSETH

I believe that marketers will save the planet. I'm not a fatalist, but I think the world needs change—desperately. Economic disparity, social injustice, and environmental crisis are pervasive. As much as we'd like to pretend they don't affect our daily reality, they do. We all know something needs to be done, so why does it seem that society as a whole is so apathetic to these and other pressing issues? Far more importantly, what can we do to change it?

History gives us some clues.

Those who have dramatically altered the course of history for the better—Gandhi, Martin Luther King, Mother Theresa, Jesus, etc.—have all been master marketers. We may not traditionally think to apply that label to them, and they may not have self-identified as marketers, but they were among the best marketers the world has known. Let me explain.

Let's start with the definition of marketing. While many people only see marketing as promoting something to sell more of it, I see it as the management process of moving something from concept to consumer.

Marketing: the management process of moving something from concept to consumer.

Those historical figures mentioned above were marketers. They moved ideas, from concept to consumer, to achieve great outcomes. There are some distinctions that I'll touch on later, but, for now, let's explore how avatars throughout history mirror modern marketing professionals.

MARKETERS KNOW HOW PEOPLE MAKE DECISIONS

While some marketers focus on the tactics and mechanics of marketing, all truly good marketers know how the human brain works. We invest hours and resources into understanding the decision-making process as a whole. We know, as many do, that people make decisions based on emotion and justify those decisions with logic. So, we study specific emotional triggers that will lead people to take the desired action—which usually involves buying our product—and then we craftily present logic to appeal to the rational brain to mitigate buyer's remorse. We read research papers that detail the heuristic models of the brain to identify the path of least resistance to engineer a desired outcome. We know what words to write, colors to use, and sounds to employ to create the necessary emotional and physiological states in potential customers to get people to do exactly what we want.

This knowledge is a super power of sorts. To borrow the wisdom of Uncle Ben in Spiderman: "With great power comes great responsibility." It's critical that we yield these marketing super powers responsibly. Comparing modern marketing strategies with those of master marketers throughout time, it's clear that we are selling ourselves short.

In essence, we need to use our super powers for good, not evil.

How can we tap into the same knowledge base and skillset as those who have shaped history for the better, and still find ourselves pushing products to people who don't really need them? The answer to this question is the very heart of purpose-driven marketing.

WHAT IS PURPOSE-DRIVEN MARKETING?

One of my earliest mentors was Stephen Covey, author of *7 Habits of Highly-Effective People* and other seminal texts. Prior to meeting Dr. Covey, I had been working in Internet marketing for several years and had created relative success. However, he taught me something that shifted my paradigm completely. He said, "Joseph, if you want to be successful, learn to integrate the spiritual with the secular." I didn't fully comprehend it at the time, but I came to understand that he was talking about a deeper, more profound level of success than the typical metrics known to marketers—something beyond conversion rates, ROI, and profit. To be spiritual, he taught me, is to see—and be driven by—something that transcends us as individuals. It's about seeing something bigger than ourselves.

What he taught me mirrors what we learn in the familiar parable of the three stonecutters.

On his journey, an old traveler came upon a stone quarry where three stonecutters were working. He asked the first, "What are you doing?" Without even looking up, the weary laborer replied: "I am cutting stone, and I am getting callouses on my hands." To the second, he asked the same question, "What are you doing?" The second man stopped, looked the traveler in the eye and said, "I am earning an honest day's wage so that I can support my family, whom I love." To the third, he asked the same question, "What are you doing?" and the third man responded by lifting his gaze high toward the heavens and saying jubilantly, "I am building a cathedral to glorify the Most High."

We can do the same things but get different results when we're driven by different reasons.

What they were doing—cutting stones—was the same, but why they were doing it was vastly different. One motive was menial, one was noble, and the third was spiritual. The third man was working for a cause far bigger than he, or any one person, could complete on their own.

Purpose matters greatly to what we're doing as marketers.

HOW ARE MODERN MARKETERS
DIFFERENT FROM GANDHI?

So we know how they're the same, but let's explore how modern marketers are different, using a practical example. To understand how modern marketers differ from the historical greats, we should explore a third category: therapists. Psychologists also understand how people make decisions. They know what drives us to do the things we do.

However, they use that knowledge differently that most marketers do. For example, consider the drama cycle.

THE DRAMA CYCLE

This simple diagram explains the root of all drama we experience in our lives. The narrative is that of the standard fairy tale: the damsel in distress (victim) is captured by the evil dragon (villain) and is helpless until the knight in shining armor (hero) rescues her. Now, one may contest that this specific narrative is sexist, but the actual roles transcend gender—we all experience them on a regular basis.

Anytime we feel a problem is out of our control, we slide ourselves into the victim role. Whoever or whatever is causing the problem is the villain, and whatever is our imagined solution (winning the lottery, finding a better mate, etc.) sits in the hero role. We see it in dating: "Oh, my ex-boyfriend was such a lazy jerk. If only I could find someone who was motivated." We see it in politics: "Candidate X is the one who caused all the problems you're facing. Vote for me and I'll fix everything." It's not surprising that the drama cycle dominates modern advertising: "If you're using one of those 'other brands,' you aren't getting the quality/price/service that you deserve. Switch to our brand!"

The thing to note is that these are only roles. They are completely fictitious; they exist only in the mind. When we eliminate drama, we reclaim our own power and look at 'problems' objectively, free from disempowering, blaming roles.

Both marketers and psychologists know the drama cycle well. The difference is that whereas therapists would seek to remove people from this triangle, marketers would drive them deeper into drama. While therapists seek to liberate people from the negative effects of their emotions, marketers would enslave people to their emotions. This has got to stop.

TRANSACTIONS VS. TRANSFORMATION

The same knowledge can be used in different ways. Just as the difference between marketers and therapists is only a minor distinction (in theory), so the difference between marketers and the world leaders who've left a positive mark on the planet is also a minor distinction.

Like marketers, they also understood human behaviour, but like therapists, their purpose—what drove the use of that knowledge—was different. While marketers use the knowledge of how people make decisions to engineer transactions, true leaders use it to engineer *transformation*. They both change behaviour, but they do it quite differently.

You can change human behaviour in two ways: addressing disciplines or addressing disposition. You can change someone's behaviour from the outside by motivating them through external pressures—like sales that trigger scarcity reactions, fear, etc. to create a transaction. Or, as George Sheehan so succinctly pointed out, "What changes our values changes our behaviour." True leadership—true marketing—changes people from the inside out. It's transformational. When you change someone's behaviour, you have them for a moment, but when you change the way someone sees the world, you have them for a lifetime.

This concept is not just idealism. It's essential to improving sustainability in our marketing efforts and business practices as a whole. Far too often we sacrifice long-term goals (what we want most) for short-term profit (what we want in the moment). If we pursue money and profits at the expense of the more important things, or compromise our values or timeless principles, we've sold ourselves short, and sold ourselves out. Instead of taking the path of least resistance that we are accustomed to, we need to start embracing the path of greatest influence.

When keynoting at conferences, I often show a picture of Usain Bolt's world record sprint and I ask the crowd, "How far did he run?" People answer that he ran 100 meters, which, I point out, is actually incorrect. He, and the other racers, actually ran about 110–115 meters. However, we only measure the first 100 because only the finish line 'counts.' What we don't realize is that he didn't run merely *to* the finish line; he ran *through* it. You don't set a world record by hitting the most obvious metric (the finish line) and then stopping instantly. You have to set your sights further. You have to have a more sustainable vision. That's why racers run 115 meters.

Let's consider the finish line as a metaphor for profit. As marketers, we need to shift our paradigm to go beyond the finish line—chests lifted, looking beyond profit. We need financial gain for sustainability but if we stop there, we stumble. When our goal becomes maximizing profit, we focus on efficiency rather than effectiveness. We treat people like resources instead of like members of the team. We sacrifice ethics. We compromise on the environment. What is our social mandate? That's our 115 meters. Profit is our 100 meters. Profit should not be a goal; profit is a by-product of doing business properly.

3-STEP BLUEPRINT FOR CHANGING THE WORLD

If we are to have the same impact as those who have changed history, we would do well to follow their blueprint. Whether we're talking about Gandhi liberating a nation, Dr. King eliminating racial oppression, Mother Theresa fighting poverty, or Jesus creating a movement that would last 2000 years, we can see that they all had three things in common:

1. *A Big Idea.* We aren't just talking about innovation here. It isn't about a "eureka!" discovery, or a new product or service (although it may include those). What we're talking about here is the expression of something timeless and eternal. Something *spiritual.* What concept or principle would you be willing to live for? Or die for? Your *Big Idea* is a purpose or idea that transcends yourself—or any one person—as in individual. It's something we are committed to seeing accomplished . . . even if it doesn't happen in our lifetime. A *Big Idea* has the power to change people's behaviour because it transforms the way they see the world. It's something that people can buy into, that they can feel a part of, and that will unite them despite differences that may have otherwise kept them apart. Think of how Gandhi brought together both Hindus and Muslims in the idea of a united India.

2. *A Clear Message.* I teach PR & Marketing at the University of Winnipeg. In one of my discussions, I hold a picture of Dr. Martin Luther King delivering his famous speech at the Lincoln Memorial on August 28, 1963, and ask "What is his message?" The students respond unanimously with the words "I have a dream" and then paraphrase the part where he described children being judged by the content of their character and not by the color of their skin. Though we may not all know the words to his speech, we almost universally understand that his message was about equality and unity. He was able to articulate his Big Idea in way that that transcended the perceived barriers between people and united them for a larger cause. A clear message explains in very few words what could easily occupy a library. A clear message is communicated in a way that nearly all people can understand. It stirs emotion. It is said that a good teacher is able to understand those who don't easily explain themselves, and explain to those who don't easily understand. A Clear Message does the same.

3. *Evangelists.* To push a worthy message forward, you need an army of advocates for the cause. Dr. King didn't get 250,000 people to Lincoln Memorial on his own efforts. He had an entire host of people working on behalf of the cause. These are people that subscribe to our Big Idea, that understand the Clear Message, and have the passion to share it with others. With the evolution of the Internet and social media, we live in an unprecedented time to build our army of advocates. While many see social media as merely an opportunity to build an audience to consume the content we publish, transformational marketers tap into the viral effect by creating a message that people will share with their audiences as well.

In addition, savvy marketers also realize that not everyone needs to buy the product for our campaign to be successful. Short-term, profit-focused (100m) thinking will evaluate a marketing campaign based on whether a prospect who sees our message buys what we are selling. Purpose-driven marketing understands that even someone who doesn't buy our product can still be an advocate on our behalf if we give them content worth consuming and spreading.

When building your army of advocates, focus on finding people who will spread your message, not just buy your product. Smart marketers understand that if they get someone who will buy into the way of thinking your Big Idea espouses, they will be a future customer and a current advocate for you right now.

USING MARKETING TO PROMOTE UNITY

The world changers I've mentioned used these three tools to engineer large-scale transformation, but they also had one other thing in common: their words and actions all underscored the profound truth that *we are all one*. Despite our many differences, we need not be divided. Any line of thinking that results in an 'us vs. them' – racism, economic division, or an accusatory marketing campaign – is based in scarcity and lack. Our differences shouldn't drive us apart, they should be celebrated. Truth thinks in terms of "we" and "us." It unites us, rather than divides us.

The world doesn't need another unique selling proposition, it needs organizations and individuals that will step up as leaders and inspire the world to be a better place.

Change begins now, let's get in the game.

About Joseph

Meet Joseph Ranseth - Speaker, Author, Purpose-Driven Marketer.

Joseph Ranseth has been a pioneer in Internet marketing since 1999, specializing in high-impact Social Media campaigns since 2007. He has been featured for success in viral marketing by industry publications such as Advertising Age, on national television including Fox News, CBS, etc. He has also been recognized several times by the Huffington Post for using social media to inspire the world.

Joseph is the founder of Vine Multimedia, a digital marketing agency with a social purpose. Designed with social benefit in mind, Vine's business model allocates a significant amount of time to helping non-profit agencies and returns company profit back to the community either directly or through social awareness campaigns.

A popular speaker, Joseph has appeared on the TEDx stage and in numerous industry conferences, passionately sharing the principles of purpose-driven marketing and transformational leadership in the digital age. Drawing on the examples of those who have shaped history, Joseph invites all individuals and businesses to improve their communities along with their bottom line through socially-minded marketing practices.

Joseph also shares his expertise in teaching PR & Marketing at the University of Winnipeg, and is a frequent guest lecturer at other institutions. His ability to combine powerful principles with practical application resonates with the up-and-coming generation and has inspired many entrepreneurs and leaders, new and seasoned alike.

An active volunteer, Joseph believes that the best way to change the world is by starting locally. He sits on committees for several local charities, including the United Way of Winnipeg. He is on the board of directors for the National Autism Association in the U.S. and several local charities in Winnipeg. His favorite volunteer role, however, is that of Big Brother.

Living on a small farm just outside of Winnipeg in an almost off-grid home that has no television or Internet, Joseph enjoys spending time with his wife Tricia and their beautiful daughter, Winter.

For more information on Vine Multimedia –
Visit: vinemultimedia.com
Or to book Joseph to speak visit: JosephRanseth.com.

CHAPTER 19

CREATING YOUR REALITY

BY DR. KERRY WHITE BROWN

Where there is no vision, the people perish.
~ Proverbs 29:18, KJV, Holy Bible

It has often been said by countless coaches, philosophers, leaders and teachers that if you want to accomplish anything in life, you first have to possess the vision, or some describe it as the imagination. In *Think and Grow Rich*, Napoleon Hill discusses the importance of the imagination (the vision). Hill says, "Man's only limitation, within reason, lies in his development and use of his imagination." Consequently, this leads me to believe that we can have the life we want to live – by getting in the game of life by first having the vision of what kind of life we want to live. The famous Walt Disney makes it even more lucent by saying, "If you can dream it, you can do it."

I can remember growing up in a large family enjoying the love and support of my family, but not having the lifestyle that I desired for myself. I envisioned having much more than I was afforded as a child. Even at 9 years old, I dreamt of having a nice big house, a nice car and money in my bank account that I wouldn't have to be concerned about not having enough. I wanted to acquire things that I had only seen in passing, on television or what I read about in books. The crazy thing is that at that tender age, I had a desire to obtain those things in my lifetime. You see, I was forming my life's vision early on. You probably want to know what is this vision I'm speaking of and how do you make that a reality. All of this vision talk is merely about creating the life you want to live in your thoughts and imagination first, then creating that same vision in the physical realm.

All the forms that man fashions with his hands must first exist in his thoughts; he cannot shape a thing until he has thought that thing.
~ Wallace D. Wattles

You see, somehow, I managed to make my dreams come true. Everything that I dreamed of as a child has come to pass. The only "problem" is that my dream is constantly evolving. As I accomplish one dream, I dream bigger dreams.

After climbing a great hill, one only finds that there are many more hills to climb.
~ Nelson Mandela

The question still remains, how do you create the reality that you want? There are seven (7) basic steps in creating your dream life.

1. The very first step is simply deciding what it is you want your life to be like, look like and feel like. It is amazing how many people have not really sat down and sincerely thought about what they want out of life. It is therefore a must. If you want to accomplish a goal, you must first define the goal that you want.

2. Visualize your life as you would have it. Make sure you create all the details involved in your desired life. Where will you live, what will you drive, what are the colors involved, what type of business will you be in? Make certain that you put all the details in your vision.

3. Write down your desire. Everything that you just envisioned, write them down so that they really become engrained in your subconscious mind. Most people don't have a defined vision or goal for their life and even those that have thought of a goal, have not written it down. Brian Tracy goes on to say that people with clearly written goals accomplish much more in a shorter period of time than people without clear, written goals. According to Tracy, writing your goals down is so powerful that it increases your chance of success by 1000%.

4. Reviewing your goals help you on a daily basis. It's one thing to define a goal, visualize your goal, but your goal must be reviewed on a daily basis to make changes if and when necessary and most importantly, just to keep track of where you are in achieving your

goal. Reviewing your goals also help to keep you focused and not be sidetracked by what's going on around you. Reviewing your goal helps you to stay "in your bubble." If creating a vision board helps to keep you focused – then do that. Put pictures and/or drawings of everything you can imagine from your vision onto your vision board.

5. Take well thought out action to keep you moving in the direction of your goals. Some days will be harder than others to stay in your bubble, but every little step forward moves you closer to your goals. In the book, *Action! Nothing Happens Until Something Moves*, Robert Ringer discusses the need for people to be proactive in making things happen. All of the vision in the world without action is merely a pipe dream. Even the Bible talks about the consequence of non-action.

> " *...Faith without works is dead."*
> ~ James 2:26, KJV, Holy Bible.

> *Contrary to popular belief, you don't need to be*
> *motivated to act. If necessary, force yourself*
> *to take action and motivation will follow.*
> ~ Robert Ringer

6. Find someone in your field that is doing what you want to do. Or, find someone who is running the successful business that you one day want to run, or has the desired lifestyle that you want to live. Seek out those individuals and mimic what they do. You don't have to reinvent the wheel. Smart people emulate those that are doing what they want to do. Identify their successes and failures. Learn from them.

> *Formal education makes you a living;*
> *self-education makes you a fortune.*
> ~ Jim Rohn

7. Have faith that all the hard work that you put in will pay off one day. Success does not happen in an instant, but it occurs one day at a time. You must realize that the only limitation that exists is the one that you set for yourself. Vic Johnson discusses the number one secret that all World Class Achievers possess. When all things are practically the same between individuals, belief or faith is the one thing that accurately explains why one person becomes a millionaire while the other barely makes ends meet. This most important thing is the mere power of one's belief. Anton Chekhov, a Russian novelist,

stated, "Man is what he believes." Johnson goes further to say that it is through your beliefs that you inevitably create the world you live in.

Thinking back to when I was a little girl, I'm not sure why, but I believed that I could become a doctor one day and live the life that I had envisioned for myself. I had no one in my family that had ever accomplished such a lofty goal, however, I just knew I could. I guess as a child, my imagination was vast and I was not smart enough, or I was smart enough, to believe that I could achieve any goal that I set my mind to. I didn't allow my humble beginnings, my lack of financial support nor my limited world exposure to pose stumbling blocks for me. I knew that if I studied hard and dedicated my time to my education, that I could one day become a doctor and so I did.

> *The only real limitation on your abilities*
> *is the level of your desires. If you want it badly enough,*
> *there are no limits on what you can achieve.*
> ~ Brian Tracy

Napoleon Hill also spoke of a burning desire. If that burning desire is there, then limitations do not exist. When the burning desire is present, you are like the energizer bunny that simply keeps on going regardless of what obstacles are in the way. A burning desire causes you to figure out a way to go around the obstacle, go under it or simply forge forward and break through the obstacle. Thomas Jefferson once said: "When you reach the end of your rope, tie a knot in it and hang on."

Dan Kennedy spoke of attending his first seminar some 35 to 40 years ago and heard the speaker say, "You are exactly where you really want to be." Now, think long and hard about that profound statement. If we truly think about our goals and visions of our future, it simply sums up to our just really wanting "Control" of our own lives. We don't want to have to be told what to do, when to do it and for how long we should be doing it. We want to be able to chart our own course in this life. I personally wanted to be able to call the shots and determine when I went to the office and when I stayed at home, spend time with my loved ones, travel when and if I wanted to, and simply have the freedom to take as many courses and go to as many seminars as I wanted to. Therefore, if it is control that you want, then make up your mind to gain the control that you desire and not give it up by making excuses for why you can't achieve your goals in life. Acquire that "burning desire" that Napoleon Hill speaks of in *Think and Grow Rich*, to create that reality that you want. You can literally create the life of your dreams.

First, simply declare what it is that you truly want – barring all hurdles and perceived limitations or stumbling blocks. If there was something that you could achieve knowing that you would not fail, what would that thing be? So, create a vision as to what that new life would look like. What sights, sounds, colors, and smells would you experience? Make this vision as picturesque as you could possibly make it, so that when you are visualizing, you actually experience your new life before it is physically manifested. Write down these goals so that it becomes a part of your subconscious mind. Re-read these goals on a daily basis to engrain these thoughts into your subconscious. Your subconscious is designed to help you achieve those things that it thinks are truths to you. Once these goals have been established, go out and act on those goals. Daily action toward your goals gets you closer and closer to your desired outcome. Go out and act as if the thing that you desire has already materialized. Some calls this "Acting as if..." Emerson says, "Do the thing, and then you will have the power." You ultimately gain momentum and focus when you finally take action. Believe it or not, this is a simultaneous process, as suggested by Vic Johnson.

After you have taken action, then study and emulate someone that has already achieved the success or has the business that you want to realize. People that have achieved world-class status don't waste time reinventing the wheel. Oftentimes, we view these great achievers as innovators; however, they are in fact adept at studying previous successes and applying new angles or slight twists to old ideas. Always remember that success leaves clues.

Lastly, have the faith to believe that your ultimate desire will materialize as long as your focus remains on the goal. Napoleon Hill says that, "Faith is the starting point of all accumulation of riches!"

All in all, it is possible to manifest your dreams. Great Achievers have achieved more than most because of how they set goals and went about achieving those goals or desires. Achieving big goals require you to dream big and subsequently become a bigger person. You must stretch beyond what is natural to you. Legendary coach Lou Holtz once said, "if you are bored with life, if you don't get up every morning with a burning desire to do things—you don't have enough goals." I love the way Vic Johnson sums up this entire thought pattern. He says that you must first know what it is that you truly want, and you must have a burning desire to command it, as dreams are the origin of your realities.

Are you pleased with your present place in the world?
If your answer is yes, what's your next port of call?
If your answer is no, what are you going to do about it?
~ Earl Nightingale

About Kerry

Dr. Kerry White Brown is a practicing orthodontist in Columbia, South Carolina. Dr. White Brown has always had a passion for art and the healthcare field. In her mind, orthodontics was the perfect profession for her to marry her two interests and help create *Sensational Smiles* that would last her patients a lifetime. She takes great care in providing the best possible patient experience in her office on a daily basis for all patients as they go through the journey of obtaining their one and only Sensational Smile.

Dr. White Brown returned to Columbia in 1998 to practice orthodontics after an academic career that reflects intense discipline and outstanding achievement. She received her undergraduate degree from Benedict College in 1991. After leaving Benedict, she entered Howard University College of Dentistry where she graduated with honors and was elected into the prestigious Omicron Kappa Upsilon National Dental Society. In 1997, White Brown received her specialty degree in orthodontics from the Howard University College of Dentistry.

Dr. White Brown is an orthodontist who takes pride in providing optimal care for her patients. She is extremely elated to be able to extend treatment to those patients who, under normal circumstances, would not be able to afford orthodontic treatment through her affiliation with the non-profit organization called "Smiles Change Lives" (an organization that identifies eligible individuals to receive orthodontic treatment). Dr. White Brown has agreed to provide free orthodontic care yearly to one child at each of her five offices located in Columbia, Florence, Orangeburg and Charleston. Lately, the number of patients receiving treatment has increased in her office due to the organization's backlog of patients waiting for treatment.

Dr. White Brown is presently a member of the American Association of Orthodontists, Southern Association of Orthodontists, American Dental Association, National Dental Association, the South Carolina Dental Association, National Association of Professional Women and the Alpha Kappa Alpha Sorority, Inc.

You can connect with Dr. White Brown at:
kerrywb@whitebrownsmiles.com
www.facebook.com/OrthodonticSpecialistsofCarolinaPC
www.linkedin.com/KerryWhite-Brown

CHAPTER 20

GUARANTEED SERVICE™ – THE KEY TO MAKING LIFETIME CUSTOMERS

BY MICHELE TROST-HALL

Real estate is one of those businesses in which the competition is high and at times cutthroat. You have to step up your game and find ways to not only bring buyers and sellers on board for the short term, but to make them lifetime customers.

We have found that what sets companies apart from their competition is customer service. In fact, we call it Guaranteed Service™, because we treat all of our customers like family, and this is not just a slogan or an empty promise. We host events throughout the year for our customers and their families. We don't just sell a house, shake a hand, and collect our commission. We found that when you commit your time and resources to making your past, present and future customers happy, they will not only look to you when they are ready to buy or sell their home in the future, they will tell everyone they know what your company stands for and encourage them to partner with you for their real estate needs as well.

EVENTS

A great way to open the doors to your company to the public is to schedule events. You invite your customers and sometimes they will bring along a friend or family member. This does three things, first it shows you care about your customer and that you are committed to them even after the sale, second it allows potential customers to meet you and ask questions, and third, your company is seen as giving back to the community.

This third reason is very important, because it sets your company apart in that you are committed to giving back and people like this idea. It makes you seem more approachable, transparent, authentic, and altruistic. All of these attributes will make people notice your company, no matter what you are selling.

Here are some of the events we offer every year:

Movie Day: Our Movie Day includes complimentary movie tickets, free popcorn, and a beverage of your choice. This event is always hosted in the Spring where we rent out the entire movie theater and we invite all of our clients (past, present, and future) to join us.

Parade Day BBQ: Every July our town hosts the Annual Fair & Rodeo Kick-Off Parade. After the parade, we invite all of our clients to join us on our back patio at our office where we provide delicious BBQ and give away prizes. We raffle off the prizes, which have included a $500 Visa gift card, a trip to Las Vegas, children's bikes and a Kindle Fire.

Pumpkin Pie Day: We will be inviting all of our clients to come to our office and pick up a free pumpkin pie for Thanksgiving.

Kid's Club: In our kid's club, the children of our clients enjoy a free meal at Pizza Ranch™ on their birthdays, along with a free Dr. Seuss banana split from JC Burgers™ and a free 6" tile from Pottery by You™. They will also be eligible to receive discounts at area roller rinks, photography studios, restaurants and a Martial Arts Academy.

In the past, we have invited our clients to visit Santa at our office while enjoying hot cocoa and cookies. In addition, we have invited them to a pumpkin patch where they can pick out a pumpkin free.

We are always looking for new events we can do and make our offerings even greater. You might think these are expensive, and while there is a cost, we are able to get bulk discounts, and to us, it is a large part of our marketing budget. We find these dollars generate more leads because they are directed toward our target market.

SPECIAL PROGRAMS

People love the idea of getting something extra, and they especially love getting it free. This is why we have added value packages to our normal real estate services. We researched what the competition was offering, and we decided we could do better. We offer services and special programs no one can touch in our market.

Some of the items cost us very little to nothing to implement, and while other items have a slight price tag attached, we have found these extras draw in business better than any advertisement in a newspaper. When people hear about our Guaranteed Service™, Seller's Advantage™ and Buyer's Advantage™ program, they become very excited.

BEFORE YOU BUY/SELL PROGRAMS

We know that living in a digital age people do a lot of their shopping and decision making online before they ever talk to a live person. We also know that it is one-on-one contact that makes a sale happen, and so we have combined these ideas in our website.

We offer potential buyers and sellers all types of services and resources before they even talk to us, but in order for them to access these services, they must fill out a simple contact form. When we receive the form, we wait a bit to allow the potential client time to browse through the hundreds of items they now have to explore and read. We do a follow-up phone call to see if they have any questions. We are not doing the hard sell, we are just there to help them – that is the Guaranteed Service™.

Here are some of the offerings we have on our site, and we offer hundreds more:

- Professional access to tools normally only real estate agents have access to.
- Resources containing ways to save money, buying, selling, and building.
- Ideas for how a buyer can make an offer that a seller will not turn down.
- Ways to use the Internet to search for homes and how to avoid pitfalls.

- Tips on how to get the right mortgage for your budget.

- Ways you can make your home more sellable without paying a fortune.

- Resources on how to buy a Foreclosure home.

- Local school details and federal reports.

- Crime rates in the areas you are looking at buying.

- A step-by-step guide to purchasing a home with the best offer for you.

- Over 20 financial calculators that are easy to use.

- Email Alerts of new listings.

Having all of these resources on our website demonstrates we are committed to helping our clients in a way they can find answers to common and even hard-to-answer questions online 24/7.

These resources make us the experts in real estate, and this puts our potential clients at ease. We know what we are talking about, and we are showing both buyers and sellers how to save money and make money.

DURING THE SALE

We let our clients know about all of the exciting offerings our company offers to everyone that walks in the door. These are special offers in addition to all of the events and resources I have already mentioned.

Buying and selling a home can be a very stressful and emotional process, and people want to feel that their agent is working for them and trying to give them every perk and advantage. Here are some of our offerings that lessen the financial burden as well as the stress that the buyer or seller may be experiencing. If people have a negative experience, you will lose not only that sale, but also any further business from that person, their family, and every person they know or have reach to. In this digital age, those can mean hundreds or thousands of lost leads. One bad customer could tank your business, so make them feel special and appreciated.

This is what we offer all of our clients to show our appreciation:

Home Warranty Program – Many lenders will require a home warranty, and we work hard to get the seller to pay for this mandatory warranty, but if we cannot then we will pick up the cost of providing one for you.

On Staff Mortgage Consultant – Instead of sending you all over town looking for a mortgage with no idea what to expect, we provide a mortgage specialist to meet all our client's needs and to answer all of their questions. It can be a tricky and scary process, and so it is relief to have someone to talk to right in our office. We work hard to get our clients the right mortgage.

Certified Home Buyer and Seller Advisors – it is not enough that our agents just have their license; we make sure they have earned certificates from the National Association of Expert Advisors (NAEA). Being nationally certified eases the clients doubts, because out team has 70+ years of combined negotiation experience, which means the client will get the best terms, conditions and price for their new home.

- **Sell it For Free** - We go the extra mile on this one and really put our money where our mouth is. If our client is not happy with their new home, for whatever reason, we will list their house free for up to 12 months.

- **Extra Keys** - It can be aggravating to move into a new home, walk into the kitchen, and see one key on the counter. You have a number of people in your family that need a key. We help with a vendor coupon for an extra set of keys. One more stress eliminated.

- **Moving Van** - Imagine you have bought the house, and the closing went a bit faster than you expected. When does that happen right? So, you are frantically looking for a moving van, and you begin to get quotes that rival your closing costs. We have a van for that. You can use our own in-house moving van free. You can check that off the list.

- **Spanish** - We have a staff member that speaks Spanish. You have no idea how that has broadened our market and put people's minds at ease when approaching us. We want to serve all markets possible, so having a multi-cultural team only makes sense.

- **We will Buy Your Home** - If we list a client's home and it does not sell within a specified amount of time, we will buy it. We are confident in the market, and we know families do not want to wait forever for their home to sell, because they may have already bought a new home. Taking the burden and worry away, makes for very, very happy customers. We know how to sell homes, so we know we will be able to sell the home quickly.

It is so important that the buyers find their perfect dream home. Sometimes that means building a home and so we provide exclusive access to new construction in six different neighborhoods and we have good relations with local builders and contractors. We do all the heavy lifting for our clients and are with them every step of the way with our Guaranteed Service™. You cannot go wrong providing a client with extra layers of confidence and value in what you offer.

In addition, we have a Home-Hunter service that provides backstage access to MLS listings and really great deals including foreclosures. Allowing the client to sit with us and review MLS listings allows them to find homes that may not have even been shown by an agent yet. They get a jump on finding the perfect home. There is nothing more frustrating than inquiring about a home that is already sold.

AFTER THE SALE

Our Guaranteed Service™ only begins with the sale because we offer all types of services and incentives afterward. I have already mentioned the kids club and the special events. We also offer the Raving Fan Club membership. This is a card that provides a client access to special discounts and services from local businesses such items for the paint, carpet, cleaning services, restaurant discounts, haircuts, hardware, home décor and many more.

We want our offices to be a community hub. We want people to come by and see us, because we know this keeps our name on the tip of their tongue whenever someone talks about real estate or who is a community leader. In this spirit, we offer the use of our office copier, fax, notary, conference room, and many other services.

Building trust and rapport with a client is worth gold in the bank, because not only will they come back to you in the future, they become your greatest marketing asset and can bring in more solid leads than any other marketing strategy you can deploy.

CHAPTER 21

RISK IT!

BY RACHEL PAPPY

"I didn't know what I was going to do." Big teardrops streamed down her soft, supple face. Years of heartache were etched deeply into her skin, betraying a lifetime of pain.

Mariamma was a woman who had faced grit with a spark in her eyes and never let on to the pain, sacrifice, tears and heartache she had endured.

Even from a young age, she was a humble and obedient child. Her home was located in a tropical paradise full of beaches and farming at the Southern tip of India, but she wanted to escape. In her teens she persuaded her strict father to allow her to travel to the Northern half of the country to study nursing. But nursing was not a profession that her father considered acceptable. He wanted her to become a respectable teacher like him. Mariamma would be the first of her siblings to pursue a bachelors degree and she and her father fought over her choice. She was not adventurous by nature, but always focused on maximizing her potential. In the end she won the fight and moved to the other side of the country, far from home, to nursing school.

After she graduated, with her Bachelor's degree in hand, she landed a job in a big city to further capitalize on her nursing degree. Her friend's husband was going to show her and her sister around town, but he broke his leg, and he sent his youngest brother to show the ladies the sights. The brother was an adventurous man named Jacob Mathew. Mariamma was barely 20 years old and Jacob was a Captain in the army who drove a motorcycle. They lived in a land and a time where dating was taboo and marriages were strictly arranged by one's parents. But this practical and responsible young lady could not resist the sweet mystery of this unexplainable attraction.

When Jacob told his parents he wanted to marry Mariamma, they firmly said no. He was a prized son. Handsome, successful, and from a good family with acres and acres of income-earning rubber trees, he would invite a generous dowry (payment) from a bride that wanted to marry him as was the tradition. But a love marriage would mean no payment at all. Likewise, Mariamma's parents were disgraced to learn that Jacob had been secretly writing their daughter love letters as this was considered utterly shameful. They were insulted by this breach of custom and would not give their approval for their marriage.

And so their brilliant, responsible daughter who always did her father's bidding was faced with the painful decision of getting married against his will. With a heavy heart, she made a difficult leap of faith, and said yes to Jacob and no to her culture.

Mariamma quickly settled into married life. As was standard in the culture - they had servants and nannies who took care of all the household chores. They had one beautiful daughter, and lived in the lavish quarters assigned to Jacob as a Captain in the army. They lived a life of luxury, prestige, and ease. The army in India was a profession that was greatly respected and those in the army were treated like royalty everywhere they went.

Soon after their daughter was born, a friend from a country called America wrote letters to Jacob and Mariamma and advised them that this country was greatly in need of nurses. It was the early 1970s and Jacob and his wife debated over the wisdom of moving to this country called America. They knew nothing about it and knew very little English. Their friend in America advised them that the opportunity to pursue anything was available in this new country, it was a country founded on Christian principles, he said there was no caste system, and the universities and technological advancements were among the top in the world. He urged them to think of the future of their children.

The decision was difficult. They lacked for nothing as it was, but the promise of endless possibilities was enticing. But should they leave their good life, their heritage, and their culture for an uncertain future?

They learned only Mariamma would be able to go to America and not Jacob or their daughter because the hospital would only sponsor the nurse and not her family. The United States laws also only allowed immigrants to come into the country with eight dollars, so they would need to determine how she could survive until she was paid. It seemed unthinkable and was beyond anything they had ever imagined.

Practical Mariamma, now just 25 years old, did not enjoy a good spur of the moment adventure. As she prayed , she could not fathom moving without her 2-year-old daughter. How could she leave her daughter behind? But how would she take care of her? She didn't even know where she herself would sleep at night.

Jacob and Mariamma thought and prayed and asked God if this was His plan. They thought of the endless possibilities America may provide for the future of their children. A nation without a caste system and the difference it may provide to raise their children in a country founded on Christian principles and religious freedom. An opportunity for their future children to obtain a first-rate education!

Mariamma finally applied to the hospital in America and the hospital sponsored her to join their staff. With no knowledge of what she was jumping into, she hugged her two-year old daughter with tears. It broke her heart that her two-year old daughter did not understand that mommy was hugging her to leave her, not for the weekend, not for a week, but for an indefinite amount of time and she didn't know when she would see her again. It would be over two years later when they would finally reunite.

That woman, Mariamma, was my mother, and she had left my older sister in India. She remembers that heartache with tears even to this day 40 years later.

She got in the game. Sometimes it involves tough choices.

When my father first came to America he was excited to become an entrepreneur. He began by renting out one taxi to drive passengers from the airport. He soon purchased several taxis and oversaw a series of drivers. After the luxury cars moved in and upended the taxi business at the Detroit Metro Airport, Jacob opened a supermarket in Detroit. After a fair number of robberies in his supermarket, he opened an auto mechanic shop.

He was a remarkable player in the game, never stopping for a second to consider what it would be like to stop playing.

But one day the game changed. It was a day like any other. He was preaching at a prayer meeting in the living room of a friend, when suddenly he stopped mid-sentence, in the middle of a verse. Suddenly his entire body started profusely sweating and he was drenched instantly from every pore in his body. He was frozen standing in place, and couldn't get a word out. The house was full, people sitting on all of the sofas, dining room chairs, and every inch of the floor. I was sitting on the floor, a few feet in front of my dad and watched him frozen for nearly a minute until I realized something was medically wrong. They helped him to sit and then quickly carried him to a bedroom to lay down. Someone called 911. I came to the bedroom and he smiled at me and asked me to pray for him. I was 12 years old. I prayed and then the EMT workers arrived and rushed him to the hospital in an ambulance.

We reached the hospital a short time later. Just before they pulled back the hanging sheet in the ICU for me to see him, they told me that he could still hear and they told me to try not to cry. They said a blood vessel had ruptured in his brain and then they pulled open the sheet hanging from the ceiling that kept his bed private. I had expected him to be sitting up in his hospital bed and ready to joke with us. But he was not. His eyes were closed, his body was still, and he was hooked up to machines that you could hear and see forcing his breathing. He was in a coma. Tears immediately overflowed from my eyes and streamed silently down my cheeks. I sharply breathed in and held back my cry. Don't cry. Daddy will hear me.

My dad was in a coma for several days before he went brain dead and they pulled his life support. *Even the Greatest Game has an End!*

He was 49 years old. For the greatest players, their legacy survives long after their game has ended.

"I didn't know what I was going to do," Mariamma continued with tears running down her cheeks. "I had a 12-year old daughter that had barely started life, a 16-year old son that was a handful, and a 22-year old daughter that was still in college."

Playing the game takes guts.

If the story ended there, some may call it a tragedy. But life is always a drama, and this one ends in victory.

My parents took a risk that paid off. They heard that America was the "Land of Opportunity" and their sacrifices let us prove that to be true! All three of Jacob and Mariamma's children not only earned a Bachelor's degree, but each have also gone on to earn Post-Graduate degrees. All are now married with children, and we are the joy and pride of our sacrificial mother's life. We were all able to achieve success in the U.S., all married with children, and we are the pride and joy of our sacrificial mother's life.

I live life with a sense of gratitude. I live life with a purpose. I live life with the opinion that I only have one choice – and that is to get in the game!

With the firsthand knowledge that our lives are short and decisions I must make are not always easy, my prayer each morning is to maximize my full potential and that means not standing on the sidelines, but rather making the choice to be the greatest player in the game!

For me, I always knew I was created to serve others. It was a desire deep within me and was evident in all that I did. It was the purpose for which God had created me and I was going to pursue that end at all costs. But it was only after I became an accountant that my calling in life became readily apparent. I found myself with an overwhelming desire to help those that owed taxes to the Internal Revenue Service and a desire to defend my well-meaning clients that now faced the nightmare of being confronted by the IRS! This passion gave me my purpose in becoming a tax attorney!

Once I began practicing, I knocked on ONE door- and that was the door of the best tax attorney in the state – Rod Polston. He flat out told me that he was not looking to add any attorneys to his practice. He had been a solo practitioner for years and it had served him well. I told him that he was undeniably the single greatest tax attorney in the State of Oklahoma and I wanted to join him because I knew my purpose in life was to serve clients through my knowledge of tax law. I tried to demonstrate why I would be an asset to his practice, but conceded that I was willing to take any position within his firm until he felt the need to add an attorney to his practice because I only wanted to work with the best.

I knew what game I wanted to play and I knew what team I wanted to be on.

Rod Polston did add me as the first attorney to join his practice. Since then, I have grown to become Vice President of Operations and the Managing Attorney of the largest tax resolution firm in the State of Oklahoma. My passion for my clients was recognized in OKC Biz Magazine, the Norman Transcript, and I have been honored to win the Forty Under 40 Award , as well as the Next Under 40 Award. Most recently I was humbled to learn that I had been nominated to the Oklahoma Bar Association as the Most Outstanding Young Lawyer of the Year! I take joy in all of these accomplishments because I know it is not because of my ability, but solely because this is the result of God's mighty hand at work directing my ways. I count God as the driving force behind my work ethic and always remember the legacy that sacrificed to give me every advantage in this game!

Most importantly, the legacy that preceded me has shown that the best players are those who are able to risk it all and make a difficult call when a lot is riding on the line. So ask yourself, what's your skin in the game? What are you willing to risk? When you have faith and risk it all, the reward can be an exponentially greater reward!

Mariamma didn't accept excuses. She was the quiet, obedient Indian girl who hated adventure. But she found herself in a place breaking all the rules and facing adventure head on. And now she's holding the trophy as the MVP! !

About Rachel

Rachel Pappy was born and raised in Michigan. She earned the Dean's List distinction during her undergraduate degree at Wayne State University and after a career as an accountant, went on to earn a scholarship to attend law school at Oklahoma City University. During her first year of law school she was elected by her fellow classmates to serve as their Class President and was subsequently elected to serve as the law student chair for the Oklahoma Bar Association Law Student Division to represent on behalf of all law students at all the law schools in the state. During law school, Rachel Pappy was also exclusively selected as the winner of a coveted award from the Oklahoma Bar Association for her commitment to the practice of the law. Rachel Pappy has been active in various state and federal political campaigns, and was previously selected by the Mayor of Oklahoma City to serve on the Board of Directors for the Oklahoma City Department of Health and Human Services. Rachel currently serves on the Norman Chamber of Commerce for the Norman Next Board of Directors, as well as on the Board of Trusted Advisors to the Greater Oklahoma City Chamber of Commerce. Rachel is a current member of the distinguished Ginsburg Inn of Court and is regularly invited to teach numerous tax seminars all across the State to provide tax advice to various professional organizations including CPAs and other attorneys.

Rachel is currently the Managing Attorney and Vice President of Operations at the Law Offices of Roderick H. Polston and is licensed to practice law in various state and federal courts throughout Oklahoma.

Rachel Pappy is an active member of her church and regularly volunteers in the community. She has been awarded with the Mercedes-Benz Forty Under 40 Award, Next Achievers Under 40 Award, and has been featured on the cover of the *Tulsa Business and Legal News*, in the *OKC Biz* magazine, and in *The Norman Transcript* for her outstanding contributions to the community and the practice of the law. Most recently she has been nominated to the Oklahoma Bar Association as the Most Outstanding Young Lawyer of the year.

Rachel Pappy brings years of tough negotiating to the table and has been successful in negotiating for thousands of clients over the years, which has resulted in the release of levies, garnishments, stopping foreclosure proceedings against assets, and assisting clients with properly purchasing, setting up, and selling their businesses.

When she's not in the office Rachel loves spending time with her husband and three children. More than any of her other successes, she values the opportunity to teach and encourage her children to maximize their potential and become God-fearing men and women who utilize their strengths and talents to glorify His name in all that they do! She is a firm believer in a no-excuses attitude and her clients and family benefit from her relentless pursuit of achieving personal excellence in all that she does.

CHAPTER 22

WHAT'S YOUR DIGITAL DNA™?

BY LINDSAY DICKS

How to get into the Search Engine game by building your Digital DNA™ and becoming a trusted expert.

Q: What's the first thing anyone does when they have a problem they need to solve?

A: They go to Google (or another search engine of their choice).

Q: When they find a company, what's the next thing the searcher does?

A: They "Google" that company to see if they are legitimate or not.

A recent survey by Dimensional Research says that an overwhelming 90 percent of consumers use online information to decide who they're going to buy from. Like it or not, the "Google University" plays a HUGE role in the way we find solutions to our problems today. AND, like it or not – what Google says (whether true or not true) is perceived as fact.

What happens when someone searches for you online? What does your Digital DNA™ (the search results for you) say about you? Is it flooded with 3rd party credibility that you are a trusted, credible expert and displays your blogs, articles, press releases, photos, videos, social media profiles and more! Or does it simply display your website and the other 9 search results that have nothing to do with you – or worse, there is something negative displayed or you're not there at all?

Today's biggest misconception with social media when it comes to its use for businesses is that someone is going to tweet a sales opportunity and a viewer will:

1. See the tweet and

2. Purchase immediately off that link. If that happens for you, you are very lucky because I can tell you, that isn't the case the majority of the time.

More importantly, today, Social Media is used as 3rd party credibility of who you are and what you do; it helps brand you as a trusted expert in your industry so that when someone Googles you, 3rd party verification is displayed. This is your Digital DNA™ and can be comprised of many things including your website, blogs, articles, press releases, photos, videos, your social media and more.

So what's the key to building your Digital DNA™? Plan and simple, content and more content! And I don't just mean the content on your website. I mean keyword rich, relevant, content that is syndicated online. Social media is just one of the tools that can be used to spread the word, the more the better!

There are MANY different methods you can use to distribute content online, many more than I can cover in this chapter- so let's talk about the three biggest.

I. SOCIAL BOOKMARKING

One of the best ways to share your content online is through social bookmarking. You're probably already familiar with the process of "bookmarking" something on your computer – a website you visit often, perhaps your bank or MSN. This process is simple – you're creating a virtual bookmark so that it's easy to find the website or web page that you were looking for. That's bookmarking.

Social bookmarking is just what it sounds like—bookmarking, gone social. In other words, when you bookmark a website, others can see it as well. So if you've found a great new sports blog, for example, social bookmarking would allow your friends to see it and check it out for themselves. These bookmarks are also easily indexed by Google, thus social bookmarking your own blog through some of the stop social bookmarking sites like Digg, Delicious, Reddit, Technorati or StumpleUpon can help improve your Digital DNA™.

Here are 3 tips for making social bookmarking work for you:

1.Tag effectively!

The most important thing about using social bookmarking for business is tagging your content properly. Each social bookmarking community has its own way to tag posts to make sure you understand the rules for each. Understanding how these tags work can help ensure the most exposure for your post.

2. Don't just use one social bookmarking site.

Using a variety of social bookmarking sites allows a very natural linking structure as far as Google is concerned. It also provides a variety of ways that searchers can find your content and your website, thus opening up your funnel for how visitors come to your website.

3. Headlines are important!

One of the keys to creating shareable content is getting the viewer to read the content in the first place. How do you do that? Your headline! Make sure your headline grabs the reader's attention and gives them a reason to read more. Using your keywords in your headline is also very beneficial.

II. PRESS RELEASES

Another great way to improve your Digital DNA™ is through press releases. The pickup of press releases online is very different than the pickup of a press release in your local newspaper. Online pickup is a direct reflection of the content or keywords in the press release. So putting out a press release online about YOU and your business is a great way to develop your Digital DNA™. Some of the best websites I have found to distribute online press releases are: www.prlog.org, www.pitchengine.com and www.prbuzz.com.

Here are a couple easy tips to making your press releases most affective:

1. Include quotes

Including quotes in your press release adds a human element to your press release and can also break up the rest of the copy within the press release to make it more scannable to the reader.

2. Link the press release back to your website

Provide the reader with access to more information by placing a link at the bottom of the release for more information. This allows readers who are interested in you and/or your company to easily get to your site for more information. This link is also good for SEO (search engine optimization) purposes as well.

3. Include your keywords!

Don't forget the importance of keywords and make sure you sprinkle them throughout your release. Remember, online pickup is a direct reflection of the content or keywords in the press release. If your goal is to get these press releases to be picked up as a part of your Digital DNA™ then YOU are very important in the release. PR rules say that after the first time you are mentioned in the release every mention after that should only be your last name. Online – no way! First and last name always – unless you're Madonna and people only search by one name for you. ☺

III. SOCIAL MEDIA

The biggest objection I hear about Social Media is that "my clients are on Facebook or Twitter." And while for some, I might agree with you. Social Media, for businesses, is about developing your online appearance as a trusted, credible expert so that when someone "Googles" you and your Facebook account pops up as result, what the searcher finds supports that you're a trusted expert. So that means two things:

1. If you're not on social media then it's going to be a lot harder to develop dominant Digital DNA™, and

2. I completely agree with you that all those random cat pictures and quotes that have nothing to do with you or your business are not only not important – they may actually be harming you – BUT there is content that IS important.

So what IS important for a searcher to see? You want...

1. Content that you have written that helps establish you as an expert – this can be blogs or articles that you have written, press releases that you have written (or written about you) or white papers and specials reports about specific topics in your niche.

2. Content that <u>others</u> have written that you share to help establish you as a thought leader. Yes, I did just say <u>share content that is not your own</u>. Why? Sharing other (good and relevant) content helps it to "not be all about you." You become a thought leader in your industry for all things related to your niche and followers will look to you for valued information. I do this in my own business with my weekly *SEO* and *SMM Alert*. Every Friday I post a list of the blogs I have read that week that are relevant to my niche that would be of value to my followers. In turn, I have created a great following that looks to me for any new and valuable information that's happening in my industry. This alert has helped to build me up as a trusted expert and thought leader.

3. Content that engages the user and elicits a response. Just like having CTAs (calls to action) are VITAL on your website, they're also super important within your social media posts. If you want a user to comment, pose a question and tell them to comment. Engagement within your social media relies solely on you publishing content that elicits a response.

Now, wash, rinse and repeat. There is no social media rule (or etiquette) out there that says if you have shared it once, you cannot share the same content again. In fact, I encourage you to do so. The way that Facebook now has their newsfeed setup, if you haven't shared something within about an hour of me jumping on Facebook I will never seen your post – and I can assure you on Twitter I'm not scrolling down far enough to see it either. Which means, if you think you have 4 pieces of content to share in a month – you really have at least 8 or 12 pieces because you can re-share that same content 2-3 times!

Here are some tips to sharing content on Social Media:

1. Schedule your posts
News doesn't stop and neither should your posting. That means post at times that are during "normal business hours." This means scheduling tweets and status updates to go out after hours and on the weekends even when you're not "in the office." Also, many have found that posting on weekends helps them reach an audience that they normally wouldn't get in front of during the week.

2. Don't just like and follow...comment!

If you think that following a ton of people it is a good idea, well...
it is! Keep in mind that what's better is directly communicating
with them. A like or follow acts as a wave whereas an actually
comment can make people feel special. Don't hesitate to let others
know how much you really like their content.

3. Create a weekly schedule

If you struggle with trying to come up with things to say each and
every day, developing a weekly schedule may help. Coming up
with a schedule once a week (or once a month if you're feeling
ambitious) can help you think ahead and decide what you'd like
to post. If you have more flexibility, you can push things down
should current events pop up and require immediate posting.

4. Develop series

Lovers of what you do follow you for a reason. Keep them coming
back! A weekly or monthly series gives them something to look
forward to. Using hashtags like #MoneyMonday or #TipTuesday
helps the series become recognizable and can bring in new fans.

5. Host giveaways

Everyone loves freebies! Treat potential fans and current fans with
a sample of your product or a gift card that can be used anywhere.
If it's in the budget, monthly giveaways can lure in new fans and
the great content that you push out can keep them.

Developing a content strategy will take time, thought and consistency.
But understanding and controlling how you are represented on the
Internet is the single most important online business strategy today.
What does your Digital DNA™ say about you? Does Google say that
you're a trusted, credible expert? If not, you're missing out on business
until they do.

About Lindsay

Lindsay Dicks helps her clients tell their stories in the online world. Being brought up around a family of marketers, but a product of Generation Y, Lindsay naturally gravitated to the new world of on-line marketing. Lindsay began freelance writing in 2000 and soon after launched her own PR firm that thrived by offering an in-your-face "Guaranteed PR" that was one of the first of its type in the nation.

Lindsay's new media career is centered on her philosophy that "people buy people." Her goal is to help her clients build a relationship with their prospects and customers. Once that relationship is built and they learn to trust them as the expert in their field, then they will do business with them. Lindsay also built a proprietary process that utilizes social media marketing, content marketing and search engine optimization to create online "buzz" for her clients that helps them to convey their business and personal story. Lindsay's clientele span the entire business map and range from doctors and small business owners to Inc. 500 CEOs.

Lindsay is a graduate of the University of Florida. She is the CEO of CelebritySites™, an online marketing company specializing in social media and online personal branding. Lindsay is recognized as one of the top online marketing experts in the world and has co-authored more than 25 best-selling books alongside authors such as Brian Tracy, Jack Canfield (creator of the *Chicken Soup for the Soul* series), Dan Kennedy, Robert Allen, Dr. Ivan Misner (founder of BNI), Jay Conrad Levinson (author of the "Guerilla Marketing" series), Leigh Steinberg and many others, including the breakthrough hit *Celebrity Branding You!*

She was also selected as one of America's PremierExperts™ and has been quoted in *Newsweek*, the *Wall Street Journal*, *USA Today*, and *Inc.* magazine as well as featured on NBC, ABC, and CBS television affiliates speaking on social media, search engine optimization and making more money online. Lindsay was also recently brought on FOX 35 News as their Online Marketing Expert.

Lindsay, a national speaker, has shared the stage with some of the top speakers in the world, such as Brian Tracy, Lee Milteer, Ron LeGrand, Arielle Ford, David Bullock, Brian Horn, Peter Shankman and many others. Lindsay was also a Producer on the Emmy-winning film Jacob's Turn.

You can connect with Lindsay at:
Lindsay@CelebritySites.com
www.twitter.com/LindsayMDicks
www.facebook.com/LindsayDicks

CHAPTER 23

MARKET YOU! — HOW TO SELL AUTHENTICALLY, GET YOUR IDEAL CLIENTS AND MAKE MORE MONEY

BY AMY DAWIDOWICZ

Many of us, at one point or another, live our lives as entrepreneurs, whether we are business owners, CEO's, or leaders looking for clarity as to what makes us different from others in our business world. And as leaders, what we don't often see is that OUR vulnerability is what sets us apart from others who are likewise in our field.

It's YOUR personal story that is so POWERFUL to people – that vulnerability of you connecting your story to the product or service you're selling – that becomes your WHY. This then motivates us to move faster, work harder or produce more. Or perhaps just keep going. It is amazing when we get that sign that a chapter has closed in our book—only to write the next chapter. And that next chapter, which is the "unknown," is what creates fear and makes us that vulnerable little doe that feels so fearful of that change – the new unknown. But it's also in that softness where vulnerability creates a power ...something that sets us apart from everyone else. It is that exact ingredient that is supremely unique to you.

This is exactly what is most beautiful about your mission. Maybe it is the very reason why you created your business. The sole purpose you created to get your word, product, and service out there to a hungry audience starved for your exact type of insight. That energy is your magic. It is almost cyclical, isn't it? It all began with a thought then formed a feeling, and then an emotion—something that goes into an anabolic or catabolic state, only to result in an action. This then evolves into a memory, which we store in our brain or the amygdala. And then that program develops into a story. Interesting, right?

In business, we might assume this situation happened before and so it must happen again in that same way, and we don't take that next step because of fear, worry or disbelief. This is a tune that our mind records and plays. It becomes a feat that we must overcome. Yet, at its origin, it taps into our cellular tissue and allows us to be vulnerable. This is a growth of emotion—the root of that vulnerability is fear—fear of being seen, fear of failure, and fear of success. You get the point.

What if we were just completely authentic and genuine to society about our intentions? What if we simply admitted that we're human? What if we just allowed ourselves to communicate this way and told everyone – Not by dumping on them (stories that go on and on), but really had an integration, a culmination of thoughts – and we're being true to our process of marketing ourselves?

It's interesting because we are all in the business of "marketing" – whether you know it or like it. This is our reality. This is how to get more clients now, to increase sales. Now is the time to grow your profit margin. Now is the key ingredient to all this power of how you tell your personal story. Have you ever hid a pill in peanut butter so that your dog didn't know you were actually giving it medicine? That is the same with marketing your product or service in a story. You get emotional buy in and then slip what you're selling into the storyline to feed your potential customer the best possible solution. Whether they know it or not, they have already bought in.

At one time, I had it all – the Ken-doll boyfriend, the mountain home with a sunrise-to-sunset deck. It was a fixer upper, but it was a beautiful home on 6 acres of land with 330 plus acres to the left of the house so you couldn't see neighbors or anything but woods and mountains for that matter. It was solitude and quiet and a place of peace where you could hear your own thoughts. But I couldn't figure out why the cars, the house, and the boyfriend who spoiled me didn't make me happy.

I didn't understand why my many businesses and professions didn't keep me occupied. I was on this journey to find this peace, an easy and effortless way to be in the business of life.

So, I decided to take an assessment that would give me clarity about my energetic profile, with results I could see...not feel. I went to a conference where beforehand we took this assessment online to get our results at the conference.

On the last day they gave us the results in hardcopy and asked us all not to look at the results. Well this girl has been waiting too long to find out the block that was stopping her from finding that professional, financial and personal freedom— there was no way she was going to have to wait any longer. This is not the way she does her business. She is a 'get-them-in, get-them-out satisfied and clear,' and that's all she wanted in return.

So, I opened my results and looked at them. I could understand them, but not to the degree where I understood how and why I was still feeling the way I was. It seemed like the results had this magic button that could press and unlock all the world's secrets, which, in turn, would bring them flooding to me. But they didn't. So, I grabbed the creator of this assessment and asked him to read me my results. He asked me if I had ever taken this before. I said no. And he went on to say that my resonating energy level is really high and that I must be pretty successful. I responded saying, "Yes, I am, but I still feel this yearning...a sadness, or I feel loneliness. But I have everything. What is it about?" He started to look through my results again. And he said to me, "How is your relationship?" I said, "Well, its okay." But deep in my psyche my thoughts were screaming, while my conscious brain was stating that it was strange, but I didn't answer a question about relationship. I though this was more about energy and leadership and about how I can lead myself in order to lead others. "Why are you asking?" I replied.

He responded, "I've heard you speak about the holistic picture of a relationship to business. This involves every ASPECT of your life, right? This means all your relationships—not just business ones. So, if you're at all distracted it could pull you off and out of that success trajectory, which is what it sounds like is happening." I responded again, saying, "Well, yes, because success equates to fulfillment, and there wasn't much of that."

I thanked him and walked on. By the end of the day my mind was still on the results. I hopped in the car, set my GPS homeward and started in for the highway. As I was lost in thought, I looked to my left and saw a cluster of trees. On my right was a body of water and a gas station. I kept on toward the highway and a bit later I saw a cluster of trees and on my right a body of water and then a gas station? Huh? I looked to the GPS. It said it was a few more minutes to the highway, so I kept on. By now, I'm reeling in my thoughts, asking God what to do about all this and what is my next step?

As I looked up, I saw that same cluster of trees, the same body of water, and to my right, that same gas station. Now, I m pissed. I pull over and I realized I literally *and* figuratively was driving around in circles. But that's when it hit me: I was driving around in circles in both my business and in my personal life. I was playing small and wasn't allowing myself to grow, because I thought making the challenging decisions I had to make was going to make things more difficult. I knew then that I needed to literally point myself—or, rather, my car, in a brand new direction in order to get off the hamster wheel. I knew that it might be challenging, but I likewise knew that it was going to be more challenging if I *didn't* do it.

Three months later:
My main focus was on one business – a new creation from all of the others and put all my focus toward that. I left my house, found an apartment, and then tripled my income making six figures in less than three months in a small, sparsely populated city. This clarity was about listening to the messages that were coming across. That I have everything inside me to be the successful entrepreneur but need to be in line with my integrity and with what I am doing here in the world.

When I tell people this specific story they then understand that without a foundation, they too can build or re-create the personal, professional and financial freedom in their business they deserve and long for. Now I use that story to sell that assessment because I am living proof and my clients success stories are too! Do you see where I am going with this? Attaching a story to a product or service helps people to be put in your shoes. They connect on that emotional level and follow your lead because you created a solution to your issue and can to theirs as well. Got it!

The trust of our clients is attained through that of connecting on a deeper emotional level. Story telling is this delicious and enticing way to hide your message in your motive for your clients to digest your message on an emotional level. Think about it. Everyone has had or knows someone who has had a relationship that has taken them of their trajectory. And everyone is looking for clarity in one aspect of their life or another. So don't you think the outcome of this story will help me sell my assessment because I made six figures in the clarity I received from it? Think about it, an emotional connection to my audience and them to me, and them to the outcome and benefit I received that they too can have if they sign up. Get it?

But truly this is the most non-salesy way to inspire people in to action. We all want others to thrive and not just survive. My motto is I'm only as successful as those whom I surround myself with, so if you're coming with me then lets go ...cause you won't fail in working with me. I am the best and I work with the best to be the best at who they are and what they do and the service they provide. Now, who doesn't want clarity on that?

But do you think this didn't come at a price? Well yes, I had to move (I know people don't like change), there was some upset in my apple cart and his, there were many financial hiccups and time consuming lawful documents to sign, a house to sell AND it didn't matter. The life I live now reflects one of courage, confidence and success in all areas not just business because of this and what does that reflect to others? I walk my talk.

You see, story telling is hiding the pill in the peanut butter to get your clients back on track. It's not sneaky, it's actually you being more transparent with your clients, which is what we crave these days. We have been lied to, not told or surprised with political and financial woes. This is why it's a beautiful thing to share yourself with someone and help them attain the miracle you can offer.

As seen in *Forbes* Magazine, *"The emotional part of the spectrum gives our consumers something to relate to, creating the "human" side of our brand. This is not only more engaging, but builds trust with our*

**http://www.forbes.com/sites/groupthink/2013/12/19/how-you-can-master-the-art-of-good-story-selling/

*consumers. The pragmatic side builds trust and rationale for purchase and it's important to build both sides of the equation." ***

The beauty about emotion is if it migrates into our limbic system we connect like the flip of a switch. BUT if we don't, we will immediately shut off or allow for distraction. Similar to our default setting, right? This is why things don't get accomplished or the issues we've faced time and time again aren't resolved. And maybe we say, "Nope. I don't connect with that" being it much more challenging to attain the trust of a client. It's similar to how we screen people, the customers you want to buy from or work with. Do we connect? (meaning - do we know, like and trust them?) If not, its not a good fit. How great is that. It's not something to be practiced, it just is!

So why don't we use this method all the time in not just "Story-Selling" but in all that we do. Well simple, we need a good story that connects and aligns to our purpose, message and what we are marketing. It can be challenging, because like the amygdala, that emotional center of the brain, we can get confused in the remembering of an experience and lose ourselves in the midst of our story. And then we've lost our audience. It is important to understand there is a strategy that I teach in "how to sell your story".

Anne Loehr of The Blog states, *"It's not easy to "find your story" for a corporate environment. It takes a certain willingness to be more vulnerable when looking to instigate either laughter or emotion from an audience. Understanding how well it really works can be a tremendous motivator."****

But once you have found your story and learn how to connect it to your elevator pitch, sales speech, product or service, you're golden and you have gained the respect and attention of your ideal client. This is a proven method that works. Just look at the bible, without the religious connotation. This is one big story of life and these stories have been pasted on for eons and eons as a guidebook in how to live life. Has it not grabbed the attention of millions of people over the generations? This is the culmination of stories that ministers, pastors, etc. use to gain

---

***http://www.huffingtonpost.com/anne-loehr/its-story-time-corporate-_b_5698595.html

the attention of a large audience, then collect money for the church's continuance so you hear more stories. Brilliant, so why are we not using our own personal stories to illuminate what we are marketing?

Do you see how strategic sales using the tool of storytelling has been used for decades as a powerful marketing tool? It is so important to not only your business financially, but in the development of relationships and the expansion of your business. It a connection of the dots; so, if you are lacking or missing a link between your business and marketing strategy, I suggest this method as one to adopt.

> *I've learned that people will forget what you said,*
> *people will forget what you did, but people*
> *will never forget how you made them feel.*
> ~ Maya Angelou

"SO I'M LIVING MY LIFE NOW..."

About Amy

Amy Dawidowicz is an entrepreneur and lifestyle catalyst. As a professional business and life coach, her work involves one-on-one coaching, innovative group programs, and motivational speaking. With years of experience, Amy guides committed individuals, courageous entrepreneurs, CEOs and high achievers into the fulfillment of ideal personal, professional and financial goals.

The road to achievement is about taking chances, and Amy knows this first hand. She is often quoted as saying, "I take a leap of faith and grow wings on the way down." One of the ways Amy helps people with their growth is by discerning the strategies of her clients, thereby generating more success in their business. The tools she has discovered along the way allowed her to triple her income in just three months, and that power allows her to shares these strategies with clients.

With a Bachelor's in Psychology and a Master's in Education, Amy has become an authority of many modalities. By combining an IPEC Coaching certification, 17 years of energy medicine and Reiki mastery with 200+ hours of yoga certifications—not to mention 8 years as a successful entrepreneur, Amy has quickly evolved into *The Spiritual Entrepreneur.*

As a gifted storyteller with years of relatable experience, Amy's mission is to inspire entrepreneurs. She does just that by traveling from conference rooms to festival stages, with an approach centered on the philosophy of sharing—not selling. Her authentic approach and unique story quickly gains the hearts of her audiences.

Whether on stage, one-on-one, or by keystroke, Amy acts as a catalyst for others success by igniting audiences with a keen perception that allows her clients to engage on a visceral level, and creating a bond that propels them on a path of prosperous accomplishment.

Inspired by enlightened individuals like colleagues Maribel Jiminez, David Neagle, Ted McGrath and Sheevaun Moran, Amy thrives on motivating others to facilitate the discovery of one's self so their story will draw the perfect clientele.

You can connect with Amy Dawidowicz at: Amy@AmyD.me, via Facebook at: www.facebook.com/amyd.me, or tweet to her at: twitter.com/chooseevolution

CHAPTER 24

GOOGLE+ HOLDS THE MAGIC PASSWORD TO GOOGLEDOM – YOUR COMPANY CANNOT SURVIVE WITHOUT IT.

BY JEAN R. LANOUE

A few years ago, Google changed the social media world with Google+. Their entrance into the social media arena may have seemed quiet, but it was one that was very important. Google+ is the entrance to YouTube, Gmail, Google Drive, Google Local and Hangouts and more. Google is the number one search engine by far. Can you guess number two? YouTube is the second most powerful search engine. Did you know that Google owns YouTube? If you wish to make it as a business, it is crucial to have a Google+ account with a complete profile to generate the type of traffic you need for your business to grow.

Google+ is a combination of Facebook and LinkedIn. You can have the social aspect of Facebook but you can (and should) add your complete resume like on LinkedIn. Google+ may seem to be just another media platform but is actually your social fingerprint. There are Google+ communities where you can join in conversations and get answers to questions, just like the groups on the other platforms. There are even

Google+ user communities so you can learn how to use it properly.

So, what makes Google+ so essential? Google+ is Google and really that is all that needs to be said. To get your blog and website found in a Google search, it is essential to have a Google+ account. Sure there are other search engines such as Yahoo and Bing, but Google stands head and shoulders above all of those other search engines combined, so not being "verified" by Google is not a wise move.

How does Google+ boost your SEO? To begin with, when you have a completed your profile, it shows up in search engine searches looking like a Yellow Page ad. You remember the yellow pages, those giant books that arrived once a year, and were kept by that ancient device that is now euphemistically referred to as a landline. It is so hard for the newer generations to conceptualize that phones used to be devices that were shackled to the wall and had to be shared with other people.

GOOGLE+ IS THE YELLOW PAGES OF THE DIGITAL AGE

Smart companies paid for advertisement space in the Yellow Pages, because during the dominance of the Yellow Pages, there were no Internet or search engines. People had to flip through key words printed alphabetically, on very thin, yellow paper in a very heavy book. If they wanted a dog groomer, they looked for the heading and then there was a list of names of businesses. Some of those were just a single line with a phone number, with no description of their product; while others were quarter, half or even whole page advertisements that had the logo, the name of the business and usually a list of services. These businesses were called first. Not buying that ad space meant that their business was delegated to the fate of the names and numbers in the front of the book, called the white pages. You could only find a listing if you knew the exact name or number of the person or business and in some cases, their address.

During a Google search, your profile will appear on the right of the screen with information about your company, who runs it, the founders, where it is located on a map and much more. The cost is free when you complete your profile. That is prime real estate for free.

Another nice feature that increases your exposure is that Google will index all of your public posts from Google+. That means when someone is searching on a topic for a blog post you wrote using that keyword, your blog will appear. The higher the rank, the higher on the list it will appear.

It was frustrating when you would have to wait weeks for Google to index a submission you made. Now you can share those web pages on Google+ instantly and they will be quickly indexed on the Google search engine.

The phrase "Google+ is a ghost town" is often said to me. It may not have caught on with the teens and tweens, but unless they are who you are trying to reach, then it doesn't matter that they're not there. Actually, it is quite helpful that the space is not so cluttered. Your posts are much more likely to be seen. It is almost impossible for your business page posts to be seen on Facebook anymore unless you pay. And a couple more interesting points for those that need statistics:

- 22% of Americans use Google+, equal to the number that use Twitter.[1]

- 1 Billion user accounts, 540+ million active users across Google platforms, 300+ million active in the Google+ stream alone.[2]

To Begin

If you want to start setting up Google+ and to try out some of the features, you have to start by setting up a Gmail account. This is a personal email account and is required with a Google+ account. Be sure when you are setting up this account that you are using your real name in the fields when it asks first and last name and not a handle or a business name. There will be time for that later in the process. For the user name, which will be part of your email, try to get your domain name.

Once you have set up your Gmail account, you will have automatically set up your Google+ account. You see access to your Google+ account up in the right hand of the Google.com page. Open it up and explore your profile. You can add a photo, personal information and much more.

---

1 (Elliot, N., Why Every Marketer Should Use Google Plus. Forrester. March, 2014. http://blogs.forrester. com/nate_elliott/14-03-31-why_every_marketer_should_use_google_plus)

2 (Nayak, V., Google+ Reaches 1 Billion Users Mark: +1 Button Is Viewed 5 Million Times A Day. Dazeinfo. January, 2014. http://www.dazeinfo.com/2014/01/30/google-plus-users-2014-statistics-social-media/)

Circles

Once you have created your account, you can begin adding people into what are referred to as Circles. When people in your Circles add new content, you can be notified and view it. There is not a mandatory reciprocal relationship with Circles, meaning that just because you add someone to yours does not mean that they have to add you to theirs, although you want them to. When you post new content, pictures, blog posts, etc., those people that have added you to their Circles can automatically see your new content. They can also be viewed publically unless you set up the sharing protocol to be only viewed by certain Circles. This allows you to separate business from personal.

Other Features

In addition to Circles, there are Communities; these are special interest groups of people sharing common content. Say you like photography, there is probably a Community for that. You can look at people's content "+" it, comment on it, and share your ideas. The more you participate in Communities the more likely people are going to be interested in your page and therefore you are directing potential leads to your business.

Google Hangouts is another popular feature in which people can conference video chat with people. These can be private or public affairs, and it is like hanging out with people at the local coffee shop even though they can be half way across the world. You use Google Hangouts as a teaching platform or a group discussion on matters that mean the most to you and your clients. These can be recorded and automatically placed on YouTube, which is connected to your Google Plus.

Pages

You are given the ability to create business pages, and this is where putting your website URL is so important. The setup of the business profile is similar to what you did in your personal profile. There are two important things you need to do here, as it will determine whether or not your website is captured by the Google search engine.

The first is to make sure you verify your email account. This is a simple process in which Google sends a confirmation email, and you click the verify button. This places a check next to your email address on your profile. It assures Google and others that you are a real person and not a robot.

The second process is verifying your website. Google generates a little piece of HTML code that you place on your webpage. It takes Google a couple days to crawl your webpage, and then your site is verified. Now your cool Yellow Pages-type profile will pop up in keyword searches.

Once you have set up a page, have 10 or more followers, a profile picture and the page is at least two weeks old, you can claim a custom URL that matches your brand. This makes it even easier for your page to be shared and to be discovered.

Now it's time to engage.

Plus One
Because your content is shared publically, visitors to your site can add a "+1". This is comparable to "like" on Facebook but it does more, because for every "+1" it can push your content higher on the Google rankings. The more people that like you, the more people can find you.

This all points to greater exposure through a higher Google ranking. There is no other social media tool around that can impact you directly in the way Google+ can. It can be a tricky process for someone doing it on their own because of two factors:

1. You do not have the time to set up and maintain a Google+ account. Let's face it, marketing takes time, but it is necessary in order for your business to survive.

2. You do not have the skills to make it happen. People may be experts in many areas, but that does not automatically make them a Google+ genius.

In both cases, you need someone that is a Google+ genius and has the time to maneuver you through The Google+ matrix. This is just one of the services I provide for my clients, and their customer base and sales soar. While it might be free to sign up for Google+, it costs money and takes a certain knowledge base to leverage it the way your business needs to.

Content is the Key
Are you worn out with all the steps for getting your website verified and added to rank on Google? It can be confusing when you begin having to add codes to webpages, and knowing the difference between personal

and business pages. It is all-important but it can be overwhelming. Hiring a professional agency such as Digital Marketing Genie, takes all the guesswork out of the process. It is important for it to be set up correctly, and with content that will attract new customers to your site.

Content is the next consideration, as what you post will say a lot about you and your company, so, not any content will do. It has to be engaging, interesting and have a call-to-action with the proper mix of SEO. Great content will get shares, +1's and people adding you to their Circles and looking at your website.

What type of content am I referring to?

- Ebooks
- Whitepapers
- Guides
- Blog Posts
- Webinars
- And more...

Can you create this type of lead generation content? Again, this is an area where Digital Marketing Genie can really help, because we know how to produce content that is attractive and fills a niche people will be interested in. In order to make people know who you are and keep your Google ranking high, you have to be present – that is, you have to be a part of the Google+ Community in a very active way – producing content, commenting in Communities and +1'ing other people's content. This means that while you are working at your business, someone else has to be you online. We have specialists that do this for you. You can't be everywhere at once, so why not just duplicate yourself, and let our team do the heavy lifting.

Content that Drives Action

You can use Google+ posts like digital breadcrumbs that draw your potential customers down a path toward a much more substantial piece of content they can access by opting in to your mailing list. They fill out a simple form and they are given a special report or Ebook and you have now generated a new lead. Easy as pie, if you know how to make pie. What you cannot afford is not generating new leads for your business.

The best way to get the most value out of your Google+ business page is to publish great content often. When you share content through Google+, it helps Google to index it quicker on their search engine. You may already be publishing content to Facebook, Twitter, and LinkedIn, so be sure you are also publishing that same content through Google+. There are services that can assist you in publishing to all of your social media channels on a schedule. There is a Google+ app that allows you to post directly to Google+ and it will share it to all of your other social media sites.

Tips to Make Your Google+ Pop

Here is a list of some simple tips that can help you make your posts pop, while at the same time save you time:

1. You make your posts more interesting by dragging links, photos, and videos directly into your share box.

2. You can mention other people by adding a + or @ in front of their name, and this will create a link to them.

3. You can share information directly to people through Google+ by sending a post to them and being sure that you disable "reshare."

4. If you +1 on a post, it will not list on your +1 page, you have to use the +1 on the web.

5. Your Circles are color coded when you post:

   • a green box means that that particular group of people are not in your Circles but may view your post (Public).

   • a blue box means that only people in that particular Circle can see your post, unless it is shared.

This makes it easy to send private posts to friends and family, and for other posts – you can share with everyone. You can add whatever particular Circles you want for each post.

Invest In Yourself

You have to spend money to make money, and sometimes people are reluctant to invest money in generating leads. Google+ is a fantastic platform for lead generation, if it is leveraged the correct way. Time is money, so why not hire a professional to do the work for you. If you gain one lead, you will probably be close to paying for your investment, and then any other leads that are generated are profit, so it only makes sense to invest in your company.

About Jean

Jean R. Lanoue helps her clients maneuver through the ever-changing digital world. As a small business owner herself, she understands the many hats that a business owner wears. She started her first business in her twenties and has been helping businesses grow ever since.

Jean has been utilizing social media channels to generate blog traffic by building trust and loyalty, even before social media was cool (2007). She started working in the digital marketing field to gain knowledge about marketing her own business. She learned very quickly that there was a lot of information being shared about how to market online, but not many agencies wanted to help accomplish the tasks. She continued taking every available course and getting her certifications. Then her blog became more and more successful. As she talked about the opportunities that had come her way, people started asking for help. Thriving on helping other businesses grow, Jean decided to help them – including medical practices and law firms – to market their message and brand using digital media.

Jean R. Lanoue is the founder of The Social Jeanie and Digital Marketing Genie. She has always had an entrepreneurial spirit and has owned several successful businesses. She is also a business professional with more than 20 years of experience doing marketing, training, accounting and management in the corporate world. She is an author, a national speaker and has been recognized as one of America's PremierExperts®. She is a Cydec, Google & Constant Contact Partner and holds a certification in Inbound Marketing.

Traditional marketing is broken. Buyers are taking control. They're tuning out old-school marketing that's impersonal. The true power of digital marketing comes from your ability to create a community based around your company, medical practice or law firm and engage in digital conversations with your customers, clients or patients. Social media is a powerful tool when combined with other inbound marketing tools such as email and call-to-action offers on powerful landing pages. However, digital marketing does take time – that's something that's frequently in short supply for many business owners. Realizing the pressure and time constraints that business owners were under, Jean created a done-for-you service. Her company manages your complete digital presence for you, to help your business grow by providing quality, relevant content, and engaging over the social media networks and your blog; so you can spend your time managing your business, medical practice or law practice. Jean and her team work together with you to build a powerful digital marketing campaign for your company, focusing on ROI. They customize strategies based on your needs and objectives after a thorough evaluation. They learn about you and your business first. Then, find your potential customer on the best online channels.

You can connect with Jean at:
jean@digitalmarketinggenie.com
https://www.facebook.com/SocialJeanie
https://www.facebook.com/digitalmktggenie
https://plus.google.com/+Socialjeanie
https://plus.google.com/+Digitalmarketinggenie
http://www.linkedin.com/in/jeanrlanoue/
https://twitter.com/SocialJeanie
linkedin.com/company/digitalmarketinggenie

CHAPTER 25

FINALLY IN THE GAME!

BY DEBORAH BROWN

THANKSGIVING TRANSFORMATION

My love for volunteering led me to a homeless shelter one Thanksgiving morning a few years ago - an experience that rocked the foundations of the perception of my life, how I viewed the struggles of others, and I began to consider that I could do something that would have a positive effect on other people's lives. I was there to help serve the day's breakfast and assist with the preparation of dinner. As much as I was there to serve and feed the homeless, I found that I was the one really being fed though not the tangible nourishment of food. A seed had been planted, one which would greatly influence my future path. In the midst of handshakes and some laughter, the residents shared their stories, experiences, the circumstances that brought them there and the current challenges they faced. Despite the physical nourishment they received, what seemed to be most impactful for them was that someone cared about their story – they were being heard. Many of them felt like they were invisible ghosts of society. People would pass them every day, avert their eyes so that they would not look directly at them, and would often ignore a simple "hello." They were the invisible denizens of the streets that not many people wanted to acknowledge even existed, let alone be interested enough to sit and have a conversation with them.

As I drove out reflecting on the events of the day, I admittedly felt an internal conflict. I was happy that I had spent the day volunteering and helping make people's lives better, even if they were small changes, but now I was returning to my better life just miles away and leaving it behind, because these people needed help year round. Was just one day enough to make a difference to change a life? It was then I realized that I wanted all my interactions moving forward to be a source of hope and inspiration, while leaving the other party feeling they were heard, seen and that they mattered. People should never feel that they are living a cellophane life in which others may be looking at them, but not truly seeing them for who they are inside. I concluded that all people, from those who were down and out living on the streets to the CEO of a large corporation, needed the same things – to be seen, to be heard, to be loved, to be appreciated, and to have a sense of acceptance and belonging to a community. I could be that person who enhances lives through my ability to listen, show authentic empathy, and provide positive solutions.

It was not as if I treated people indifferently before, or that this was even a huge departure from my natural personality, but the difference now was that it would be done with deliberate intent and awareness. This had profoundly shaped my life on several levels, both personally and professionally, and years after that November day, it has created a wondrous and fulfilling path for my life. The small act of being present for someone can lead to confidence, which leads to hope, which results in a vision of possibilities they had never imagined.

MUSINGS OF YOUTH

As a young woman in my 20's, I was fleet-footed and was recruited out of college into a Management Consulting firm as an Analyst in the IT industry. I was a jetsetter living 100% out of a suitcase, while working for a great company alongside some of the most brilliant people I had ever met, gained great experience, had some of the biggest organizations as clients, and was well compensated. As a fresh, young graduate, I embarked on an exciting journey, and I could never imagine a day in which I would not love flying and living in hotel rooms around the country. These were the thoughts of the 25-year-old me.

As seven years passed, the routine of long hours and multiple cities was less charming and balance of life became an enigma. Friendships suffered, special family moments missed and healthy living habits were non-existent. Most weeks I was working between 60 to 80 hours, and it became clear that I was making a living but not truly living. My life was full, but not fulfilled. As I grew older, my values shifted along with my priorities.

There was this feeling growing inside of me that even though I loved my job and all the promotions and salary increases, I was missing something. There was a piece of the puzzle that would give me a sense of complete fulfillment, but I was struggling with what exactly it was.

I dug deeper inside myself for answers. I knew it could not just be the money or the promotions that kept me working the way I was, and that is when I made a connection. It was that promise I had made to myself on that fateful Thanksgiving Day. I realized that the most fulfilling part of my job was the interactions I was having with other people – the personal connections. I felt great joy during the opportunities that I had to mentor my team, train junior colleagues, and resolve interpersonal conflicts. I looked forward to working with challenging clients, and I was good at giving feedback to colleagues about their interpersonal situations and scenarios. I truly enjoyed working with people and helping them overcome their obstacles.

They say that you cannot see the picture if you are in the frame. Life was fast-paced and the years flew by – I was moving up the ranks, my salary was growing and professional opportunities were getting better and better – from the outside looking in, I had nothing to complain about. I did not have the perspective of seeing what I could do to push that missing piece into my life – the one piece that would change the entire game for me. It took four more years before I finally jumped into the game and took control, and the best part was, I did it totally on my own terms and set the tone for my life moving forward.

LIFE ON MY TERMS

I have learned to take calculated risks, that is, not only do I look before I leap, I take a few steps back. Imagine you are trying to cross a gap between two ledges, and between them is a dark, bottomless chasm – do you step up to the edge, bend your knees and hope your bunny hop will get you across? Or, do you step back a few steps, assess the jump and begin running in order to gain some momentum before leaping?

I took time off from my career. I spent a year finding myself, exploring what that missing piece was, and then formulating a plan to bring that piece back into my life. During that time, I did a lot of volunteer work and a variety of things for my own personal enjoyment and growth—

trainings, classes, seminars, and just about anything that was not professionally related…I was doing it. It was my time to breathe, stay on the ground and experience stability.

This gave me those few steps back in order to get some introspection. My own journey of personal development, self-awareness and discovery led me to my personal commitment to live life on my own terms going forward. This determination to not only 'get in the game' but create my own rules for the game, resulted in a clear vision of my definition of a balanced life and the person I wanted to become—physically, professionally, spiritually, emotionally, financially and socially.

My passion for working with people and adding value to their lives in some capacity led to the birth of my company, Optimal Leap, Inc., which is dedicated to helping people discover and create their own vision for their optimal life and supporting them through the journey of stepping into that reality. Its mission is not only to help people leap to their best, design their best life, but to also leap to greater levels of themselves than they first even imagined – understanding that there is always another level that is attainable. I am passionate about helping people achieve the level of fulfillment they desire for their lives – their own unique recipe for a balanced, fulfilled life.

LESSONS ON THE ROAD TO A NEW LIFE

I have learned some important lessons along the way toward the life-path I now stand upon. I realize I have not completely figured out what I want to be when I grow up – mostly, because this image of self is in constant flux. What I value today may not be the same thing I will value in ten years or beyond. I am constantly learning, evolving and growing, and I do not believe that process ever stops. Our lives are active, not stagnant, so when it is time to move to that next level, express that next passion, we do eventually have to face that chasm, which is nothing more than our fear of change, and leap over it into a new, exciting life. What I have learned is that:

1. There comes a time when you have to take a real hard, honest look at your life and ask the questions:
   - "Is this what I want?"
   - "Am I happy with who I am today and where I am headed?"

- "Am I living a fulfilled life?"

- "If I had the opportunity to do it all over again, would I be here today? ...who I am today? ...doing what I am doing today?"

2. You have to accept who you are today, the entire package including all of the good and bad parts. You have to accept that humans are flawed and that, like everyone else, you are making your way through life the best way you can and that is enough. Accept that you are a unique individual that is constantly learning and helping others learn along the way. Give yourself a break - we are all in this together.

3. You have to be willing to take a risk for the sake of the greater good. This may be financial, relational, etc., holding hope and your vision in focus. Sure, the leap can be scary – but you are betting on yourself. You have to have faith that on the other side of that fear is a new life that you will not only survive, but you will conquer.

4. You need to have a mentor – whether formal or informal. ... People with whom you have the freedom to dream big and who have the ability and the desire for you to take it a step further and make it even bigger than you imagined. ...People who hold that vision for you during those times when the light on your side is dim and in the moments when you get short-sighted.

5. Commit to amazing and wowing yourself! With this mindset, there are no limits; there is no room to place limitations on yourself as you are constantly raising your own bar.

6. You have to spend time or dedicate time to creating your vision. This should be written down in a place that you can frequently visit, and is easily accessible so that you can keep abreast of your personal progress toward it.

7. You have to identify the gap between 'the you of today' and 'the you of your design for tomorrow' and determine what it will take to get there. Write down the goals associated with this as well as the people and resources needed to get you there.

8. You have to walk before you are able to run. Realizing that things do not happen overnight but that progress is made with each small step. Be aware that there will be times when you

have to take three steps backwards in order to take a giant leap forward. Building momentum forward will carry you through.

9. Mindset and the quality of your self-talk is half the battle. It is important to have already won the game in your mind. Albert Einstein said that whatever plays on the screen of your mind is a preview of life's coming attractions.

10. Say 'yes' and figure it out later. I heard this from several mentors and this directive has helped me to make some of the boldest moves I have made in my life.

11. Zig Ziglar stated, "You do not have to be great to start but you have to start to be great." The most important step is the first step. The action of taking that first step, any step, sets in motion other events that will navigate and lead you to where you ultimately should be or want to be. I started out with quite a bit of uncertainty and very little clarity as the entrepreneurial track was new territory for me, but deciding to make that first step made all the difference as opportunities and resources showed up along the way.

In order to 'get in the game' and bring balance and fulfillment into your life, you have to be aware of and define what the game is and means to you. The game, from my perspective, is about making the bold move to pursue your passion and insatiably going after your goals regardless of what the environment or the circumstances tell you, and being authentic in your pursuit. Sometimes you have to step outside your immediate sphere of influence to discover what is available to you. Sometimes it takes being pushed beyond that threshold of pain to make a change, but once you do turn that corner and you have clarity, that clarity is true power, and that power leads to fulfillment and freedom.

I will leave these questions for you to ponder. Tomorrow morning when you wake up, will YOU be headed to the job you HAVE TO GO TO? Or will YOU be going to the passionate career you GET TO GO TO?

The real question is, will you pursue your passion and create that vision for your best life now or later?

About Deborah

Deborah Brown works with clients to define and design their lives to incorporate their personal as well as professional aspirations. As a senior ranking consultant in the IT industry for 14 years, Deborah knows firsthand how difficult it can be to attain work-life balance and what happens to your spirit when you give all you have to the job. Her personal desire for fulfillment, and witnessing so many other professionals experiencing similar challenges, were the impetus and inspiration for creating her company, Optimal Leap, Inc.

Deborah is a graduate of the University of Miami where she obtained two Master's degrees in Biomedical and Industrial Engineering. In her corporate career, she worked in Management Consulting where she had the opportunity to lead teams and support their advancement. Deborah holds her Project Management Professional (PMP) certification and has managed large scale projects for Fortune 500 companies. Some of her clients over the years included Best Buy, Walmart, Target, AC Nielsen and Johnson & Johnson. She now embraces the philosophy that quality of life and playing full out is the biggest and most important project there will ever be. While Deborah's project management and business skill set is vast, her greatest expertise and passion revolves around relating to people. Her desire to combine her knowledge and experience in these areas serves to deliver the best results to her clients.

With a thirst for knowledge as well as personal and professional development, Deborah uncovered her deep desire and ability to support others in reaching their next level of success. She entered the coaching profession, specializing in life and transformational coaching, with a dedication to guiding her clients and partnering with them on their journey of realizing their full potential. Deborah has done Advanced studies under the International Coach Academy, based in Australia.

Deborah launched her company Optimal Leap, Inc. with the goal of having her clients leap to their best, to give them a supportive environment and permission to design their life's vision through the 'Optimal You' framework. The coaching, consulting and resource partners through Optimal Leap support individuals in defining, developing and fulfilling their visions. Deborah's coaching is designed to excavate and pull the vision from the inside out.

Deborah, originally from Jamaica, currently resides in Florida where she wholeheartedly embraces the warm weather. In her spare time, she enjoys volunteering for causes that are near and dear to her heart and traveling which allows her to explore new countries and cultures.

You can connect with Deborah at:
Deborah@OptimalLeap.com
www.OptimalLeap.com

CHAPTER 26

ON 'BEING' A LEADER

BY WERNER BERGER

We are all born with the capacity to become great leaders, yet we find Leadership, one of the most important qualities on earth, to also be among the scarcest. My experience as a corporate consultant and high altitude climber[1] taught me you cannot train leadership; it has to be developed. Leadership is more about who people are 'being,'[2] than the skills they possess; and 'being' cannot be taught nor trained. Most people, placed into a cauldron of experiences, good or bad, will be molded, regardless of their character, or their former state of being.[3] And, herein lies the hope for leadership development for corporate and global success.

Researchers have put forth a multitude of characteristics of highly effective leaders. The main question – which of these can be trained and which has to be developed? Anything labeled as a skill, although important, does not correlate to the essence of Leadership. To be effective, each of the descriptors must include a deep knowledge, appreciation and acceptance of self. A lack of the latter is the reason $114 billion spent on leadership training[4] has fallen far short.

Effective leadership is defined by congruency of actions, not by title. Ask: do your actions come across as appropriate to the situation or

---

1. Werner is the oldest person in the world to have climbed the highest peak on each of the seven continents (incl. Mt. Everest).
2. Beingness has been in conversation since the days of Aristotle and Heidegger with definitions like "dasein," conscious existence and character.
3. Example - Vietnamese POWs.
4. McKinsey & Company.

simply as a vain attempt at engaging a learned skill? Ultimately, actions are an indicator of character - a way of being; what's inside; the kind of leader showing up! FOLLOWING, you will find structures related to the building blocks and attitudes of exemplary leadership.

WIN/WIN

Motivation is linked to, "What's in it for me?" Our two dominant desires are avoidance of pain and the gaining of pleasure. Simple. Why then do so many, if not most of today's leaders, who purport to be in the Win/Win game, fail so miserably. Ilya Pozin, Staff writer, Forbes Magazine, "The top reason employees hate their job is, 'Their boss sucks.' As a result, employee passion for their working life is long gone." Don't they understand the concept of Win/Win or are they simply incapable (or, not yet capable) of implementing it? Further, a Fortune Magazine study concludes, "95% of North American managers say the right thing. Only 5% do the right thing. That has to change!"

In any environment, Win/Win can be measured by the level of satisfaction of any two entities: you/me, manager/employee, husband/wife, parent/child, etc. If both partners are satisfied, we have a Win/Win. Clearly, other options are, one wins, the other loses, and both lose.

The question, "In the short term, we have four (4) possibilities. How many do we have in the long term?" Please think of this and formulate an answer prior to continuing.

Answer: only two. The statistics quoted suggest most corporations operate in the Lose/Lose cycle. Disgruntled employees rarely offer high performance. This is the antithesis of what the 'leader' wants and, unfortunately, the tendency now is to blame the 'mis-hire;' never thinking, every time I point at someone I have three fingers pointing back at me.

Clearly, what is missing for the 95% is an inability to "be" the leader who embodies and successfully strives for Win/Win.

Your task, relative to people who are significant to you, is to assess your relationships, then enter into communication to escalate the possibilities.

PERFORMANCE WITH FULFILLMENT

Similar to Win/Win, two additional dimensions lead to work excellence, Fulfillment and Performance... again leaving four possibilities.

Every leader worth his salt will have teams functioning in the High Fulfillment/High Performance (HF/HP) zone. This is where synergy, work ethic, pride and motivation reign. Leaders spend at least 55-60% of their time supporting HF/HP individuals, 25-30% on LF/HP, 5-10% on HF/LP and, if any time is left, on the LF/LP group. With the last group, time should be spent on transitioning them out, or into situations where they can thrive.

FIVE QUESTIONS

It is only natural for individuals to have numerous questions when participating in any group. Five[5] dominate, and when their answers satisfy the questioner, high satisfaction and high performance become possible. The questions are, in sequence:

1. Why are we here?

2. What is expected of me?

3. How am I doing?

4. What's in it for me to give my all?

5. When I struggle, who do I go to for help?

Each correlates with familiar corporate terminology, namely:

1. Purpose

2. Goals/Expectations

3. Feedback

4. Rewards/Recognition

5. Support

---

5. The Wilson Learning Corporation, Eden Prairie, Minnesota

Answers to these five questions should be readily available, yet this optimistic view is not supported by reality.[6]

Authentic, high and open Communications are critical to change. Basic skills include Listening, Questioning, making Restatements and utilizing Empathy appropriately. Unfortunately, the most common workplace complaint is, "My boss doesn't listen." WOW! And, then he expects people to perform at a high level?

Your challenge: to ensure words, tone and body language are congruent; all sending the same message, i.e., aligning 'being' with 'doing.' When at odds, authenticity and trust evaporate.

STAGES OF TEAM DEVELOPMENT

As with every leadership competency, there is a gap between Knowing and Implementing. For example, leaders must know and shepherd their team through five stages of team development, if they wish to reach a stage of Collaboration.[7]

The leader has a clear vision of what is to be accomplished and, needing a team, she enters

Stage 1 — Membership. She recruits and engages.

Stage 2 — Sub-Grouping. This commences when the team members start working together. Cliques form based on many variables; how things should be done, priorities, who should be doing what? etc.

Effective leaders understand this is simply a part of team formation. They also know when it's time to draw the antagonists together… too early leads to disassociation, too late to entrenchment.

Stage 3 — Confrontation. To function fully, differences must be resolved. If not, divergences may lead to disruption or even worse, escalate to relationship breakdowns.

---

6. A recent Gallup study reports, "'Bosses from hell' are giving U.S. workers the Monday blues. Gallup's 2013 State of the American Workplace report had grim findings, including that 70% of those surveyed either hate work or are completely disengaged, and perks don't help." Many other studies suggest the disenchantment rate is much higher.
7. As articulated in the book *Managing For Excellence*, by Bradford and Cohen

Courageous leaders, knowing that conflict is not necessarily bad, do not shirk from this responsibility. Assertively and compassionately, they step into the 'fray,' knowing Task-related conflict could lead to improvements; and, conflict associated with Relational Concerns, once resolved, generally leads to increased trust.

Stage 4 — Once disruptive issues are dissolved, the team enters Stage 4, Individual Differentiation. Aligned individuals can now get down to business. Each works effectively on his/her piece of the 'puzzle.' The orientation, "I'll do my job, and I trust you will do yours." What's still missing is a real sense of 'being in this together.'

Now the leader encourages members to share strengths and weaknesses, praises good performance, deals with non-performance, challenges members to take on tougher decisions, ensures information flow, coaches problem solving, and encourages consensus on major issues. She knows, higher levels of autonomy can lead to synergistic interdependence and shared responsibility.

Stage 5 — Collaboration is achieved when everyone has 'the other's back,' members are internally driven, appreciate individual strengths, and openly and non-judgementally, accept each other's shortcomings. In this stage, the team-experience is elevated, as is the success of the venture.

Here the leader faces a delicate balance, shifting between visible leader and fading into team member. She has ensured her people have the knowledge and skills to act, make decisions based on defined parameters, participate fully in all aspects of challenge-resolution, and take responsibility for the results they produce.

PHASES OF GROWTH

People are different! The rookie leader has learned about behavior styles, and how modifying his communication is important to establishing and maintaining rapport. Unfortunately, this level of flexibility cannot be attained unless the leader has internalized a Win/Win orientation. Any manipulative intent is quickly spotted.

Beyond style flexibility, a further level of complexity enters the picture; namely, the developmental phase of the project and/or its people. Every living organism, plant, animal or human, goes through three main and distinctly different growth phases on their path to maturity. If any aspect of these phases is disrupted, growth is delayed. What cannot be accurately predicted is how long the developmental process will take. My experience shows the main obstruction to a smooth and rapid transition from phase to phase is the leader's inability to adapt to the changing needs of his people.

Not only are attitudinal orientation and awareness key, the ability to modify how and what is communicated as the project and people mature, becomes critical.

Phase 1: The leader has an idea, or an assignment, to build a system or product. He assembles a team. Note, now it's his show, his idea and if his helpers are rookies, he will communicate very differently than with veterans.

To the rookie he tells what he wants to have done, states expectations and sets milestones. Nobody objects to his 'tell' orientation, since this phase is very leader dependent.

Phase 2 starts after the invention of a successful prototype and/or production process. Effort is now directed at accelerating output.

This shift in team dynamic demands a change in the leader's approach. If he keeps up his 'tell' orientation, team members feel 'bossed' and become disgruntled. This does not mean the leader has to abandon all 'tell.' There are times when 'tell' is required; the main shift is from 'tell' to both 'tell' and 'ask.'

With progress, another shift occurs. First, it was about output; later, it's a demand for improved quality. Who better to support and design this than a group of inspired front line employees?

Thus far, the progressions have been reasonably smooth, predictable. Soon this takes a dramatic twist; a twist most organizations fail to master, and hence, simply end up as forgotten statistics,[8] or they limp along as under-performers.

The transition to Phase 3 is the one that tests every leader and can

---

8. Example: The number of Fortune 500 companies that existed 50 years ago is now below 40.

only be successfully negotiated by those who live and breathe the aforementioned. You see, the transition is characterized by high tension and a sense of overwhelm, overwork and over-extension.

If nothing changes, Phase 2 gradually peaks, plateaus, and then declines; mainly, because actions tend to become repetitive, and stagnation and boredom set in. Something has to change; especially since competition and markets change. Yet, in a competitive environment, where everyone is struggling to compete, people are already over-worked. Change demands inventing new systems and new ways of interacting with each other.

The leader's role shifts to consultant, mentor, supporter and cheerleader, inspiring the team to focus on new possibilities and even greater cooperation.

The heavy workload, and striving to re-invent themselves, causes stress and overwhelm; still, the leader delegates more decision responsibility to the team. Timing, leader support and transition speed are vital.

A successful transition is marked by renewed energy, camaraderie, inspiration and a boost in performance. How the leader communicates has again shifted, mainly to making suggestions. Determination, passion for what is possible, a degree of humility and high levels of appreciation for 'his' people, help speed the process and its success.

LEADERSHIP DEVELOPMENT

When I graduated with honours from an MBA program in 1965, I had the notion I could rapidly rise in the leadership pool of a major consumer goods company. Fate intervened and instead I took over the running of a small business. Three years later, I bought it and within a few more years, had grown it by 742%. I was working around the clock, missed much of my young family's development, and eventually started thinking, "If my people would only do what they were hired to do, my life would be easier. I should fire most of them, rehire the best, and have stringent criteria for re-engagement." Hmmm!

Something was off. Being recognised for superior customer service, specialty products, and growing as a company was a great start, but not enough! My degrees, and the 15-year-school-of-hard-knocks had not developed me into the type of leader I had imagined. My life was void of fulfilment and of a true sense of team. My passions, energy and commitment could only take me so far, and, at age 43, I decided the struggle and effort were no longer worth it. I sold the business and stepped into an uneasy retirement. I was too young and too energetic to roam the pasture. I had no firm plans for my future.

Then, my real growth started. I went into intensive training to become a corporate consultant. I could relate to the struggles of the executives I was coaching, loved seeing their enthusiasm for learning, got rave reviews. But, there was again something missing . . . not just for me, in fact, for our entire industry.

Billions of dollars are being spent on training each year, and with the best technologies and seemingly sound curriculums, we were seeing very little change.

Ah-ha! "*Training* does not work, especially by itself; and almost never, when it comes to leadership." But then, how did some leaders become so great? A few learned it in their formative years, others by being thrown into situations of leadership development that became osmotic. On rare occasions, this happens in home environments; in others, by a process of self-discovery, and predominantly in unusual and trying circumstances. In my case, I learned more about myself and critical leadership skills and aptitudes experientially on lengthy physically-challenging treks; and especially, in humility instilling environments that demanded high and authentic communication, clear focus, unwavering commitment to a desired outcome and deep empathy for my fellow adventurers. My education in classrooms, the daily pressure and demands of my own business, and even my consultancy training, paled in comparison. For this reason, I launched New Wave Leadership and TransformationalTreks. com and am still humbled by the success of these ventures.

The orientation of this writing has been to reinforce the absolute foundation blocks for highly effective leadership. From personal experience, what has to be added is the internalization of these concepts to the point of being second nature. The skills need to become grounded, internalized, intrinsic. Without, quasi-leadership will remain mediocre; with, we will have the dawn of a new era of leadership, and a scarce commodity will have been reversed to the advantage of all.

About Werner

Werner Berger is a Corporate Leadership Consultant, High Stakes Adventurer, and Health Advocate. He emphatically states, "Leadership is absolutely essential to a successful life and planet, and yet, when you look at the state of the world, and the degree of discontent amongst our workforce, you quickly realize leadership is seriously lacking." His purpose as a corporate consultant is to *transform corporations into opportunities of unprecedented personal fulfillment and success.*

Uniqueness counts and this is exactly what Werner brings to his work:

- He has consulted internationally since 1984; from small companies to ones as large as Clorox Canada and AstraZeneca.

- His consulting experience leads him to conclude, "Leadership Training does not work. . .by itself. Leaders have to be developed."

- He has been Master Trained (certified to train other leaders) by prestigious Wilson Learning Worldwide, in 13 different technologies (including Leadership, Management Development, Consultative Selling, and Exceptional Customer Service).

- He is the oldest person in the world to have climbed the highest peak on each of the seven continents (the 7-Summits).

- He is the first, and to date, the only person to have ever flown a kite on the top of Mt. Everest.

- He is the recipient of the 2012 Pennsylvania, AARP "First Ever Life Re-Imagined Award."

- He firmly believes, "If you do not have your health, mental, physical and emotional, you have nothing."

- He currently takes corporate leaders on Transformational Leadership Experiences to places like Mt. Everest Base Camp, Nepal, the top of Mt. Kilimanjaro, Africa, and across the ancient Inca Trail to Machu Picchu, Peru. Every single client, thus far, has returned from these adventures with the comment, "It was a Life-Changing Experience."

- In 2018, he is launching a Global Peace Initiative and states, "Most people say they'd love to live in peace; of course, on their terms. All this means is, there is no global alignment to a common outcome. Missing is open and honest communication, mutual respect and trust. So, let's get to work."

Werner: "I challenge you to dream. Dream of happiness and "mountains" you wish to climb – even the ones you think you can't. Join me in stepping out of your comfort zone into a world that is brighter, more fulfilling, and more enjoyable. When your old and restrictive beliefs get shattered, you discover a world of infinite possibility. Step into your birthright and become the leader you are destined to be."

To reach Werner Berger:
Werner@MeetMeAtTheTop.com
www.TransformationalTreks.com
www.NewWaveLeadership.com

CHAPTER 27

MORE TIME, MORE MONEY - THE ART OF LEVERAGE

BY GREG WATSON

Have you ever wondered just what your life would look like if you had more time or more money? Have you ever wondered what your life would like with more of both?

MORE TIME + MORE MONEY = FREEDOM!

So, how can you get more time and more money into your game? The answer to that is "Leverage."

"Leverage" is a term often ascribed to financial transactions, or in exerting influence over other people, but in its purest form, leverage is simply about using a small object to lift a large object, and it's effective, as long as you are using the right tools. Leverage allows you to accomplish things that otherwise you could not do as effectively by yourself, to Get In The Game at a different level, and to play a bigger game.

- In an engineering sense, you can use a block and tackle to lift an engine block out of a car, but it's fairly unlikely that you could do that yourself, without some sort of help, is there?

- In a financial sense, you can use certain financial instruments (shares, options, futures etc.), as well as borrowed funds, to control a much larger asset base (to both your own benefit and those around you) than you would be able to do otherwise.

- In a personal sense, you can use leverage to get control of more of the precious commodity that we just can't create more of... Time.

In essence, Leverage is about creating your Freedom Team around you to create your abundant life.

There are just two key concepts which, when understood and applied consistently, can help you to create your abundant life through leverage. They both revolve around the concept of "Team", and allowing others to engage in your life to achieve better outcomes – for everyone. In all things, if we create a situation where everybody wins, we create a sustainable model for action, and in this case, a sustainable model for living. I'm going to run through these concepts with some examples to demonstrate how they can work for you.

Over a period of time, I have progressively applied these concepts to my personal life and my business, and extended that through to my family as much as possible, so that now we have a vision of our future that is not clouded by doing "stuff" that we either don't like doing, or that we aren't particularly gifted at doing. It doesn't need to be rocket science – it just needs to make sense. If you want your life to make sense, I reckon they will work for you too! Let's step in and explore our two keys to *More Time, More Money.*

I. THE POWER OF PERSONAL EFFICIENCY

Personal Efficiency is key to obtaining any level of personal leverage, particularly as it relates to time. This is about getting the right person doing the right job – and creating efficiency in your abundant life. It also recognises that you should really only be doing the things that you are best suited to doing, not necessarily everything that needs doing.

Businesses and communities have been using this type of success mantra since the beginning of time. Utilising people's individual skillsets to build an effective team accomplishes so much more than just getting everyone to do everything, and this applies from simple agricultural and subsistence communities through to the corner store, and from a manufacturing or service business to the global economic community that we are a part of today. This division of labour really is the most simple of economic efficiencies, and if we apply it to our personal lives in the same way, we can free up time and create freedom, whatever that means for you.

This whole concept revolves around getting the right person for the job, to free you up to do the things you are both good at, and enjoy. It also enables and empowers other people to do the things that they are good at and enjoy, so everyone wins!

Many of us grew up in households that were defined by a lack of abundance, and some of those generational prejudices are passed on down the line. For me, I grew up with my grandmother and father, and later with my father and stepmother. My grandmother grew up during the Great Depression of the 1920's and 30's, in a small rural community in Australia where their family ran the local hotel. Their necessities were always met, but there was never any great wealth, and the focus was on "getting by" with what you had in those generally frugal times. She carried that through to being a parent, and my Dad grew up in a household that was wealthier, but had a "save for a rainy day" mentality based on fear of lack, not an abundance mindset. My upbringing as a little bloke was similar – we would watch our pennies, live carefully, be thankful for small mercies, and generally be content with what we had. You would fix things that were broken, and save money by doing things yourself, but there was never much left over.

This led to people being a "jack-of-all-trades" at home, even though they worked in a specific field from Monday to Friday. My Dad worked in banking during the week, but on the weekend, he was a gardener, a carpenter, a painter, a brewer, an excavator, and a leathersmith, amongst others - and my friends' fathers would become motor mechanics, woodturners, fencers, pool cleaners, and roofers. My grandmother (probably like yours) was a baker *par excellence*, a seamstress, a nurse, a laundry woman, and a hairdresser. Most of this was done in the interests of being frugal (apart from genuine hobbies, of course), and because that was the way things were done in our family, and plenty of others, perhaps yours as well.

Realising at some point that I was still wrapped up in the paradigm that had been fed to me as a little bloke, something we have put in place for our family is an Outsourcing Plan. We do the things that we really love to do. For me, around the house, that is cooking and gardening – I take great joy from feeding my family and friends and growing my own produce.

But there is someone else who is much better at ironing clothes than I, someone who is much better at cleaning toilets than I, someone who is much better at mowing lawns than I. In the same way, when my car needs servicing, I don't change the oil myself – I take it to a mechanic, and he does it (and does a far better job than I ever could, incidentally). But I don't see my mechanic if I have a hole in my tooth – I'll see the dentist about that. And I don't take my car to my dentist to get fixed – the person who is the right specialist gets the job, and that's the case with everything.

Wouldn't it be a better way to get someone who is really good at what they do to help you with what you need, so you can do more of the things that you're really good at doing? We decided to do that.

So, how can you create more time, more money, more freedom in your life so you can play the game at a different level? Here's a simple Five Step method for you to follow.

Step 1 – Work out what you're going to do with the time you've created (before you create it). Are you going to spend some of it on your work or business to create more financial freedom? Are you going to spend more time with your family? Are you going to spend more time bass fishing? What is it that **YOU** want to do? You need to know what you want to create before you create it, so begin with the end in mind.

Step 2 – Take an Inventory of everything you do at home. Seriously – EVERYTHING you do at home. You might do this over a week period, a two-week period or even a month, but at the end of the exercise, you should have a very clear idea of the tasks on which you are actually spending your time.

Step 3 – Work out what functions you could readily give to someone else. (Ironing, cleaning, lawn mowing and yard work are probably some of the most obvious). Keep the ones you like doing, for a start. Take money out of the equation, and just look at what it would be possible to outsource.

Step 4 – Decide what resources you are prepared to put towards your Freedom. Money is the most obvious solution – to pay people to do the things you don't want to do, however for some people or families, it may not be practical to take a big chunk out of your budget. So, the other part of this equation is to work out what you can trade your own skills and time for. So, if you are a mechanic, you might be able to trade an oil change for the guy down the road who mows lawns, or the lady across the street who is an accountant, and so you still create that win-win situation.

Step 5 – Implement the Plan! A plan is only as good as its implementation – you need to step out and take action to create the time and money you want. Do It!

One of the simplest things for our family was just to employ someone to clean the house for us for a few hours every two weeks. We like to have a clean home, but we don't particularly like scrubbing toilets and floors, so it seemed logical to get someone to do that for us so that we could free up more time to do what we wanted to do.

The mindset starts with your personal life, and extends to almost every other part of your life. Sharpening your ability to be more efficient in your everyday life will also flow into other areas, and one of those key areas is your financial efficiency. As an expert in investor finance strategies, I deal with this in a professional capacity every day. The amount of leverage that is available to you in the financial world is just incredible, if you can understand how it can work for you. Personal Efficiency is the key to creating *More Time*, but Financial Efficiency is the key to creating the *More Money* part of the Freedom equation.

II. THE POWER OF FINANCIAL EFFICIENCY

This form of leverage, Financial Leverage, is one of the prime adages of the wealth building industry - using Other People's Money (OPM) so that you can fund part of your own investments, and reap a higher return on your own input. So, how does that work? Using OPM allows you to control much larger assets than what you could otherwise control, and it enables much greater returns on your own money.

Here's a simplified example looking at what is possible across a few different asset classes:

Let's say you've got $100,000 – and you invest it in a bank deposit or CD. Rates vary from country to country and time frame to time frame, but at 3%, you'll make $3,000 per annum. That's all you'll make – a 3% return.

However, if you invested that $100,000 in say shares or managed funds (with a long term buy and hold strategy), a bank might lend you a dollar for every dollar you put in, so you've now got $200,000 working for you. The long term rate of growth in western share markets averages around 10% per annum – so your average return might be somewhere around $20,000 – which on the $100,000 you originally invested, is 20%,[1] compared to 10% without leverage! Is that sounding better? Let's take it one step further.

Let's now look at residential property. Prior to the GFC (Global Financial Crisis) in many places around the world, you could borrow up to 100% (or more) of the value of residential property – that's *infinite leverage*. Of course, the risk inherent in that approach was part of the reason the world plunged into financial turmoil in 2009. However, it is still worth examining from the perspective of leverage. Whilst 100% leverage is not accessible in most markets around the world today, banks in Australia will still lend up to 90% (and in some cases 95%) for purchasing residential property. So, taking the 90% example, for every $100,000 you've got in cash, the bank can lend you $900,000, so you can potentially have $1 million invested in property (or in multiple properties).

That's your small object lifting a large object – a million dollar object! Historical statistics shows that the Australian property market doubles in value every 7 – 10 years, which is around 10% per annum. That equates to a return of $100,000 per annum on the $1 million you've got in the market,[2] which is 100% on the funds you invested yourself.

THAT is the power of financial leverage, and that's why many people prefer property investment in Australia over other forms of investment – simply because of the amount of leverage that is possible over the long term.

Apart from these examples, there are many other ways that you can achieve financial leverage, including through the use of share options,

---

1. This assumes that dividend returns cover the cost of debt finance.
2. This assumes that rental returns cover the cost of debt finance for investment properties.

exchange traded funds and futures markets in currencies, commodities and bonds, however there are different risk profiles attached to these types of instruments. So, from a financial leverage perspective, you MUST have the right professionals on your team – a finance broker, financial planner and accountant/CPA at the very least – to make all the pieces stick together.

Your challenge now is to go forth and practice the Art of Leverage in your personal life, in your business life, and in your financial life, to create *More Time, More Money* so that you can truly live that abundant life and achieve the Freedom that you deserve. Go for it!

About Greg

Greg Watson is a seasoned finance expert who specialises in helping his friends and clients create more time and more money in their lives by successfully leveraging their personal, professional and financial lives. After 15 years on the corporate ladder in Australia, in the year 2000 he stepped sideways out of corporate life to start his own consulting business, later transitioning into a mortgage broking and financial planning franchise before establishing an independent brand, The Investor Hub, in 2011.

Greg's philosophy is for creating win-win in every circumstance, and creating lasting partnerships for his clients with both himself and other professionals, to ensure that clients are supported and served with absolute integrity throughout their freedom journey. Greg focuses on sustained relationships that bring lasting benefits to everyone involved. In keeping with his philosophy around personal leverage, he is very much an advocate for appropriate specialists advising clients on their specific area of expertise, rather than creating a one-stop-shop or one-size-fits-all mentality.

His objective is to create more prosperity through the application of leverage in all aspects of people's lives. To date, he has helped hundreds of people improve their position through his financial services businesses, and he is committed to expand that reach both as that business continues to expand and through programs designed to educate people around the possibilities for leverage in all aspects of their lives.

Greg holds both Bachelor and Masters Degrees in Economics from Australia's Macquarie University, specialising in monetary and financial economics, as well as subsequent professional qualifications in mortgage broking and financial planning, and is an accredited Mortgage Adviser. He also has an eclectic professional resume, including business, economic and banking analyst roles at the Australian central bank and other financial regulatory bodies, Chief Financial Officer of an independent mutual bank, and 15 years as a consultant and mortgage broker in his own businesses.

Greg is married to Dinah (who is also his partner in both businesses), and they live in Nelson Bay, Australia. Together they have three children - two adult sons, and a teenage daughter. Greg's favourite pastimes that he likes to pursue with some of his leveraged time are fishing, gardening and cooking, as well as a life-long obsession with the gentle sport of rugby union.

You can connect with Greg at:
gregw@theinvestorhub.com.au
www.twitter.com/GregNWatson
www.facebook.com/MoreTimeMoreMoney

CHAPTER 28

FRIENDSHIP MAKES CUSTOMERS FOR LIFE

BY BRIAN STENNETT

I always wanted to be like those hopefuls on the show Shark Tank, to be an independent business owner. I have the opportunity now as I grow my business, but I realized I had it in me all the time, I had certain skills and ways that I do things that have created lifetime customers. I am in a different industry now than when I started as a cars salesman, but I have brought those same customers along into my new venture because they trust me, and no matter what I am selling, they will want to be a part of it. Here are the top tips for creating Lifetime Customers.

1. FIND MENTORS

When I started in car sales, I had never sold cars before. I identified some of the top salespeople in the region that were selling twenty, twenty-five plus cars a month and I said to myself, "What's going to be the quickest way to shorten my learning curve?" I decided that taking them out and treating them to lunch would allow me to ask about their experiences, have them share some pitfalls or success tips. This was the quickest way to selling twenty-five cars a month. Seek mentorship from people in the area that you're trying to succeed in. You don't have to recreate the wheel; you just need to figure out how others did it.

I would ask, "What has made you successful or what tips can you share if I wanted to be as successful as your are?" That's how I've learned everything that I've learned. I just ask people, "Hey, I'm new at this. I want to be successful, and you seem to be successful in your field. Is there anything you could share with an eager young guy like myself that will enable me to maybe miss some pitfalls or to become as successful as you? Maybe not as successful as you, but I'm sure you can lessen my learning curve."

They often insisted on paying for lunch; they just enjoyed talking to me. I found that many people will be a mentor to you if you ask them. They're not probably just going to run up to you and just tell you what you want to know. You have to show some initiative and ask them.

2. IMPLEMENTATION

After you go out and meet with your mentors, and you will begin to collect nuggets of wisdom, because usually those people love to share their experience, so be ready to write some good notes. Begin to implement one or two of those ideas and you should see some immediate results. I've always been a life-long learner, and so I am always on the search for better ideas and new mentors.

3. TRY IT OUT

In every opportunity I've had in sales, I usually write down a 100 to 200-name list of people that I know and ask them if I could practice on them. By doing so, you will become comfortable with trying new sales ideas, and get some helpful feedback. You may even be lucky enough for it to turn into a real sale. Try to practice as often as possible.

4. BE OPEN MINDED

Try to listen to other people's ideas because you could learn something important. Leave judgment at the door. I try to encourage my teenage child to try to learn something new every day. Write it down, because later on, it may make more sense to you.

5. GET EDUCATED

Attend trainings, and read books written by experts. I go to seminars where I can pick up information from successful people and this helps me stay current and learn new sales and business techniques.

6. STAY POSITIVE

You have to have a positive attitude, because if you are a pessimist you're probably not going to be good at sales. People are attracted to positive people. If you find yourself being negative about the company you are working for or the product you are selling, you might want to consider moving to another company or line of work.

7. YOU ARE ALWAYS SELLING SOMETHING

We are always selling no matter what role we are playing with people – whether as a car salesman or as a mom or dad. There are days I have to sell my son why he should clean his room. I could do it brute force and give him an ultimatum. The problem is when you use brute force on someone, you may win that sell at the moment, but you risk buyer's remorse.

8. DON'T USE BRUTE TACTICS

Brute force does not have a positive lasting effect – because being a good salesperson does not mean you are good at selling a particular product, it means you are great working with people and could sell them anything. If you can just present some good information to someone in a way that they receive it and they understand it, then their brain can work on it to really decide whether they want to buy something or not. There is a minimal risk of buyer's remorse, and they feel respected, which means you have created a customer for life.

I have a colleague who played football, and has a very aggressive approach. He uses the 'you are dumb if you don't buy from me' method. Now, is he successful at it? That is a matter of interpretation. The top leaders in my region ask me why my quote volume is so low. However, I am converting about 90% of people that I meet with.

I present ideas in a manner where my clients can appreciate it. I do not beg people to buy from me. I present tailored solutions that would fit their situation based upon the information they gave me. A high percentage of the time, I end up doing business with them. If you take care of your customers, they will take care of you by buying from you now and in the future.

9. DON'T PUSH, KNOW YOUR CUSTOMER'S NEEDS

If you just sit down with your clients and show them you care, you create customers for life, rather than focusing just on pushing a certain product.

When I used to sell cars, my sales managers would say, "Hey if we sell a Chevy Camaro today, there's an extra thousand dollars in commission you can earn." They wanted us to push every client, even if they were a husband and wife with four kids and they needed a min van, the sales management wanted us to try to push them into the Chevy Camaro. I did not do that and even rebelled against that. The management did not like it, but I made solid sales nonetheless, and I still have great relationships with my customers years after I sold them their first car.

They used to call me an order taker, which was not a positive term. Many of the sales managers were never sales people on the floor. They were college graduates who would read sales books and base everything on numbers rather than on people. They would say, "You just do whatever the customer wants. You're just an order taker." This meant I would do what the customer wanted to make them happy, rather than pushing my sales managers agenda.

I was the top salesman at the dealership and I accounted for 40% of the dealership's bottom line. Go figure.

10. YOU HAVE TO CARE ABOUT THE CLIENT

To be successful in sales, you have to care about the client. It has to be about them. If you make it about you, then you make experience temporary success, but you will ruin relationships. Once they find out you are a fraud, and that you only cared about the sale, not them, then you are done. They will not come back and they tell other people to stay away as well.

I really become energized talking to people and building lasting relationships. As a little kid, I always wanted to be a doctor. If someone in the family would get a scuff or a cut or something like that, I would run and go get medical supplies like methylate, iodine, and bandages and patch them up. I love to just sit and hear people talk about their stories or learn things from them, and I had a dream of being that type of doctor. When I grew older the thought of going to college for seven to eight years after I graduated from Penn State seemed like a long time for me, but I still wanted a career in which I could connect with people.

I got into the sales field and learned a lot when working for a car rental company. I started out in a suit and a tie to pick customers up, wash their cars, and stuff like that. I worked my way up to assistant manager and through all of that; I would just always ask people about their life and their story. In doing that, I found that people enjoy when someone shows a personal interest in them.

11. MAKE CONNECTIONS IN THE COMMUNITY

Go out into the community and help others, because other people notice. You might not think by sharing your story or just going out into the community and meeting people has an impact, but it does. By helping people and telling them what you're doing, you can become an inspiration. You may think you're bothering people but you're actually not – you're uplifting, and you're showing them that you care.

I was recently at the local VFW and they were having a benefit to get flags for the town's renovations. I went out to help them in their effort and I was wearing a polo with my company logo. A woman runs up to me and says, "Hey, are you Brian Stennett?"

I said, "Yes."

She said, "We have not ever met, but I am the one that assesses clients when they sign up for services for our company."

"Oh, wow." I replied. "I'm glad you said something to me. It is a pleasure to meet you."

"I'm just so proud of you." she said, "Your clients just rave about your service and I've been telling people that I just wanted to meet you in person."

She knew my mother and told her the same thing, "I'm just so proud of him and everything he's doing. His clients just rave about him, how when they call him or text him, he answers right away. He always gives someone an ear or listens – no matter what he is doing. It makes a difference."

When I sold cars, I would tell the client, "Hey. Our transaction does not end here today. Actually, we're creating a life-long friendship and I'll check back in with you every three to six months." And then I would say, "If I get to be too much or I'm bugging you, please just tell me and I'll stop. I really thank you for allowing me to take care of you and I want to service you long-term."

12. WORK ON CREATING REFERRAL BUSINESS

That is the magic touch; just that little extra will build a customer base, rather than relying on constantly acquiring new ones. I give them my personal cell phone number and I get texts. I got a text last night from the Fire Chief in Mt. Union. He came to me from a referral from the local restaurant that I frequent. The girls take good care of me there.

I sent them a thank-you card for great service. I usually take digital photos with my iPhone and then I put them in an e-card telling them I really enjoyed the meal and the service. I do love good service. These simple gestures have garnered me a ton of referral business. How much does a smile and thank you cost?

My managers say, "You're a great salesperson."

I don't know that I'm a real salesperson. I just like people. I listen to them and I give them my word that if I can help them I'm going to take care of them. That's all I do, and it leads to sales. But I really don't consider myself a salesperson – I'm a friend, and friendship creates customers for life.

To summarize, my mentor Jim Rohn says, "Start today where you are, the timing is never gonna be perfect, but just get started!" or just 'Get in the Game!'

About Brian

Brian Stennett Sr. is a sales professional, entrepreneur, insurance agent, and most importantly, a single father of two young men.

Prior to becoming an agent with Nationwide Insurance in November 2012, Brian was the dominant senior account executive in Central Pennsylvania for the Car Sales Division of Enterprise Rent-A-Car. Brian was awarded numerous sales and customer service awards during his seven years with Enterprise.

In 2008 and 2011 he was awarded the Enterprise Excellence Award in Recognition of Superior Sales Achievement. In 2008, 2009 and 2012 he was #1 Senior Account Executive in Central Pennsylvania, and in 2010 and 2011 he was the #2 Senior Account Executive In Central Pennsylvania.

Brian's entrepreneurial drive has led to his recently opening two agencies in central Pennsylvania in the towns of Bellefonte and Howard. In 2014, he was awarded the prestigious Nationwide Champions Conference Agent, which is given to only a Select Group of top agents across the country that have met rigorous sales and customer service goals. His short-term goals are to open a couple more agencies in the next 12 months, while his long-term goals are to open an agency in all 50 states.

Brian graduated from Penn State University in 2004 with a BS in Business Administration – Management/marketing, and Entrepreneurship. "We Are Penn State – Go Nittany Lions!"

Brian is very involved in his community where he volunteers, and his greatest goal is to be the best father he can be. Brian loves to cook and especially grill, and he has the bragging rights in his community of being the winner of the 1st Annual Mount Unity Chili Cook-off in 2014.

Contact Brian Stennett Sr. directly about insurance or other business advice at: brian.k.stennett@gmail.com.

You can also find him on the web through the following links:
- Facebook Business Page - www.StennettInsuranceAgency.com
- Agency Website – www.BrianStennettAgency.com
- LinkedIn page - www.linkedin.com/in/stennettagency
- Twitter page - www.twitter.com/bkstenn
- Pinterest page - www.pinterest.com/brianstennettsr/
- Google page - https://plus.google.com/104871272535056449021/
- Instagram page - http://instagram.com/bkstenn

CHAPTER 29

SAY "YES" THEN FIGURE OUT...FOUR STEPS TO BECOMING A GAMECHANGER

BY LORAL LANGEMEIER

I'm known world-wide as "The Millionaire Maker" and it's for good reason. Over the past ten years, I've helped thousands of people become millionaires by sharing practical information through my proprietary Millionaire Maker Blueprint. I've spoken on thousands of different stages worldwide and have become one of the foremost experts on building and sustaining wealth.

I've personally built multiple companies, worth millions of dollars, and I'm committed to helping people achieve their Financial Freedom Day. I believe everyone has the potential to become a Game Changer in whatever they do. There's nothing that I have that you don't have. We share the same 24 hours in our days and the same 7 days in our weeks. I say this to motivate you. I want you to know that anything is possible when you take action and surround yourself with the right team.

That said, my success wasn't handed to me on a silver platter. I made a conscious decision to "get in the game" at a young age, and over time I became a leading Game Changer in my industry. You can decide to become a Game Changer too. Unfortunately, I meet thousands of people from all over the world and everyone has an excuse when it comes to why they don't have the business and life they want.

When it comes to success, there is no excuse. Changing the game starts by changing yourself. Anyone, and I do mean ANYONE, can become a Game Changer in their industry while becoming a millionaire at the same time.

When I graduated from high school, I became a certified personal trainer. As my company became more successful, I was approached by a large oil and gas company who heard about my business. I worked with Chevron for years and designed 272 gyms and fitness plans for their employees on offshore drilling rigs. I was able to do this because I said yes, then figured out how.

In fact, the moment I said yes to this contract, was the moment I started living my life by the mantra of "Saying yes then figuring out how." To this day, I continue to say yes to new opportunities, then commit to figuring out how to turn them into successful businesses.

Let's dive into the four simple steps to becoming a Game Changer in your industry.

Ready? Go!

THE FOUR STEPS TO BECOMING A GAME CHANGER ARE:
- Step #1: Get In The Game
- Step #2: Stay In The Game
- Step #3: Create A New Game
- Step #4: Lead The Game

Let's take a closer look at each step...

1) GET IN THE GAME:
"Getting in the game" means stepping up and taking control of your life. Only when you lead your life and become accountable for your own success, can you then become a Game Changer in your industry.

To get in the game you first have to DECIDE you want to get in the game. Next, you have to COMMIT TO ACTION.

Life is made of decisions and you can decide to step up and play a new and bigger game at ANY time. All you have to do is decide. It really is that simple. What's your decision? Are you saying "Yes" or "No?"

I want you to think of the great business leaders who inspire you. The only difference between them and you is that they decided to take action and made the commitment to see their idea or vision through to the end.

Once you commit to getting in the game, the next step is to take action. You might be thinking to yourself, "Loral, I get it. I can decide to get in the game but I don't know how to get in the game. If I knew how, I'd already be playing."

I get it. I've been there before, but I chose not to stay on the sidelines for long. I chose to get in the game and I made a commitment to learning how to play along the way and this involved finding the right people to bring on my team.

In fact, I can say with 110% confidence that everything I've accomplished in my life (both professionally and personally), has occurred because I made the decision to "Say yes, then figure out how" by finding people who knew what had to be done.

The other KEY component of taking action is sequencing.

Sequencing is knowing what to do and when to do it. I'm the only coach who knows how to do this, because I created this concept. Now I coach people world-wide on the proper sequencing of their Cash Machine and I lead people to Millionaire Status.

I have one question for you and I want you to answer it right now... Are you ready to get in the game and play?

Fast Action Step: Go to Facebook and declare to the Live Out Loud community that you're "Getting in the game by taking action and saying yes, then committing to figuring out how!"

It's a liberating experience to decide you're moving forward with the attitude of figuring it out along the way. You can find my Facebook community here: https://www.facebook.com/liveoutloud

2) STAY IN THE GAME:
To become a Game Changer in your industry, you need to "stay in

the game" no matter what. You Stay In The Game By STAYING IN ACTION. This is where a lot of people fall to the sidelines. They decide to get in the game, but they don't commit to always "saying yes, then figuring out how."

When you commit to "saying yes, then figuring out how" you're committing to staying in action at all times. When you stay in action, you gain momentum. This positive momentum can be turned into fuel that can then be used to propel you towards your goals.

When you stay in action, you also build your money muscles. Money muscles are similar to the muscles in our bodies. When you don't exercise, your muscles atrophy. They shrink and become weak. Most people have atrophied money muscles because they haven't exercised them properly. When you strengthen your money muscles, you increase your endurance and sustainability.

Sustainability is KEY to running a successful business. You need to have the staying power to make it through the tough times, learn from them and move forward full-steam-ahead.

The simple formula for staying in action looks like this:

- Take action. (Build your money muscles!)

- Analyze the results you received from the action you took.

- Identify what's working for your business and what needs to be adjusted.

- Implement your key learnings from step 3.

- Repeat. (Increase your sustainability!)

"Staying in action" is a practice and similar to any practice, it takes time to master. You will hit roadblocks and there will be times when you question your ability to continue on. What sets great leaders and successful business owners apart from the rest, is their ability to stay in action and move forward no matter what.

No one achieves greatness on their own. It takes a team of experts to make success happen.

I owe my success largely to the mentors (members of my expert team) I've had along the way. They not only helped me stay in action when times were tough, they also helped me to "say yes, then figure it out" as I built my businesses.

Now I'm committed to mentoring action-takers around the globe so they can achieve their Freedom Day too! You can learn more about the mentoring and coaching services that my team of Millionaire Makers and I offer at: www.LiveOutLoud.com.

Fast Action Step: Build your momentum by following these steps for staying in action:

1) List the recent actions you've taken to drive you towards your goal.

2) Analyze the results you received from each specific action you took.

3) Identify the actions that are working for your business and what needs to be adjusted. Continue doing what works and adjust what's not working.

4) Implement your adjustments and key learnings.

5) Stay in action and do it all over again!

Bonus Fast Action Step: Share the top three action steps you're taking this week in the Live Out Loud Facebook community. "Living Out Loud" about your goals is one of the quickest ways to build momentum for success.

You can find my Facebook community here: https://www.facebook.com/liveoutloud

3) CREATE A NEW GAME:

When you commit to getting in the game and staying in the game, "creating a NEW game" is easier than you think. Creating a new game is taking any business idea or service and offering it to the masses in a distinct way.

Distinction is KEY because it sets you apart from your competitors. Too many people shy away from a crowded market place because there's too much competition. I believe a crowded market place means people want to buy what you're offering. This is a good thing!

When you create a new game that is distinctly different than what everyone else is offering, you set yourself up to be a Game Changer. You also set yourself up for making fast cash!

My signature event is called 3 Days To Cash and I guarantee everyone who attends will make money if they do what I tell them to do. I also guarantee that people will become Millionaires within 3-5 years when they do what I say. These are distinct promises that I have never heard from another coach and speaker. They're unique to me and they add value to my business.

So how do you create a new game? The simplest way to create a new game is to apply the knowledge you learn from being in constant action. When you stay in constant action, you're receiving constant feedback from your surroundings. When you gain constant feedback, you gain a new perspective. Your new perspective is what allows you to create a new game. You now have something to offer that is uniquely yours.

I decided to create a new game and now I'm an international Bestselling Author, Speaker, Coach and Entrepreneur.

I remember when I decided to step up and create a new game. I was working for a well-known financial literacy author and coach. Over time, I noticed there were certain parts of the "financial conversation" that weren't happening. This is when I decided to implement my new perspective by taking action and creating my own business. Live Out Loud was born and it became the platform that allows me to take action and grow my business while helping thousands of people do the same.

Fast Action Step: It's time to identify your unique perspective. What do you do differently than others? What key lessons have you learned from taking action? What do you offer that is unique to you or your business? Take a few minutes and write down anything that comes to mind.

The notes that you take today are going to help you create the new game you'll create and play tomorrow!

4) LEAD THE GAME:
Now that you've created a new game, the final step is to "lead the game".

Leading the game is easy. You lead the game by teaching other people in your industry how to create games of their own. Both Kevin Harrington and myself are leading the game in our unique industries and now we've joined forces to lead together.

Whether you realize it or not, you already know how to do this. When you commit to "saying yes, then figuring out how", surrounding yourself with mentors and staying in constant action, you're ready to help others do the same.

THIS is how you become a Game Changer.

Fast Action Step: I want you to grab your journal and a pen. I want you to commit to "saying yes, then figuring out how", staying in constant action, applying your new perspective to the present and surrounding yourself with the right mentor(s).

Write a commitment statement. Date it and sign it, then put it somewhere where you'll see it multiple times a day.

Remember, becoming a leader in your industry is attainable for anyone who is willing to:

1) Get In The Game

2) Stay In The Game

3) Create A New Game

4) Lead The Game

All you have to do is DECIDE you want to play, then join the game!

About Loral

Loral's straight talk electrifies audiences and inspires powerful action from live stages and television programs ranging from CNN, CNBC, The Street TV, Fox News Channel, Fox Business Channel-America's Nightly Scoreboard, *The Dr. Phil Show* and *The View.* She is a regular guest-host on *The Circle* in Australia and has been featured in articles in *USA Today, The Wall Street Journal, The New York Times, Forbes Magazine* and was the breakout star in the film *The Secret.*

With unquestionable candor, she is quick to speak truth that leaves no doubt about her point of view.

"Get off your lazy assets."

"Millionaires don't leave money to chance."

"Companies make money. People get taxed."

"You are here to do something better."

"Change and engage your relationship with money. Start first by hanging out with people who have it."

"Entrepreneurs change economies."

"Entrepreneurs solve problems and need needs."

"What problem do you solve and what needs do you meet?"

"Say YES and figure out how to get it done."

Growing up on her family's farm in Nebraska, Loral was never content to sit at the little kids table for holidays or special occasions – even as a nine year old. The Big Table was where the important conversations were happening, and she quickly took her place – even if it meant sitting on someone's lap. Today, she and her team call smaller players in money matters to take their seats at The Big Table as the conversations around money shift perspectives and livelihoods for the better.

Loral Langemeier is living proof that anyone can have the life of his or her dreams through hard work, persistence, and getting things done in the face of opposition. Loral began her career working with the Chevron Corporation right out of college. It was clear to her early on that there was more to life than cubicles and trading her time for dollars. Despite her own fears and persuasion from friends and family against it, Loral quit her job to become an executive coach. Virtually overnight, Loral quintupled her income while working much less. With her newfound freedom of time and accumulation of wealth she founded Live Out Loud, Inc.

As a single mother of two children, she is redefining the possibility for women to have it all and raise their children in an entrepreneurial and financially literate environment. Loral is dedicated to helping men and women from all walks of life to become millionaires and enjoy time with their families.

Legacy is something very important to Loral. She is a frequent donor to charitable groups including The Boys and Girls Club of America, The Lake Tahoe Bear League, An Empowered Woman Foundation, Life School and Family Resource Centers. She has developed special programs for women and children and, in 2012, raised $40,000 for the founder of the Make-A-Wish Foundation. She also runs Serve Out Loud, a program aimed at providing discounted education in financial literacy to United States Veterans.

To book Loral to speak, make quantity purchases of her best-selling books — *Yes! Energy: The Equation to Do Less, Make More; The Millionaire Maker; The Millionaire Maker's Guide to Wealth Cycle Investing; The Millionaire Maker's Guide to Creating a Cash Machine for Life and Put More Cash In Your Pocket* — and learn more about her perspective-shifting and proven wealth creation training programs, visit: www.liveoutloud.com.

CHAPTER 30

THE HIGH COST OF NOT HIRING A PROFESSIONAL

BY KEVIN ROBERTS

You sign for a registered letter, and sit down and open a rather thick envelop. You notice it is from the IRS, and your stomach drops. You see some rather large numbers, and words like penalties and fees and under that are even larger numbers. You thought that you filed the taxes for your business correctly using a free online program. It was not free after all, and now you owe thousands of dollars on a deadline. Your successful business could now be closing their doors, all because you ignored the advice of hiring a CPA.

Small business owners do not often realize that one of their greatest expenses they will encounter are taxes, and they often make the costly mistake of trying to handle it on their own. This can lead to mistakes, and mistakes lead to audits, penalties, the close of their business and in extreme cases, jail time. It is that serious.

Many new businesses fail in the early years from poor management and lack of attention to financial basics such as record-keeping and reporting. This is very preventable if you follow some basic strategies.

I. CHOOSING A LEGAL ENTITY

One of the first things a business should do, whether at its inception, or ready to grow to the next level, is to select the type of legal entity under which they wish to conduct their activities.

You should begin by asking yourself some questions:

1. How do you intend to finance your business? Do you have the capital to finance it on your own or will you need investors or partners?

2. How much personal risk are you willing to bear? This is so important, because certain types of legal entities can actually protect your personal assets should you ever be unfortunate enough to be sued successfully.

3. Taxation? There are different tax structures that can provide specific tax shelters. It depends on the size and type of company you intend to build.

4. Who else is involved? This goes back to question number 1. Do you have partners who you share with in the creation of a product or service? How many partners are going to be involved?

5. Any legal restrictions imposed on your business or type of business? This may take some research, but certain types of business require certain types of legal structures. You should find out early in your decision-making process. A mistake could create serious consequences both short and long term.

There are a number of options that are discussed below. The decision to choose a legal entity will have a significant impact on the way and how much you are protected under the law, and the way you are affected by income tax rules and regulations. Each type of legal entity has its benefits and drawbacks, and each is treated differently for legal and tax purposes. It is incredibly important to set up your business as the specific type of entity that it not only aspires to be, but in reality is. Many business owners make mistakes at this step by identifying themselves a certain way and then developing a business that contains aspects of a different type. By doing this they set themselves up for legal problems and situations where they are not complying with what the law requires of them.

There are five basic forms of business organizations:

1. Sole Proprietorship

A sole proprietorship is a business owned and operated by an individual or a married couple. It is not considered to be a legal entity in its own right, but rather an extension of the individual or individuals who own it. The business owner owns the business assets personally and is responsible for the debts or other liabilities of the business. The income or loss from a sole proprietorship is combined with the other earnings of an individual (or married couple) for income tax purposes.

A sole proprietorship is the simplest form of business to own and operate because it does not require any specific legal organization. It just needs to obtain any required licenses or permits.

2. Partnerships
Partnerships can be structured as general partnerships or limited partnerships.

A **general partnership** is comprised of two or more individuals who go into business together. It will usually file a fictitious business name statement to operate under the partnership name. Each of the individual partners owns the company assets, has responsibility for its liabilities, and has authority to run the business. The authority of the partners and the way in which profits and losses are shared can be established by partnership agreement. Responsibility for liabilities can also be documented in an agreement, but partnership creditors typically have recourse to all the personal assets of each of the partners for settlement of partnership debts.

A **limited partnership** is comprised of one or more general partners and one or more limited partners. Limited partners do not take part in running the business and are not liable for the debts of the partnership. However, if a limited partner does take part in running the business, they become personally liable. All the general partners are personally liable.

The rights, responsibilities, and obligations of both the limited and general partners are typically detailed in a partnership agreement. Whether you have a limited or general partnership, it is important to have a signed agreement. A partnership is recognized under the law as a legal entity, and as such, has rights and responsibilities in and of itself. A partnership can enter into contracts, obtain trade credit and borrow money. Most creditors will require personal guarantees from the general partners when dealing with a small partnership.

A partnership is required to file both Federal and State Income Tax returns. However, a partnership does not generally pay income tax.

Partnership income or loss is allocated to the individual partners and the partners report their shares of the net income or loss on their personal income tax returns.

3. The C Corporation

Corporations are regulated by state law which permits them to function as separate legal entities. A corporation has legal rights and is responsible for the corporation debts and filing income tax returns and paying taxes. Typically, owners or shareholders of a corporation are protected from the liabilities of the business. However, when a corporation is small, creditors may require personal guarantees from the principal owners before extending credit.

The first step is to prepare **Articles of Incorporation** and **By-laws** which are then adopted and filed; these govern the rights and obligations of the shareholders, directors and officers.

Corporations must file annual income tax returns with the IRS and their state's tax agency as well as other states where they do business. The elections made in a corporation's initial tax returns can have a significant impact on how the business is taxed in the future. Regular corporations (i.e., those that have not elected S status — see below) are referred to as C Corporations.

It is advisable to seek the assistance of an experienced lawyer and CPA when incorporating your business as there are a number of critical decisions to be made which will have far-reaching and long-lasting impact. Don't try this by yourself.

4. The S Corporation

An S Corporation is treated like a regular corporation with one exception — an S Corporation pays no income tax. The net income or loss from the S Corporation is combined with the other income of the stockholders on their personal tax returns. There are special rules governing the deductibility of S Corporation losses, which are generally limited to an individual's tax basis. The tax laws regarding tax basis are quite complex.

S Corporation status is attained by filing Form 2553 which must be done in a timely manner. The decision as to whether to elect S status requires appropriate consultation prior to incorporation for new businesses or before filing the election for existing corporations. There are regulations regarding which corporations are eligible to be taxed as S Corporations. If a corporation was previously taxed as a C Corporation, there are additional tax considerations that may subject the S Corporation to a tax liability.

5. The Limited Liability Company (LLC)

A Limited Liability Corporation (LLC) combines the liability protection of a corporation with the favorable tax treatment of a partnership. If an LLC has two or more members, it can elect to be treated as either a corporation (either C Corporation or S Corporation) or a partnership for income tax purposes and then files the appropriate tax forms. The default tax treatment for multi-member LLC's is partnership. A single member LLC can disregard the entity and treat itself as though it were a sole proprietorship.

An LLC is an incorporated business organization that generally protects the owners from individual liability for the organization's obligations and against vicarious liability for the negligence and malfeasance of others. Management may be flexibly structured to allow owners (referred to as members) to apportion management authority as they see fit. Partnership classification is assured under some state statutes and may be attained through proper structuring in others.

Creating an LLC is as simple as forming a corporation. **Articles of Organization** must be filed with the Secretary of State; they are similar to the articles of incorporation used to form corporations. Filing fees are much the same. It is still advised that you seek the appropriate legal and financial counsel to assist you in the process.

An **operating agreement** defines the rights and obligations of the members, including how profits, losses, and distributions will be shared. Most LLCs will have limitations on the transferability of members' interests and the ability of members to carry on the business after a member ceases to be involved.

Members are generally not liable for the debts and other obligations of the LLC, but they are liable for:

• The amounts the members have agreed to contribute to the LLC.

• Under some statutes, the amounts distributed to the members.

• Any negligence or malfeasance the member individually commits or that the member supervises.

This generally means that members are not liable for the contracts and general liabilities of the LLC or for any mistakes or improper actions of others in the name of the LLC.

One of the major advantages of an LLC is related to tax. If properly structured, it provides the benefit of one level of taxation; as with partnerships, any income generated by the company is passed through to the owners.

II. EMPLOYEES

If you chose to be a sole proprietor, filing your taxes will be similar to the way you have been filing your individual taxes for years, and your CPA can help file these simply and quickly.

If however, you decide to hire people to work for you, then you are taking on a totally new and complicated tax liability- employee taxes. You have to figure out how much to withhold from each employee, and your company will have their own liability for each employee as well. Consult your CPA and be ready to handle this new structure before you begin.

III. KEEP GOOD RECORDS

Once you figure out the type of legal structure you are going to choose, then the real fun begins. The surest way to keep your taxes on track is to think about them year round, not just in the month of April. This means you have to keep some exemplary records of anything you spend related to the business. If you don't know the best way to do this, ask you CPA, because they know what is needed at tax time, and what records will assure you are taxed accurately and with the maximum benefit to you and your company.

Note: *Bad records = Bad Consequences*

IV. SAVING MONEY

One of the biggest challenges new business owners face is taxes, because if they worked for someone else's company most of their life, taxes were generally taken care of for them. Before you ever receive a paycheck, the company has deducted the amount of taxes from your paycheck and has sent the correct amount to the IRS.

As a business owner, you are responsible for this liability and adherence to filing dates on your own. You have to get into the habit of setting aside money every month for your taxes or at the end of the year, you could find yourself in a pickle. The IRS does not care that you did not know the laws or dates for filing. That is up to you to know, and the penalties of being late on submitting your taxes are steep. If you do not pay your tax liability, the IRS can freeze or even sell off your assets. A CPA can take all of this pressure off of you, because they can help set up accounts that assure that your tax liability is being saved and when it comes time for filing, they can do it for you.

V. WHEN DO I FILE?

The question of when you file for your company depends on your legal entity. It is a different process than what you have been used to with your personal taxes, and so missed dates can mean penalties.

Can't keep up with the dates? Then hire a CPA that can keep you on track, so that you can concentrate on other aspects of your business.

TAX CALENDAR	
Significant filing dates for a corporation using a calendar year-end are summarized as follows:	
DATE	RETURNS
January 31st	Sales tax return* Payroll tax returns Annual Form W-2s issued to employees Form 1099s issued to payees
February 28th	Form W-2s filed with social security administration Form 1099s and 1096s filed with IRS
March 15th	Corporate income tax returns
April 15th	Estimated income tax payments Individual income tax returns Partnership and LLC income tax returns
April 30th	Quarterly payroll tax returns
June 15th	Estimated income tax payments
July 31st	Quarterly payroll tax returns
September 15th	Estimated income tax payments Partnership and LLC income tax returns on extension
October 15th	Individual income tax returns on extension Corporate income tax returns on extension
October 31st	Quarterly payroll tax returns

VI. DEVELOP A TEAM

Having a team of outside advisors is vital — including a CPA, lawyer, bank manager and insurance agent — and make sure your advisors are willing to be engaged and proactive in helping you. You do not need spectators — you need coaches!

Effective CPA's and Advisors help individuals and families with tax compliance and tax planning. They assist owner-managed businesses with their accounting, tax and consulting needs so that they can focus on running their businesses. They provide individuals and families with comprehensive, holistic wealth management and preservation, so that they can achieve financial independence and meet their life objectives and give businesses, individuals and families the information they need to deal with their tax debt resolution issues. In short, these advisors keep your business solvent, keep you out of legal trouble, and ultimately keep you out of jail!

About Kevin

Kevin Roberts is an entrepreneur in the financial services industry and a Certified Public Accountant operating a wealth management and CPA firm in the Louisville, Kentucky area. As an experienced CPA for 18 years, Kevin educates clients about strategies regarding their belief and utilization of money combining tax strategies with wealth preservation strategies. Kevin understands that the greatest inhibitor to wealth creation and wealth preservation is taxes. He is more than a tax preparer; he is a partner in your wealth preservation and wealth creation stages of your life.

As a Certified Public Accountant, Kevin is tasked by clients to consult about new businesses and provide advice on entity formation. He understands that small business creation is the backbone of the American dream for thousands of Americans starting their own business every day.

Kevin grew up in the almost-mountains of eastern Kentucky playing any sport centering around an orange ball that was to be thrown through a metal hoop. Attending Georgetown College in Georgetown, KY, Kevin graduated with honors with a dual degree in accounting and finance. Kevin was one of the rare breed that knew what he wanted to be when he grew up...he wanted to work with money and become a CPA since the ripe old age of 14.

Kevin currently operates Roberts CPA Group PSC, Discount Tax Centers LLC and Lifetime Wealth Design LLC out of offices located in Louisville, LaGrange and Versailles in Kentucky. The combined operation currently serves about 1,300 individual clients and 200 business clients, providing a high level of tax preparation, planning and financial services, and educating clients about the utilization of money and wealth preservation.

Kevin resides in Oldham County with his wife of 20 years, Jennifer, and is the proud father of Alexis, 17 and Harrison, 15.

Kevin can be reached via office phone at: 502-426-0000, via email at: kevin@roberts-cpa.com or online at either: www.Roberts-CPA.com or www.SmartMoneyCPA.com

CHAPTER 31

CULTIVATE YOUR X-FACTOR: THE UNRAVELING OF SPECIALNESS

BY KRISTI GOVERTSEN

As I stood there, center-stage, with the house lights down, and the footlights blinding me, I took a deep breath and started to sing, "The sun'll come out... TOMORROW...bet your bottom dollar that tomorrow... there'll be sun..." Yet, the word "singing" does not accurately describe what came out of my mouth. It was flat, or sharp, or flarp (flat and sharp), or shat. Yeah. It was the last one sharp, flat, and sounding like sh*t. Not that I would have ever used THAT word in THAT moment.

First of all, I was 11 years old, and not yet versed in swearing like a longshoreman. Secondly, I was center-stage in my very first audition for a role in the local community production of *Annie*. And I was bombing. I was bombing from the first note to the last, and I knew it. I felt it. I heard it. And I saw it on the sympathetic eyes of all the adults in the crowd as I stepped down off the stage determined not to cry. While I find determination to be excellent for a great many things, using it to will myself not to cry has never, ever, never worked...never... and the tears streamed down my face as I sat silently in my chair watching as all the other girls took their turn at the song.

At the end of that phase of the audition, all the kids that made it into the musical were announced (and to no one's surprise, I was not selected), and four of the girls were asked to stay for an immediate callback for the lead role of Annie. They were asked to sing another musical number from the show, so they could be compared side-by-side, with the winner going home with the coveted part in the show. One by one, each took their turn, and each was phenomenal. Pitch perfect. Darling. Spunky. Cute as a button. Basically they had everything you could possibly ask for in a pack of auditioning Annies.

By the time they got to the third girl, I thought to myself, "How on earth are they going to pick? They're all SO good." That's when girl number four started to sing. She wasn't better than the others, but she had a certain something, and we all knew it, and we all knew she was going to get the part (and to no one's surprise, she did).

I had a vivid two-part thought while sitting there that night. The first was the death of a dream, and it was, "I am never going to be an actress. Never, ever, never." The second was my WHY the dream died, and stayed dead for a very long time, "I'm never going to be an actress, because I don't have that special something that last girl had."

That second thought not only kept me out of the theater for a long time (although I eventually came back later in life to perform in a couple of community theater productions), it also kept me from pursuing most of my dreams that followed. I was missing that special something, so why would I ever even bother to dream? Those of us born without that specialness, that X-factor, were doomed to lives of mediocrity – so why even bother?

We all have a story that we tell ourselves that sabotages our success. Mine was, "I'm not special, so why even bother?" Truth be told, a story that took me to the brink of destruction in my twenties. If I could only be special, then life would be good, but I'm not, so it can't, so why even bother… and at some point I did stop bothering, and almost stopped living.

Now this story isn't about me crashing and burning, it's not about the journey of self-discovery and it's not about what riches and amazement awaited me when I came out the other side. This story is about being on the other side, and the three lessons I learned in the process.

I'm sharing these three lessons because I'm in the training industry (I'm "The Workshop Nerd,") and I meet people all the time that are using a similar story of "I'm not special" or "I'm not good enough" to sabotage their hopes and dreams every day. I see it happen with people in my audience and training rooms, and I even see it keeping other speakers and trainers from taking their businesses and lives to the next level. They're NOT getting in the game, and they have the perfectly crafted story that keeps them glued to the sidelines.

I'm sharing these three lessons so that if you are someone who flirts with this story of not being special or not being good enough, and it's keeping you from fully jumping into the game, I want to quantum leap you past the crashing, burning, and painful journey, and directly to the "other side" and into the game where you can immediately reap the riches and amazement that's available when we understand the X-factor, and its role (or non-role) in our lives.

LESSON #1

The story of "I'm not special" doesn't really matter (or my story does not actually do anything for me). What I mean by that, is the attempt to change the "I'm not special" story into an "I'm special" story doesn't necessarily get you closer to your goals.

Matt Garrigan, one of my first teachers when I landed on the other side of my mid-twenties crash-and-burn, illustrated this concept brilliantly. He said, "Imagine you have a life goal of feeding the starving children, but you decide that you don't feel special enough. If only you could feel special, THEN you could go for the goal of feeding starving children. But then you have kind of a bad day, and you don't feel special again, so you muster up all your might, and get yourself back to feeling special." All the while, you're just jumping back and forth between stories, and the starving children of the world are not getting fed:

To accomplish my goal, I have to just ignore the "I'm not special" "I'm special" loop, and go do the goal anyway. Hence, lesson #1: The story of "I'm not special" doesn't really matter. While I certainly prefer to FEEL special over not feeling special, neither story is actually getting me closer to my goals. The good news? *Neither story is preventing me from accomplishing my goals. Yay!*

LESSON #2

Scarcity isn't what makes specialness special (or I'm unique, just like everyone else).

Gold is valuable because there is a finite amount of it in the world. The same goes for other precious commodities. If there's a demand for it, and it's rare, it's suddenly more valuable.

I think people have a mindset that specialness, or that X-factor, is finite and incredibly rare, and that's what makes it special/rare. This is completely and utterly false. Let us take for example snowflakes, and all the snowflakes that ever were and ever will be. That's a lot of snowflakes. So many, in fact, I would never consider them "rare" or a finite commodity whose scarcity is what makes them valuable. Snowflakes are special because no two are alike. And that makes them ALL special. They are all made up of the same substance (water), it's just the unique crystalline arrangement of that substance that makes them special.

Every human on the planet is made up of the same substances, we are neither rare nor scarce with regard to our raw material. *However, our own blend perceptions, beliefs, talents, values, circumstances, choices, and how we manage our own raw material makes us each unique. Just like everyone else.*

LESSON #3

The notion that our specialness can't be cultivated is a lie (or my X-factor CAN and will evolve).

Our own unique X-factor or specialness can be nurtured and trained in much the same way as we nurture and train our bodies and minds. Based on lesson number #2, one might think that because our X-factor is blended with what makes us up, then there's very little we can do to make our specialness even more special.

Wrong. There are things we can do in every moment to nurture and coax our specialness to the forefront. If our specialness is made up of perceptions, beliefs, talents, values, circumstances, and choices, all of these things can be practiced, disciplined, and adjusted based on what we choose to shift. For example, let's take a look at YOUR talents. Your talents make you special, but if you practice and become disciplined in your talents your specialness shines through even more than it did before. It was always there, but now it shines even brighter.

Another way to cultivate sharing our specialness and X-factor with the world is to exercise the following:

    a. Knowing Yourself

    b. Being Brave

    c. Cultivating Optimism

(a). Knowing Yourself:
Knowing yourself allows you to experience your own specialness. When you can identify it, you can more easily share it with the world. I work in an industry where many of my clients speak and run workshops, and at one point or another there is a crisis of confidence in what they're offering, or that their message won't stand apart from others in their field. The only solution, in my opinion, is to tap into their own unique blend of specialness, and the only avenue to do that is get back to who they are, and what makes them unique.

(b). Being Brave:
Sometimes we hide our specialness because we're scared. We're scared of being different. We're scared of being criticized. We're scared of scaring away others with our own unique blend of specialness. Guess what? Those things might happen, but they might happen even if we shy away from our specialness. That's life, and on a planet of 7 billion people, we can't help but bump into each other with our opinions every now then. You might as well be true to yourself, and brave enough to share it because life will happen anyway; having the courage to face it allows your specialness to grow and shift along with the natural ebb and flow of life itself.

(c). Cultivating Optimism:

Remember when I was stuck in the story of "I'm not special, so why should I bother?" The destructive part of this story was the "Why should I bother?" There was no optimism, only a slow trudge toward depression and death. Cultivating optimism can counter the "Why should I bother?" attitude, and I believe that optimism is made up of two components: hope and faith. Now practicing hope and faith is a tall order since both are quite intangible. The tangible practice to experience hope and faith (and therefore cultivate optimism) is to seek out and pay attention to *opportunity*. If we think of it as working backward, or tipping over a series of dominoes, it looks like this:

Notice Opportunity ➝ Experience Hope and Faith ➝ Cultivate Optimism ➝ I should bother! ➝ Because I'm special.

Think of this as the fastest path to exercising the specialness recognition muscle, and you should ALWAYS be exercising recognizing your specialness.

So let's recap:

Lesson #1: The story of "I'm not special" doesn't really matter (or my story does not actually do anything for me). My specialness neither helps me nor stops me from reaching my goals.

Lesson #2: Scarcity isn't what makes specialness special (or I'm unique, just like everyone else). We are ALL made of the same raw materials, it's what we do with those raw materials that makes us special.

Lesson #3: The notion that our specialness can't be cultivated is a lie (or my X-factor CAN and will evolve). This is done by knowing yourself, being brave, and cultivating optimism.

One last thought before I go:

My wish for you is that you unleash your brand of specialness on the world. I don't just want you to GET into the game of life, I want YOU to get into the game of life. It's YOU we need, it's YOU we're waiting for, and it's YOU and your special X-factor that make the game worth playing.

Until we meet again, Be extraordinary!
~Kristi Govertsen

About Kristi

Kristi Govertsen is "The Workshop Nerd," and is passionate about helping people create their own workshops so they can share their unique message with the world. Growing up she split her time between Missoula, Montana and Homer, Alaska as she was raised by three parents: a physics teacher, an artist, and a commercial fisherman and boat-builder. All three influences had a profound impact on her professional trajectory, as she has found that a balance of teaching, creative endeavors, and grounded hands-on work shows up daily in her approach to business and life.

Kristi began teaching and curriculum-building in 1997 when she found herself taking a job in a one-room schoolhouse in Alaska. Alongside two other teachers, she worked with thirty K-12 children whose ages ranged from 5 to 18 years old. With the responsibility of seven different subjects: arithmetic, geography, English, algebra, history, photography, government & civics, and marine biology and no formal curriculum to work from, Kristi was thrown into the deep end of the pool of curriculum and instructional design. She was hooked! While her teaching journey took several twists and turns, her ultimate passion in the world of academia was as a math teacher at the college level, where she continued to teach until 2013.

While on the academic path, Kristi also started a tutoring business in 1998. It ultimately evolved into a training company and small publishing house as her interest in building personal development workshops and writing books on personal growth flourished. This training company officially became Koi Pond, LLC in 2007, and continues to grow and expand to this day with Kristi at the helm full-time since 2012.

Kristi has degrees in philosophy, mathematics, with a Masters of Science in Teaching. While her formal education is complete, she continues to push herself continue to learn and grow every day.

Kristi is a sought after international speaker and trainer, as well as a one-on-one consultant to many speakers in the industry. Additionally, she has authored two books:

- *GO: Grounded Optimism—The Secret Formula to Creating Momentum, Finding the Meaning of Life, and Receiving Enlightenment from a Chocolate Chip Cookie*

- *Awesomeness in Motion (AIM)*

Kristi lives in Portland, Oregon where in her spare time she loves running, karaoke, and being an active Rotarian and Toastmaster.

You can connect with Kristi at
kristi@kristigovertsen.com
www.kristigovertsen.com
www.facebook.com/kristi.govertsen2
www.twitter.com/kristigovertsen

CHAPTER 32

JETNETTING™
RELATIONSHIPS AS THE 21ST
CENTURY CURRENCY

BY HESHIE SEGAL

JetNetting™ is a system, born from my not having and not knowing built on a strong foundation of caring . . . one concept, one person, one network at a time.

Everything has a season, and in the fall of 1996, JetNetting™ arrived . . . well before its time. That was then and this is now. JetNetting™ has come of age.

The core of JetNetting™ is building authentic relationships and diverse networks long BEFORE they are needed.

- Its mindset: "How may I support you?"
- Its essence: Collaboration.
- Its outcome: Prosperity.

Clearly, some forms of competition are healthy, as long as the focus is not "one upmanship." Literally, no one lives in isolation. For true effectiveness, collaboration is the only sensible path.

Based on experience and client testimonials, once you comprehend JetNetting's simplicity and functionality, you will never go back to standard networking. You will bypass the competitive greed and pushiness that causes people to shy away from business card thrusters and networking frenzies. JetNetting™ is a lifestyle and with it comes prosperity well beyond basic revenue accumulation.

Research shows (depending on the type of job), an average of 50% of jobs are found through networking. What if you could speed up the process, make deeper connections that last, come across as likable and interesting, as someone who cares, and is ready to be of service? Nothing compares to the alignment of mindsets and the potential results that come from collaboration; its outcome is unlimited prosperity.

JetNetting™ is a way of life, of being . . . any time, any place, personally, socially, or in business. What you see is what you get . . . always! It is the underlying foundation of human currency. The more its principles are applied, the greater the prosperity.

Conversely, monetary currency rarely stands alone. When it does, it is often met with an untimely end. If built on a strong foundation of relationships, integrity, support and giving, the keys to establishing human currency, money and prosperity will easily flow in and through your life.

We all know that stories sell. Being transparent, I confess, by telling you a story, MY story. I DO intend to sell you on two things:

1). Eliminating the same mistakes I made.

2). Using my shortcuts and suggestions for a faster, more prosperous future.

As you take notes or highlight the lessons, think how you can apply them to your life and commit to their implementation. My story will lead you through the grit, the guts, the realizations and the ups and downs I experienced in learning about human currency. This led to prosperity and to living life according to my principles and values.

THE STORY

September 13th . . . it began with celebrating my mother's birthday and ended with my father's death. The house was silent and empty . . . as were the bank accounts and my college fund. My father had drained all our accounts after his business partner had embezzled everything. He even cancelled his life insurance just hours before he died. As I watched the ambulance pull away, I had no idea how quickly adulthood would come crashing down on me.

By September's end, we were bankrupt. I was 16. My life had been full of hope. Now I was told college would not be an option. I could let my dream collapse or I could make it happen. My body stiffened. In that instant, I knew I would do whatever it took to go to college - and that effort was enormous. My future was mine to create and if anyone said I could not do something, my mantra became, "WATCH ME!" It made me fiercely self-sufficient. As you might imagine, I hardened in the process; accepted no whining, no excuses.

I became an accidental entrepreneur. I loved to design and embroider so when "Linda", my retail supplier, invited me to a trade show, I jumped! I quickly made friends with company owners and negotiated for Linda, often reducing her costs by as much as 75%. Later, I asked her about a discount on my purchases. "10%" . . . Seriously? I left, borrowed $1000 and started my own embroidery business. In two years, I had hundred folded my investment. I experienced dramatic growth and prosperity until the rains came, followed by flooding. I lost nearly everything, including my heart for doing retail. Time to move on.

I was introduced to Multi-Level Marketing. While I loved the business model and its potential, I disliked the way most people practiced it. Once I added my JetNetting™ process to the right company/product/leadership, the business could become a highly successful stream of income.

Years later. I am writing about "The Good Whistleblower" . . . the good, the bad and the ugly of MLM, and its powerful way to build leveraged, residual income when approached from a win/win philosophy.

The more successful I became, the less tolerant I grew of people with excuses. After all, if I could do it with all I had gone through, why couldn't they? And therein lay the challenge. I had programmed myself to win in business, not in life. I actually did not have a life. I was about to pay the price for extreme self-reliance. I vividly remember the day I returned to humanity.

On Sept. 12, 1996, I opened my eyes after surgery. The walls were white. The cubicle was empty. My daughter was not given permission to come back yet. My mind was racing. What if I needed more than the ten days to start walking again? How was I going to manage with just my daughter and the person I was dating? I was a champion at collecting business cards. I had hundreds of business acquaintances. Yet, I knew nothing about them as people! I felt so alone. What had I been doing with my life? Certainly not what a "normal" person did. Ten months later, I took my first steps without a wheelchair. A simple metatarsal repair turned into an ongoing nightmare, even at this writing.

In the midst of unhappiness and loneliness, an angel appeared. With an outstretched hand and heart, my life coach Laura helped me see the impact of having no real friends, especially girlfriends. Excitedly, and with my usual determination, I created the Girlfriend Connection and laid the foundation for JetNetting™. To have friends, I had to learn to first BE a friend. I had to do for others, on THEIR terms.

People began to turn to me for advice, for introductions. I became what I call a "Center of Influence." *(I now teach the process as a professional speaker and trainer.)* All the while, I was masking the worsening pain from ongoing corrective surgeries. I took pain-killers with increasing frequency.

What probably kept me going was the vast number of positive relationships I was developing within very diverse networks. Support was everywhere.

By 2001, after my 7th corrective surgery, my left hip required replacement. This time, I took off the mask, told people I was going to have surgery and would probably need help. Two hundred and eleven (211) people volunteered. Floored, I thought back to the empty room after the original surgery. Sterile white walls with no sign of humanity. This time the nurses had to restrict *the number of* visitors.

Years later, Social Media arrived. I was NEVER going to waste time online! I wanted to look someone in the eye, get a pulse on behavior style, observe body language . . . all the while listening carefully to words and tone of voice; were they congruent? I could not possibly do this online!

Well, eventually, I ate crow and got to work!

With my JetNetting™ system in place, I actually knew what to do . . . provide rich content, engage, reach out, advocate for others. Because I knew how to connect and easily build quality relationships, "followers" multiplied; hundreds, then thousands.

Then, without notice, my Twitter account disappeared. My social media manager set up my account, with himself as owner, and shut it down after a disagreement. Lesson learned.

Again, I took out my JetNetting™ blueprint and started building even faster. I created rules for following . . . or not. I looked for commonalities and began connecting people. At any point, and especially on Facebook, I could take a quick look at my friend's friends and see how many came through the connections I suggested; an affirmation of the power of JetNetting™. It's actually quite humbling, especially when I think back to a time of not having a single friend.

Almost two decades after that original hospital visit, I was back in the hospital. I reached out and within hours, there were thousands of posts from across the globe. People cared because I cared. JetNetting™ works.

What I once resisted has given me a global perspective on the goodness of people. While I still know it's imperative to have friends in close geographical proximity, I know the globe has shrunk via the Internet. I have friends on every continent. The foundation to any successful business is now in place. Relationships and networks are interconnected. Resources are within reach. Human currency leads to prosperity; financial prosperity follows as a natural state.

• JetNetting™ . . . being of service to others.

  • JetNetting™ . . . using connections as the keys to business and life.

    • JetNetting™ . . . producing extraordinary results with the speed of a jet in flight.

      • JetNetting™ . . . building relationships and networks of value before they are needed.

Like others who have become experts in *their* fields, I have lived JetNetting™. My system is not a theory . . . a blueprint built on paper.

It is a system of specific collaborative orientations and actions, which when worked in unison, create prosperity; internally and externally. The system is simple - just not easy - because it does require a shift in 'beingness,' in time and in effort.

Robert G. Allen, real estate guru and millionaire maker, referred to me as a one-in-a-million when it came to MLM. I was the proverbial needle in the haystack, the one who really got it. I did not realize how serious he was until one day, sitting in his home with other Inner Circle members, he talked about Malcolm Gladwell's Outliers, those who gained expertise by putting in 10,000 hours. He turned to me and said to the group, "Heshie Segal is such a person."

What did I do to get there?

Like me, you were born with a clean slate and you are where you are today because of your background: your upbringing, and your experiences. You are who you are because of the people closest to you: parents, friends and authority figures, and how they may, or may not, have filled your head with ideas, hope, knowledge and even judgment and prejudice. If you have not yet evolved into the person of your dreams, still locked in to things that have held you back, it's time to step into your own magnificence.

We have touched on money as a resource, as currency. Are you ready to create new currency . . . relationship currency, JetNetting™ currency, to create more money? It works if you work it; decide to do it, and see how your life prospers.

For some, this will be a paradigm shift, especially if your life and old ways, are not bringing you the prosperity you desire. JetNetting™ currency is built before money; often, long before. Without it, you will have less. With it, you can accrue untold riches.

My life was transformed forever when I realized my wealth was, and is, based on the relationships and the friendships I create and not on the goods or services I offer.

MY FORMULA FOR SUCCESS

The list is in no particular order because for each person, priorities will be different.

- The more you *listen*, the wiser you become.

- The more *support* you give, the more support you receive.

- Do *favors* for people (without being asked) and even more will be returned.

- Become *accepting* of others, no matter their beliefs, background, color, class, etc. Your circle will be expanded.

- Be a *resource* for others. It leads you to become a Center of Influence and with it comes easier access to people and things.

- The *loyalty* you give will be reciprocated; ten fold.

- Your *verbal word* must become as good as any signature on a contract. Do what you say you will do. You will gain trust and credibility.

- *Compliment* others when appropriate, advocate for them, believe in them . . . even when they cannot yet see their own light. Write testimonials from the heart. You will become their shining light.

- *Show up* when others do not; stay when others leave. You will never feel alone.

- *Learn the magic* of Social Media. Connect with like-minded people, celebrate, honor, give recognition, promote their events, link them to each other and share their contributions with the world.

- *Speak to strangers* and encourage them to come out and play. You will be sought-after and get invited back.

- *Speak up* and share your brilliance. You will be seen in a new light.

- *Teach* and you will learn.

• Above all, *be yourself.* Your authenticity will garner trust.

I leave you with these thoughts.

I do what I do because I can, not to get something in return. I build relationships because people are the essence of all existence. I build diverse networks because they are inclusive. I mastermind with others for richer outcomes. I work in collaboration rather than competition. I lead from abundance. No one has it all; no one can give it all.

In an earlier life, before I understood the power of quickly building strong long-lasting relationships, I lived a lonely existence in a world unto myself. Once I stepped into the JetNetting™ mindset, relationships happened and prosperity followed.

Make the commitment, take the risk to step up to the plate, shift your focus outward. Become the resource, the Center of Influence, and when you fully embrace the JetNetting™ principles, you too will experience a shift.

Who I was, I am no longer. Who I continue to become is open to the willingness with which I embrace possibilities.

Who you are is an evolving and amazing human being. Who you become is up to you. Own your expertise, your passion, your strengths. Advocate for others. With short-sighted competition, we all have less. With JetNetting™'s collaborative approach, the world becomes your playground.

About Heshie

Heshie Segal is the founder and CEO of *The JetNetting™ Connection,* a company based on building quality relationships fast, deep and long-lasting and developing the formation of diverse networks, which lay the foundation for any successful business. For the entrepreneur or small business owner, it weaves an interactive net of trusted connections; for corporations, it supports internal collaboration and creates a stronger link to customers; for non-profits, it produces a more expansive volunteer base; for Network Marketing, the results speak for themselves since it should be all about relationships. In a 1/2 billion dollar MLM, Heshie became #1 globally, for helping others build their businesses – all based on her JetNetting™ principles.

Every experience you encounter can be a game changer. Heshie gleans the lessons from her abusive childhood experiences and turns them into learning points we can all use to succeed. Sometimes it takes a twist of fate to teach us that fierce independence and going it alone do not generally produce successful results. As a professional speaker and trainer, Heshie focuses on the power of collaboration and provides the mindset and skills that make a difference. Her JetNetting™ system replaces the networking routine so many dislike; i.e. collecting business cards and gathering emails online for the express purpose of pushing business and selling before any relationship has been built, or a need established. Her mini-book, *Blink You're Judged: How to Create a Powerful Positive First Impression* is a great resource.

If credibility and collaboration, advocacy and authenticity, trust and doing what it takes to build and maintain your relationships and networks is important to you, then Heshie Segal is your go-to person. As a volunteer, Heshie has always been involved in the community, from go-to envelope stuffer, to President or Chairperson.

She is a self-starter who multiplied her very first business, The Embroidery Stop, one hundred fold in just two years. This opened the door to speaking, creating award-winning designs, and even coaching and teaching for cruise lines and multi-national organizations.

As if this is not enough, she is the one who brought children's embroidery back to the United States, into schools and hospitals, and recently founded: www. KidsBetterWorld.com, a children's movement committed to providing basic human needs to all children, equipping them with the values of diversity, self-determination, and responsibility as the path to a prosperous, joyful and humane life.

Because she loves connecting people to help explode their businesses, in 2013 she accepted the Presidency of the Philadelphia Area Holistic Chamber of Commerce.

In her free time, she loves walking on the beach and collecting rocks and shells. Heshie's greatest joy is being a beacon for change, a light unto others.

For more information or to connect with Heshie Segal:
HeshieSegal@JetNettingConnection.com
www.JetNettingConnection.com
Tel: 215-493-1640 ~ c/267-679-4550
www.Twitter.com/heshiesegal
www.Facebook.com/heshiesegal
www.linkedin.com/in/heshiesegal
HeshieSegal@KidsBetterWorld.com www.KidsBetterWorld.com
Fan Page: https://www.facebook.com/pages/Kids-Better-World/223714681057978

CHAPTER 33

DRIVE YOUR SUCCESS!

BY DARYL G. BANK & ED CARR

What is "it" that you want? That thing you always wanted to accomplish. Are you still focused on it? Maybe you've given up on it, shelved it... or promised that you would "one day." You know One Day. That day you were going to go after your dream. Work on your health. Lose some weight. Be a better spouse...One Day.

Don't forget that "one day" is the day after you die.

Are you afraid of failing to achieve your dream? Maybe, you were actually afraid of what would happen if you did. Today we dust off that dream. It's coming off the shelf. Today is that day. Today, we will focus on getting you to that place you want to be. Today, we are getting in the game.

We're going to start with the most important element to get in the game:

1. YOU

It's up to you. Only you can do it. It's you who decides. No one can do it for you. We can't do it for you. We all have "winner" in us. We all have "greatness" in us. We are all gifted. You have to find and nurture your winner. You have to pursue your greatness. You have to open your gift.

Opportunity does not knock. Life is not served up to you. Opportunities occur every day. You choose whether to act on them or not. Each sunset is littered with missed opportunities – some seen, but most are ignored.

You have to make it happen. No one can do that for you. Tell yourself - I am in charge. I am determined. Even if no one else sees it. I do. Even if no one believes it. I do.

YOU CAN accomplish all of the things you want to …just get in the game. Live for today.

2. WAKE-UP

Once you have decided to find that winner, that greatness within YOU, then you must wake up. Most people walk through life asleep. They never ask the question: Is there more? Why do some just settle for where they are and stop striving to achieve? Because most are asleep at the wheel of their own life. Have you ever driven somewhere and you didn't remember the trip? You know how you got there, but you don't remember the trip itself. You didn't remember the drive? You were asleep not figuratively but literally. You were so comfortable in your surroundings and routine you took a nap on the way. We are all guilty of this.

Study it for yourself and you will see. In this state, your conscious mind hands it off to the subconscious of routine. In this state, you are literally asleep and being driven solely by the subconscious that recognizes the dangers along the way such as traffic. If a danger is apparent, all of you is needed and all of sudden you are awake and present to react.

Another example of how being awake relates to opportunities. Almost everyone reading this has certainly bought a new car. Before you decided to buy that particular make and model, how many did you see? Chances are not many. Then you purchase yours…BAM …now you see them everywhere. It isn't that they weren't there before, you just didn't allow yourself to see them. What we wake up to, or focus on, we will find and see the same will happen with the opportunities that surround us every day. Once we are awake and looking for them, we will see and find them.

The sad reality is that many people go through life asleep. They have jobs they don't like…relationships they are not happy with…dreams that are wilted and dead.

Wake up. Don't sleep until you succeed.

3. MOTIVATION

We don't believe in motivation. You cannot motivate someone. Motivation is not remotely understood. Either you have it or you don't. We do believe you can be inspired. You can be inspired by people or events. But only you control your motivation. No one decides that for you. No one gives it to you.

During life **things** are going to happen. **Things** are going to go wrong. Sometimes, everything that can go wrong will. How will you handle it? Remember that life defines you not by what happens to you, but by what you do when **things** happen.

When misery visits you, what will keep you in the game? Inspiration. Find it.

4. BELIEVE

Can you see it? Henry Ford said, "Whether *you think you can, or you think you can't—you're right.*" Ponder that for a moment, whatever you believe, you are right. So why is it so hard to believe in ourselves?

I believe I can. Your game must begin with I believe. You must see it. You must believe you can achieve it. How will you get in the game if you don't see it, if you don't believe it? Greatness is a choice, not a destiny. Oh, you have greatness in you. You have the gift. Everyone does. The question is are you going to bring it out or let it die with you? I believe I can do what I want. I can own my own business. I can be a million dollar producer. I believe I can be a better husband, father, and son. I DON'T THINK I WILL. I BELIEVE I WILL. I KNOW I WILL.

Mark Twain said, "They did not know it was impossible, so they did it."

Belief is a powerful concept. Don't underestimate the power of belief. The 4- minute mile is one of the best modern examples. The 4-minute mile was an unachievable feat until 1954 when Roger Bannister broke that barrier. He paved the way for others to **believe** that they could do it. Two others in the same year broke the barrier after Roger Bannister showed it could be done. What is your 4-minute mile hurdle? Who do you know that has accomplished the impossible. What do they have that you don't? …belief?

5. ATTITUDE

Attitude is important. If your attitude is not positive, we have to start there. You need to change your mindset to get in the game. Keep your current attitude and I assure you your situation will be the same. You are guaranteed to get the same results when you keep thinking the same way.

> *When you change the way you look at things...the things you look at change.* ~ Wayne Dyer

The easiest way to change the way you see things is to zoom out. Your attitude will determine your altitude and therefore your view of things. From a higher altitude, you have a broader prospective and can see things coming from afar. We also must avoid majoring in the minors. What do I mean by this? There are little things that happen in business and process that can disrupt our attitude. By not being consumed by these with a microscopic view, you are able to adapt, correct and move on with fluidity – all the while maintaining an overall view and direction of your course. Your attitude and altitude sets the direction for the rest of your team too.

Soar higher today and remove the negatives from your life. Remove those people that are negative in your life. Shed the naysayers. Birds of a feather flock together...

6. PURPOSE

What are you doing? Why are you reading this book? What are you trying to accomplish. What is your purpose?

What are you waking up and fighting for? Embrace your purpose. Fight for it. Live and cry for it. Die for it. In your purpose you should find inspiration.

Allow me to share my purpose. I want to be a positive force in all I touch. I want to help others to find greatness. The greatness that already exists within them. I want to be the stepping stone to the top of their mountain.

When I die I want people to cry, not because I died, but because I won't be able to inspire them ONE more DAY.

7. OBJECTIVE

What are you trying to accomplish? What is your goal? How do you define success? Is it that thing you gave up on? Is it that dream you shelved years ago? That dream or success is the objective. We all actually have the same objective, SUCCESS. The differences are how each of us defines success. Alright, here comes another major secret. YOU get to define your success. No one else does. In fact, never allow others to define your success. Life actually allows you to write the rules so you are guaranteed a win.

8. ACCOUNTABILITY

One of the most important things you can do is create accountability. A support system. You need accountability. You, will let You down. You have no problem disappointing You. How many New Year's resolutions have died, gym memberships expired? We all have bought exercise equipment that became expensive clothes hangers. You want to get in the game? Get a partner, a coach…someone to introduce accountability. We're much less likely to disappoint that accountability…but I will let ME down. I know I will. I've seen ME do it. But, I won't let my partner down. I will not disappoint my team.

Here's my favorite Zig Ziglar comment on accountability: If you help enough other people get what they want, you will get everything you want.

9. TIME

The most valuable things in your life are health and time. In fact, you have some control over your health. But life has allotted you a specific amount of time. No more, no less. The good news is that Life allows you to choose how you use your time. How effective will you be with it?

Bust the myth of time management. There is no such thing as time management. The only choice we have is what we do with the time we have. There are only 1,440 minutes in a day. When they are gone… they are gone. You can't get them back. How will you use those minutes? You only have 1,440 minutes today to be great. How great were you today? The good news is Life always offers you a second chance to be great…it's called tomorrow. The bad news is, life doesn't guarantee you'll be here tomorrow.

This is the only time you have. NOW!

If I told you that you were going to die in 24 hours, what would you change? What would you do? What relationships would you mend? Who's that person you would call and tell them that you love them?

That thing you would change…if you would change it then…you need to change it now. There's no guarantee that there's a tomorrow. But I guarantee there is today. (…Or your money back.)

10. SYSTEM

System is an acronym for: *Save Your Self Time, Energy & Money*

Systems come in many varieties and forms – from simple to complex. You must use a system to have predictability in your business. A System allows you to analyze and know metrics on performance. Most importantly it allows you to identify your bottle necks or choke points that hinder performance.

Standards of performance have been studied in every industry. If you know your numbers you can reasonably predict your outcome. For example, if you know that you must sell 4 items of your product just to cover the cost to manufacture 25 items, then you can back into profit based on those numbers.

Most people tell themselves they are doing better than they really are. A system allows us to see the truth. By tracking and seeing your numbers you know what is real and what is not.

If you're a salesman, business is based on closed sales. You are able to predict your sales by tracking your pipeline. Your pipeline is simply those clients that you have talked with and are in various stages of closing.

Prediction is no magic, it is simply knowing your numbers. If you close an average of 1 in 10, and your average sale is $1,000. You then can set goals that are realistic. Such as, I want to earn $10,000 this month, so I need to talk to 100 people in order to close 10 at $1,000 each.

There is no magic when systems are applied. Every industry has its own set of KPI (Key Performance Indicators) or benchmarks on business. Tracking these things simply and easily in the beginning of your business, can help you to afford more sophisticated and less time-consuming ones as you grow. A simple spread sheet and tracking your measurements is a great start to knowing.

So what must we do now? You must decide to wake up. Don't go through this life asleep. Call on your own motivation and develop an attitude around your purpose with a clear objective. Surround yourself with positive people who inspire you. We must be accountable to others and with our time. Develop systems to Save Your Self Time Energy and Money – the briefest and most precise formula for success that we know!

About Daryl

Daryl G. Bank is the Managing Partner of Dominion Investment Group. For more than eighteen years, Daryl Bank has served client's financial interest through research, attentiveness, and a common-sense approach to successful relationships. This extensive experience, throughout various stock and bond market cycles, enables him to help clients structure their portfolios to meet their specific financial objectives.

Daryl was born in Norfolk, Virginia. After graduating from Indian River High School, and Old Dominion University, he pursued a Master's Degree in public policy and a Masters in Business Administration at Regent University. Daryl began his financial career at Morgan Stanley, and then joined UBS/Paine Webber in 1996. In 2003 Daryl launched Dominion Investment Group and helped Resource Bank form their investment division. From 2003-2005, Daryl opened four investment offices and formed an insurance company, as well as a property and casualty company, for Resource Bank. From 2005 to 2009 Daryl formed investment divisions for several community banks.

Recently acknowledged by America's PremierExperts® as one of the leading experts in his field, Daryl's genuine caring attitude and approach to success can be attributed to his willingness to provide information and education to all.

Recognized in the *Wall Street Journal* and *USA Today* as one of the "Financial trendsetters" along with other leading experts, across a wide array of industries, Daryl continues to make headway in the financial sector. Daryl was featured on *Bloomberg Businessweek* online and other major online media outlets, including *CNBC*.com, *MarketWatch*, *Yahoo!Finance* and many others.

Throughout 2014, Daryl has added best selling author to the list of many achievements and with his new publication, *SuccessOnomics,* in hopes to coach and guide people to success. United with successful entrepreneurs, professionals, and experts from around the world including Steve Forbes, the book shares each author's methodology and mindset for the building blocks of success in the new economy.

Daryl and his partners are committed to expanding their existing divisions while continuing to venture into exciting new territory.

Daryl hosts the radio show, *Getting Your Financial House in Order*, which is syndicated nationally over thirty stations. He serves on the Boards of DV8 Sports, Warped Inc., and is an Advisor of Project Lifesaver International. Professionally, Daryl is a member of the National Institute of Certified Estate Planners. Daryl and his wife (Catrina) live with their son (Jackson) and daughter (Vivian) in Port St. Lucie, Florida.

To learn more about Daryl G. Bank please visit: http://dominioninvestmentgroup.com,

Contact info. for Daryl G. Bank:
Tel: (757) 226-9440
Email: dig@dominv.com

About Ed

Ed Carr is the Wealth Manager for Dominion Investment Group. For more than twelve years, Ed Carr has served clients financial interests through client-education strategies. His experience in both Mortgage Finance and Retirement Planning support his goal to supply a long-range prospective and strategic plan for managing the wealth of his clients.

Ed was born in Tallahassee, Florida. After graduating from high school, he enlisted in the United States Navy where he served for twenty years and advanced to Chief Petty Officer. After an early retirement in his thirties, Ed ventured into the Mortgage Business and became a Certified Mortgage Planning Specialist.

Ed began his financial career at Capital Financial Home Equity in 2003, and was recognized as Mortgage Planner of the year in both 2005 and 2006—bringing to life his passion for finance and educational consulting.

Ed's current role at Dominion Investment Group now encompasses the assets side of a client's balance sheet – where he exercises an educational approach with clients. Ed serves as a Founder and on the Board of Directors for the Christian Business Chamber of Hampton Roads, which helps local Christian Business professionals to connect, network and help each other grow through their faith. Ed and his wife Debbie live on a small farm with three horses in Moyock, North Carolina. Their children Daniel, Amiee, Elizabeth and Laura, and a granddaughter, Madison, live nearby.

Contact information:
Edward "Ed" Carr
Wealth Manager, Dominion Investment Group
(757) 226-9440
dig@dominv.com

CHAPTER 34

FEED YOURSELF WITH LOVE AND ATTRACT MORE SUCCESS INTO YOUR LIFE!

BY KIM WILLIAMS

I want to impart some important truths, facts and wisdom to you from my own life experience that have resulted in me being healthier, happier, more alive and successful. And a huge plus: losing weight and maintaining my ideal weight now for three years. All of this occurred by changing the way I was feeding and continue to feed myself. With LOVE!

As I begin, please note that there are three basic assumptions about you that I am working from:

1) That you are serious about getting off the sidelines, getting in the game, and being healthier, happier and more successful.

2) That you are willing and able to invest the time and money to follow any or all of my suggestions.

3) That you would like to create your own special journey of change that has your unique personal signature of love on it!

And who do I love working with? I love working with business owners and entrepreneurs because they know the fastest way to grow their business is to start with themselves and their personal development. They are always proactive about making improvements because they have a vested interest in themselves and the future of their company. They know they are the engines for their companies, and without the giving of their passion and energy each and every day they could not be of service or make a difference in others lives.

In North America, being slim and healthy is a revolutionary act. It is totally counter cultural to what 95% of the population is doing. We leaders and entrepreneurs will always take a stand, be rebels and do what others won't. We're just plain brave and gutsy daredevils. When someone says, "You do it first!" they are first in line to lead the pack!!

Can anyone relate to this??

As an entrepreneur who wants to get off the sidelines and create the health, wealth and lifestyle that you want, there are so many benefits of feeding yourself with love. Three benefits to each – the body, mind and spirit – come up for me right away. The spirit benefit comes as a higher awareness of your connection with your world and your loving Co-Creator. (I say God. You may have another name to use here.) The mind benefit reveals itself as a strong connection to the energy that is in food and being able to use it as fuel for increased focus and concentration. And the third benefit, which is for your body, is improved digestion and metabolism and therefore improved immune system and health. Who wouldn't want more of that?

When I first considered feeding myself with love, I have to admit that I was very skeptical and hesitant to say the least. However, a dear friend and business associate of mine ever so lovingly pointed out how I often spoke negatively about myself and my life and peppered my stories with swear words. I also often complained of having different pain issues such as headaches and backaches, etc. She suggested that I take a look at the quality of my food and how I was preparing and eating it. With love? I thought to myself, "Humph! I love cooking and eating and I'm good at it, so how can it get any better than this?" Then she levelled the big lesson on me. "Look at your food as fuel for your high powered racing machine, your body. Imagine yourself as the owner of a million dollar Maserati race car and you are pulling up to the gas pump. Would you pump in low grade fuel and expect the car to win a race? Would you race it on empty? No! Only the best high octane fuel all the way! And how do you look at and talk to your car? With love and care? Yes! You buff it, you shine it. Only the best for your little racing machine, right? Well, now it is time to do the same for yourself, Kim!"

Yikes! I took my lesson to heart immediately and never questioned her authority on the subject. She has shed a lot of weight, kept it off, always has lots of loving positive energy, and is successful and healthy. My mission was clear. I never looked back except in gratefulness to her for telling me the hard truth I needed to hear: Feed your self with love! Love always wins. Period. The rewards for my commitment to myself just keep coming.

Ready for the 'how I did it' part? Great! I have broken down the important basics into eight sections and summarized each section with some do's and don'ts.

PART 1 - PLANNING YOUR MEALS WITH LOVE

Using a notebook make a list of the foods and meals you love. Think loving thoughts about the taste of each item. Now plan your menu for each day of the coming week. Fill in the foods and meals that you would like to eat for breakfast, lunch, dinner and two snacks. That's right. You are going to feed yourself with love at least 5 times per day, everyday, no exception!

Now make your shopping list. List all the items that you will need to create all your meals and snacks and place these items beneath the name of the store where you will shop. Think quality, think high octane, think clean, and think love! Plan to shop in stores or markets that are nicely decorated and clean. Choose small specialty markets and roadside stands whenever possible.

Do's

Bring food and water with you wherever you go. I pack a small insulated bag with nuts, fruit, raw veggies, left-over's, whatever is handy. Nothing is better than having food ready to munch on when stuck in a traffic jam or coming out of a meeting that lasted way too long! That's love!

Create your own cookbook in a binder filled with only your favourite recipes. One book, that's all. That's love! I print out on-line recipes, handwrite, or scan and print pages from cookbooks. I take out one recipe page when I cook and I put it back into my book when I am done.

<u>Don'ts</u>

Don't skip meals. Period. Remember my Maserati? Good! Now get your own car and make your plans on how you are going to fuel it regularly. This is key to increasing your metabolism and losing weight.

PART 2 - GATHERING YOUR FOOD WITH LOVE

Bring special decorative shopping bags into the store with you where you can lovingly place your purchases. When you enter the store or market look around at the staff who work there, particularly in the produce section. How are they handling the food? Lovingly? Do they look healthy? Happy to be there? Do they look up and smile as you approach? If not, don't buy the food that they touched. It has bad energy! Go shop somewhere else. You are worth it. Period.

Now the fun part..... choosing your foods with love. This is your chance for an incredible mind, body and spirit experience. Glance at your list and locate the food you want. Pick it up and lovingly look at it, feel it, smell it, shake it, and squeeze it. Repeat again before you make your final selection. Take your time. Think quality, think high octane, think clean, and think love!

<u>Do's</u>

Forget about store cameras or who may be watching you. Just smile and wink!

<u>Don'ts</u>

Don't buy or eat food that is past its due date.

PART 3 - PREPARING YOUR FOOD WITH LOVE

Set the stage for your performance. Create a loving, nurturing environment for yourself. I have powerful affirmations posted on fancy paper on my upper cupboard doors. I listen to wordless classical music so I can concentrate. I clear off my counters, clean out my sinks, bring out all the pans, mixing bowls, cutting boards, knives, and stirring utensils that I need.

Then I lovingly prepare and set aside all the ingredients that I need.

Do's

Keep your mind and your hands on lovingly washing and slicing your food.

Have a snack handy to eat and a nice stemmed glass of water to drink.

Don'ts

Don't multi-task. Stay off the phone and don't text.

PART 4 - COOKING YOUR FOOD WITH LOVE

Place your nose over the pan often while you are cooking to enjoy the aroma. Stir it often and note the texture. Put on a timer so as not to overcook. Time flies when you are having fun.

Do's

Pretend that Julia Child or Martha Stewart hasn't got anything on you!

Take before and after pictures and place them in your cook book.

Don'ts

Again, don't multi-task. Stay focused on your recipe.

PART 5 - DISPLAYING AND PRAYING WITH LOVE

Serve your food in your loveliest bowls, plates or dishes. Lovingly and carefully place your food on your plate like you are an artist creating a masterpiece. You are! Heap it up in lovely piles and colour coordinate your patterns. Garnish it with sprigs of herbs, parsley or orange slices.

Now offer a prayer of love, thankfulness and gratitude to your Co-Creator before you begin eating. Use the words "love" and "thank you" several times throughout your prayer. For example, "Thank you God for the loving nourishment and energy that this food will provide to my body, mind and spirit."

Do's

Be creative. Have fun! Take pictures!

Don'ts

Don't think there is any right or wrong way of praying. Just get it done.

Don't eat out of a pan, a can, a takeout container, or any dish that is cracked, chipped, broken or stained.

PART 6 - EATING WITH LOVE

Find a nice quiet place to eat and spread out your dishes. Get all the utensils you need and pin a large fresh clean t-towel or napkin around your neck. Remember sparks from your fuel may fly and you can avoid getting them on your clothes.

My favourite part! Can you hear the love now? No? Start making noises! I take a bite, breathe in deeply and with each breath out I say long, humming "M-m-m-m-m-m's." Before taking another bite, I say loving, warm fuzzies to myself. Try these: "I love this," "I'm an awesome cook," I'm an expert at making _____," "This tastes fantastic!", "You rock, Kim!", "I love my life!", "Thank you God!"

Do's

Let go of your seriousness. The only thing you want to be serious about right now is how you really love the food you are eating and how good you and your body feel.

Lick your plate when you are done. Yep, you heard me!

Don'ts

Don't taste good? Don't eat it. Period.

Don't eat standing up.

PART 7 - LOVING YOUR LEFTOVERS

Had enough to eat? Fuel tank full? Great! Refrigerate what's left so you can enjoy it again. I use glass bowls and containers whenever possible. I also pack portions to go or assemble a plate with everything on it and wrap the plate.

Do's

Stop eating when you are full. Tomorrow will come!

Don't

Don't keep leftovers for more than 2-3 days.

PART 8 - VENTURE FORTH WITH LOVE

This final section is for those of you who are on a path to rapidly transforming your life and making huge leaps forward in your personal development.

Here's what you do: Every few weeks, try a food that is new to you that you have never prepared before. Choose a plant-based, non-processed nutritious food. So I'm not talking here about trying poutine or deep fried pickles! Some great choices are: quinoa, fresh water chestnuts, adzuki beans, raw rutabaga sticks or chia seeds. By doing this you will expand your awareness of the abundance of food choices that are out there waiting for you. You can refresh you mind, energize your spirit, delight and love yourself just by tasting new foods.

Do's

Pick one or 2 new foods items per month to try. Research the item before you buy it.

Purchase a small amount. Ask for cooking advice at the store.

Don'ts

Don't eat it if you don't like it.

Don't give up. You may find a tastier way of preparing it some time in the future. If not, lovingly kiss it good-bye and let it go.

Next!

About Kim

Kim Williams helps her public figure clients maintain balance, structure and grounding in their private world. Being brought up in a small rural farming community, Kim naturally gravitates towards a simple and organic lifestyle. She helps her clients to nurture old-fashioned values that have been proven to bring health and wealth for hundreds of years.

Kim is a Certified Professional Co-Active Coach®, trained and certified with The Coaches Training Institute (CTI). CTI is an affiliate of the International Coach Federation (ICF) and is recognized as the most rigorous coach training in the coaching industry. In 2011, she graduated from the HealthCoachTraining® program and declared her expertise in stress and weight management. Kim believes coaching is the most powerful force for change on earth, and that everyone has the capability to transform their body, mind and spirit – and their life – into something they never dreamed possible.

She is the founder of her company, Vision In Motion Success Coaching, (2008) where she provides both virtual and in-person stress management and/or weight loss support programs. Last year Kim was excited to join Dr. Mohammad Emran with his new company, SpringCure, and assist in developing their new program: Fast-Track Coaching for weight loss. As the Lead Attitude Coach and Training Director, she is continuously developing training materials and curriculum and teaching coaches how to keep their clients in action. Her main focus with SpringCure is in qualifying, training, mentoring and leading the team of Health Coaches who assist SpringCure clients in their weight loss journey.

Kim keeps engaged in ongoing studies in nutrition, nutritional psychology, personal development and business marketing and sales. She is a regular master minder within her Live Out Loud business community and currently commits herself and her time to two groups who each meet weekly to provide support for each other with successes and wins, challenges and intentions in their prospective businesses.

Kim enjoys a healthy lifestyle through nutrition, running, yoga and meditation, and using high quality supplements and certified pure therapeutic grade essential oils (CPTG™). She is also the author of the upcoming book, T*he Last 20 Pounds: Letting Go of What Weighs You Down,* where Kim shares her personal weight loss journey and the emotional part of keeping the weight off for life.

You can connect with Kim at:
kim@canadahealthcoachkim.com
www. Facebook.com/KimWilliams2008
www.linkedIn.com/in/CoachKimW or search Kim Williams, CPCC

CHAPTER 35

BY THE STROKE
OF A PEN

BY DAWN TANGRI AND NICOLE GRANAKOS

This is the story of two women, Dawn Tangri and Nicole Granakos. Both women were driven into insurance due to the need to take care of their families. In the end, both women's stories are happy ones because they are now in the position to help others make decisions for themselves in ways that preserve their legacies and remove huge financial burdens left in the wake of unexpected events.

NICOLE'S TALE

When Nicole started working in the insurance industry, her mother was diagnosed with COPD. This is a chronic disorder that is usually not cured and can eventually lead to death. That was bad enough news, but when her mother began to think of the possible financial burden she was going to incur while she was living and after she passed, she was disappointed to hear that she would not qualify for traditional life insurance. It would mean she would have to pay a super high premium and with the mounting medical expenses, this would not be possible.

Her illness affected her husband and the rest of the family. Her medicines were costing upwards of $500-$600 alone, not to mention the rest of her medical bills. Keeping her house up and even putting food on the table was becoming difficult. Nicole helped as she could, but it began draining her finances as well. Her mother cashed in the small insurance policy she had, at a loss, even though she knew she could not qualify for any more new life insurance policies. Nicole knows that when she finally does pass, that the expenses will be out of pocket.

For Nicole, it has been quite the education, because she realizes how something like a chronic disease can sneak up on a family, and how quickly it can lead to financial ruin. A life insurance policy could have assisted with the final arrangements. Medical insurance would only pay part of the costs of her mother's medical costs. Where could they have found help with all of the other debts the family was dealing with?

DAWN'S TALE

Dawn's father was a college professor for 38 years, and was close to retiring when the unimaginable happened: his wife was diagnosed with an aggressive invasive terminal cancer. Like Nicole's family, they were completely caught off guard. Dawn's mother was diagnosed with metastatic melanoma. She never had external skin cancer, only internal. She passed within 6 months of being diagnosed, but it was long enough to drain the family's finances, because she did not have any life insurance or retirement savings.

Dawn's mother was the primary caretaker of two of her grandchildren, which left Dawn's sister in a bind of having to find daycare providers that were both affordable and trustworthy. The ripples of a traumatic event in a family can affect every one directly and indirectly, and often the greatest issues are financial ones.

When Dawn's father heard the prognosis, he was devastated because she was the love of his life and he would do anything to try to save her. He spent his entire retirement savings on purchasing experimental drugs, trying to keep her alive and/or cure her. This meant that he would have to work an additional seven years, because all of the money they had saved was being quickly depleted. Because she was a housewife, Dawn's father didn't feel like she needed any life insurance, and so they didn't have any on her. In hindsight he realized it was one of the most important things he should have done for her and the family.

In what seemed like a cruel trick of fate, he retired in 2008 amidst a national financial crisis. His retirement portfolio fell victim to the global financial crash and he was again left significantly financially strained, losing almost all of his savings for a second time. This left him more than a little concerned about his financial future. He desperately wanted to leave a legacy to both of his daughters as well as his six grandchildren. He wanted to be able to contribute to his grandchildren's college funds, while continuing to enjoy the fruits of his labor as a professor in relative comfort and security.

They say that lightning usually does not strike the same place twice, let alone a third time, but Dawn's father was not taking any chances. At her father's suggestion, Dawn became a Financial Services Representative in 2011. He felt she'd be able to help him plan his financial future with what he had left, because he was worried about outliving his retirement funds. After studying long and hard, she passed her licensure. Dawn was able to educate her father on the options available to him to provide for his family and grow his money.

Lightning did strike a third time, when Dawn's father suffered from a massive stroke that left him in a coma for two weeks before finally passing and joining his beloved wife. Dawn had fortunately given her father some sound advice that preserved his legacy. She advised him to utilize an Indexed Universal Life Policy by making a lump sum single premium payment. This allowed him to more than double the value of his money and his legacy by the stroke of a pen.

The advice Dawn had given him turned out to be a critical turning point for his legacy. He was able to leave each of his daughters a significant inheritance, properly transfer his investment properties, and provide towards college for all six of his grandchildren. All of this was possible because he made a decision to fund life insurance policies. This also allowed Dawn the flexibility to take time off from work to fly to Texas three times to manage the estate and probate responsibilities.

WHAT IS AN INDEXED UNIVERSAL LIFE POLICY?

There is a new conversation going on in the world of Life insurance, and that is the advent and use of "Living Benefits". Those are benefits that can be used while you are still alive. If Dawn's mother or Nicole's mother had vested into an Indexed Universal Life policy, they could have drawn money out of their Life Insurance payout value. This is a lump sum amount that is provided for someone that has been diagnosed with a critical, chronic, or terminal illness. If they have a policy that has a $50,000 to $1,000,000 death benefit, and they suffer a covered illness, they can accelerate the death benefit. That money can then be used anyway the policy owner sees fit.

Let that sink in a moment.

If something unexpected happens to you, you can take care of your family while you are still alive. Your unexpected misfortune does not have to have a devastating ripple effect on your loved ones. You can also preserve a portion of your death benefit, and leave a legacy. Imagine how that could have helped both Dawn's and Nicole's families—moreover, imagine how that could help yours. These are Quality of Life policies.

The reason it is referred to as an indexed policy is that the growth of the policy is based on the growth of the S&P 500. A fail safe in this type of policy is that when the S&P 500 goes down in value, they're locked in and people do not lose any money. The policies are not directly invested in the S&P 500, but they just follow the trends. When the market goes up, so does the value of the policy, it can just never dip below the base value of the policy. Can your 401K boast the same kind of safety net?

When Dawn's father bought the policy he doubled his investment instantly. He made a one time payment, and the death benefit was double that amount, which doubled his legacy. He could have earned more on the policy but he passed about a year after he bought the policy and did not need any living benefits. What other kind of investment can you double, triple or even quadruple in a short amount of time and you can access those benefits when you need them?

WHEN DO THE LIVING BENEFITS GO INTO EFFECT?

With the exception of Cancer, which has a 90-day elimination period, all other illnesses can pay out 30 days after the policy is in effect. The living benefits are not connected to how much has been paid into the policy so you don't have to be vested in the policy for years; it just draws from the death benefit.

You can use the living benefits to put food on the table, or even keep your business running, which is really important for small business owners. Before the economic fun that everybody went through in 2008, the main reasons people lost their homes or their businesses were due to a critical or chronic illness.

WHEN LIFE INSURANCE PAYS OUT

Dawn and her sister were the sole beneficiaries of their father's insurance, and they received the money immediately. The rest of his estate is still in probate after 11 months. Life insurance goes straight to a beneficiary, it doesn't go through probate. Also, it does not get taxed, and so it came to them tax-free and immediately. If you are not thinking of your estate now, and considering life insurance today, tomorrow may be too late. If Dawn's father had waited a couple more months, it would have been too late.

When you pass, many times your finances will go into probate – which means the funds are frozen by the government. Someone is assigned to the estate and all of the debts are assessed and the finances are assessed for taxes. This can take months or years. Is this something you want to leave behind for your family? You can buy insurance, have it double in value instantly and be available to your family instantly – it seems like a no brainer, right?

Before you go online and pick just any insurance company that pops up, here are some things to consider as you are shopping for an Indexed Universal Life Insurance policy:

1. Try to find an agent that will sit down with you and answer your questions. A face-to-face interaction provides you with answers to your questions and for the agent to create a policy that makes sense for you and your family. A computer cannot do that quite yet.

2. If your agent with whom you are sitting down is not willing to go through the process with you, or if you feel like they're not answering your questions, or seem to be going around in circles or avoiding questions, that could be a red flag. Dawn and Nicole spend an average of two hours in their initial consultation with a client, whether they meet in person, or on skype.

   Nicole recalls that the craziest question she ever got was about two years ago. It was a guy who traveled a lot for his business and he said, "If I disappear, and they cannot find me, how long before my wife can get the policy." That stumped her, but she found an answer for him – and in their state it was seven years that a person has to be missing before they can declare you deceased.

3. Look at the ratings the company has before you do business with them. You can do your research online.

4. Look for the flexibility in the policy you are considering. Some companies offer living benefits but the payout is monthly rather than a lump sum. Or if you become better, then you stop drawing benefits. There are companies that will say they offer the terminal illness rider, but you have to forfeit the entire policy and you only get 40% of the death benefit.

5. If you think the premium is too high, say $300 a month, you might think you are better off just putting that in a savings account in the bank. Consider though, that paying that initial $300 could get you $300,000 of insurance that you could draw on should you need it. Can a savings account offer that?

6. This is not the same thing as disability insurance. In the state of Florida, while you are working, if you become seriously ill, disability would pay you 60% of your income. You were living off 100% of your income, prior to needing disability insurance. Where do you close the gap? Eventually, that insurance will run out. If you can no longer work, where else will you be able to find money to help your family get by?

Dawn recalls, "When I married into my husband's family, my father-in-law was too sick for me to write him a traditional life insurance policy. He had too many chronic illnesses. He had three term life insurance policies through his job. As soon as he became too sick to work, they asked him to retire and he lost all three of those policies instantly. My mother-in-law didn't have any life insurance money to bury him with when he passed. When somebody says to me, "Oh, I spend a dollar a week on life insurance through work." I remind them that the policy is only good while they are working. If they want to continue that insurance they were spending $5 a month for, they could be asked to pay $500 a month to keep it."

7. Don't think because you are a single person that buying an Indexed Universal Life Insurance Policy would not apply to you. First of all, just because you are single, does not mean you could not use the living benefits should you become ill, and in fact, it may be more imperative since you are the only person with an income.

CLOSING THOUGHTS

People do not hesitate to buy car insurance, or homeowners, or even boat insurance. They will pay a premium for dental and health insurance, but they do not consider insuring their own life. If you ask most people what their most valuable possession is, they'll name their house or maybe their car. They never state that their ability to go out and earn a living is their number one possession. Without earning a living, they would not be able to own anything else. Remember it just takes a stroke of a pen to secure your future now and your legacy tomorrow.

About Dawn

Dawn Tangri helps her clients protect themselves and their families against both the inevitable and unforeseen financial stresses. Dawn has always been passionate about helping to educate people – first, as a K-12 Teacher, a Florida Realtor, and then as a Financial Representative for AIG Financial Network. Dawn naturally gravitated to all of her fields out of a love for helping people understand life and how to live well.

Dawn followed in her father's footsteps as an educator, and in 1991 received her BS Degree in Education from West Texas A&M University. She followed it with a notable 15-year teaching career. Dawn started teaching in Texas, then moved to Florida, in which she helped three new schools start their inaugural years in Orange County, Florida.

Dawn transitioned into Financial Services in 2011, and has been an award winning service provider from the start, having won the President's Trophy in 2012 and 2013. She currently holds Licenses in Florida, Texas, and New Jersey. She is currently seeking to work nationally in all States.

Dawn's driving belief in Financial Services is that insurance is a valuable resource for families, individuals, and business owners. She teaches them about protecting themselves from unforeseen illness and accidents, so that they never have to go through what she and her family have been through.

Dawn has been a State of Florida Licensed Real Estate Agent since 2003. Dawn has also combined her mission and her entrepreneurial passions with her colleague, Nicole, to create a real estate business. They realized how the dip in the economy in 2008 destroyed people's lives, and wanted to create a company that could assist people in selling their home quickly, especially in times of crisis.

Dawn also embraces the entrepreneurial spirit with each of her children, encouraging them to become business owners. One of her daughters, a junior in high school, is starting a non-profit that connects children in the foster care system with rescue animals in a pet therapy setting.

Dawn is also a member of WOAMTEC, and in addition is a member of WPN (Women's Prosperity Network), Dr. Phillips-Metro West Chamber of Commerce, Southlake Junior Women's Club, PTSA (Parent, Teacher, Student Association), and Volunteers at OCPS

(Orange County Public Schools). Dawn is a guest speaker and sponsor of the Future Investor Clubs of America.

If you wish to talk to Dawn further, use one of the following methods:
Dawn.tangri@gmail.com
407-493-2245
Dawn.tangri@aig.com
www.myagla.com/dawn.tangri
www.linkedin.com

About Nicole

Nicole Granakos has worked as a Financial Representative for AGLA (Now under AIG) since 2008. During her tenure, she won the coveted President's Trophy in 2011, 2012, and 2013. She has helped educate new employees the past four years at AIG Financial Network, and continues to create business continuation strategy programs.

Nicole's mission is to protect her family and others from unforeseen events that can, in a blink of an eye, change their lives forever. She embodies the entrepreneurial spirit and has encouraged her daughter to be a business owner from the time she was little. She has done small things such as dog walking and creating jewelry to sell.

As their children have grown, Nicole and Dawn have seen the importance for teens to understand what finances are, how to leverage them early and intelligently. They are creating a Financial Literacy Training Program for Teens.

Nicole is a member of WOAMTEC (Women on a Mission to Earn Commission), SLBRG (South Lake Business Referral Group), and the Clermont Chamber of Commerce in Florida.

If you would like to reach Nicole , you can do so using one of the methods below:
Nicole.Granakos@aig.com
www.Linkedin.com
407-228-1132

CHAPTER 36

SIX SIMPLE STEPS TO "GETTING IN THE GAME" – ROCKSTAR STYLE

BY KEVIN HARRINGTON

Are you ready to get in the game and become the Game Changer, in your industry?

If you answered yes to that question, welcome, you're in the right place.

I'm Kevin Harrington, Original "Shark" on the hit TV show, Shark Tank. What I'm about to share with you are six proven concepts that will not only help you "get in the game", they're guaranteed to help you stand out and actually lead the game by becoming the "Game Changer" in your industry.

When you're a Game Changer, you're a Rockstar.

You're not living life from the sidelines. You're not following the crowd. You're getting ahead of the crowd and you're leading the way.

If you're not living on the edge, you're taking up too much space.
~ Unknown

People are waiting for the next big hit, whether it's a catchy tune, a new TV show or in this case, a new product or service that will add value to their life.

When you're a Rockstar, you lead the game and you become a person of influence in your market. I've been a Rockstar in my industry for 30 years now and it's because I was willing to jump in, step up and lead the way. I'm the inventor of the infomercial, and since then, I've been involved with over 500 product launches that have resulted in over $4 billion in sales worldwide.

Everything I've learned about business, I learned by getting out, getting going and getting into the game. My education as an entrepreneur started when I was 11 years old. My father owned a restaurant and I was his right-hand man. At the age of 11, I worked 40 hours a week and I literally had my hands in every aspect of the business, including flipping the steaks. I had my first taste of life as an entrepreneur and I wanted more.

By the time I was 15, I owned a neighborhood driveway sealing business. In college, I started a heating and air conditioning company that employed 25 employees and was bringing in $1 million a year.

It wasn't long before I jumped into my next venture as a business broker and I started a company called the Small Business Center. I was a licensed real estate broker specializing in the sales of businesses. I rented an entire floor of an office building and I had 14 salespeople working for me. We would facilitate the purchase of businesses, then we would connect people with all of their business needs, including incorporation, accounting, advertising, marketing and selling them insurance.

This is when my business "Rockstardom" really took off. I'm going to bet that you're reading this chapter right now because you're ready for your own inner Rockstar to step out from behind the stage and start leading the way.

It's easier than you think. Follow the six simple steps below and get ready to become the Rockstar in your industry:

SIX SIMPLE STEPS TO "GETTING IN THE GAME" – ROCKSTAR STYLE

Step #1: Induce Curiosity Overload

To get in the game and become a Rockstar, you have to get exposed to new ideas, products and opportunities. You can't expect opportunities to find you and you definitely can't get in the game by sitting at home. You have to get up, get out and network. I've programmed myself to find and receive new opportunities and you can do the same.

To program yourself to receive new opportunities, you have to induce curiosity overload.

When you induce curiosity overload, you're exposing yourself to new ideas, products and opportunities. Overtime, you develop a radar for new business opportunities that are aligned with your strengths and values.

Here's a closer look at how I induce curiosity overload. It's a simple strategy that applies to anyone who is willing to get in the game. Most people I meet attend a couple of trade shows each year. I attend 35 tradeshows a year. I'm constantly on the look out for new ideas and products across all categories, including: hardwares, housewares, fishing, golf, beauty, fitness, consumer electronics, outdoor camping and more.

Here's a trade show tip that works wonders…

Search out any media opportunities you can get. If you have products you're selling, find the pressroom and tell them why they need to know about your product.

As you can see, I'm constantly on the look out for new ideas and products. I don't wait for them to find me. I became a person of influence and a Rockstar in my industry by seeking out new opportunities.

In fact, I met Arnold Morris, creator of the *Ginsu* knife, at a tradeshow in Philadelphia in the 1980's and we formed a partnership that has generated $100 million over the years.

When I'm not at tradeshows, I'm scanning the "junk" mail. In my opinion, junk mail is as valuable as gold. I receive over 1500 catalogs delivered to my home each year. I pay attention to trends and I often find new products to promote in select industries.

What are you doing to induce curiosity overload?

Are you actively seeking new opportunities by attending industry trade shows either as an exhibitor or attendee? Are you networking in your local community? Networking at your local Chamber of Commerce (and regional and national Chamber events!) is a great way to meet people, get exposed to new ideas and share your insights with business leaders.

The most important thing to remember, no matter who you are or where you're at in your business, is to get out there, get connected and stay in the game at all times.

Step #2: Shout It Out!

Rockstars don't whisper, they shout. This is exactly what you need to do if you want to stand out from the crowd and become a Rockstar in your industry. You need to put yourself out there in every possible way.

Whether you write a book, publish weekly newsletters or blog posts, the main idea here is that you're constantly sharing your expertise, your experience and your advice with your industry. The more you share, the more you gain new customers and the more you keep existing customers.

When you consistently publish online and offline content that is relevant and of good quality, over time you will become known as an authority (aka Rockstar) in your industry.

Take a minute to evaluate your current strategy.

- Do you have a website where you share content on a regular basis?

- Are you creating content to be shared on other websites and online magazines or in offline publications?

Make a list of at least 10 online and offline sources where you can "shout it out!" to establish yourself as the go-to Rockstar in your industry today.

Step #3: Create, Create, Create!

The next step to getting in the game and becoming a rockstar in your industry is to create products and 'productize' yourself.

I have a lot of friends who are doctors and lawyers and when they're sleeping, they're not making money. Taking an expertise and creating a product such as a DVD, a newsletter, a monthly membership or a club with an annual fee are all great ways to 'productize' and sell around the clock.

Think about this for a minute… How many people do you know who spend most of their lives trading time for money? Whether they're an industry expert or a professional in their field (like a Doctor or accountant), they don't make money if they're not working. This is NOT the business model most people want to create yet it's the most common business trap that I see.

Rather than trading your valuable time for money, I want you to lead the way in your field by creating a product that's based on your expertise. When you have a product, you can sell in your sleep. If you don't already have a product, go back to step one and induce curiosity overload. See what products already exist and figure out creative ways you can offer new or upgraded products, ones that are in line with your expertise.

Tony Little is the perfect example of someone who created a product based on his expertise. He had a target training system that he used with personal training clients and he took this system and created a Target Training DVD set that he then sold to millions of people around the world.

Step #4: Claim Your Fame.
As you begin to "Shout it Out!" by getting published, then it's important to "Claim Your Fame." You claim your fame by positioning yourself in the media as an expert and a leader in your industry.

This is where the power of PR (public relations) comes into play. You should constantly be putting yourself out there. Whether it's pitching radio interviews or interviews with your local television network, the idea here is to build-up your expertise by creating massive exposure for yourself and your business.

The trick here is to work smarter, not harder. You work smarter by exposing yourself to opportunities that are going to build your funnel. The more ideas opportunities you have in your funnel, the closer you are to claiming your fame.

Getting up, getting out and networking are KEY to creating these opportunities. Networks and radio stations won't find you hiding in your garage or basement. Create your media kit and start sending it out. Include your professional bio, a headshot and create an attention-grabbing story. Media outlets are always looking for great content and stories to share with their audience. You need to create opportunities by putting yourself out there.

What are you doing to claim your fame? Create a strategy and put it into action!

Step #5: Maximize Your Exposure.

You don't become a Rockstar in your industry without maximum exposure. To maximize your exposure, you need to maximize your reach and you can do this by creating smart partnerships and building a team.

The goal is to create effective partnerships that enhance your skills and leverage the strengths of the people you're partnering with. Loral Langemeier and I have partnered because we have complimentary skills that we're able to leverage successfully.

The same goal applies to your team. You want to free up your time so you can focus on getting out and creating exposure for yourself. When you have the right team in place, you can focus outwards rather than staying behind the scenes working on the minute details of your business. These details are necessary, but they don't necessarily need to be done by you.

If your genius zone is in the minute details, then you should look to partner with someone who excels at networking, sales and marketing. In most cases, entrepreneurs are innovators and problem solvers. They have the idea and a concept, but they don't have the business know-how or the financing to take their idea to the masses.

If this is your scenario, I highly recommend that you find yourself two key team players. In fact, I recommend these steps for ANYONE who is ready to get in the game and become the Rockstar in their industry.

1. Find a great mentor (someone who has already done what you're doing) to guide you through this process.

2. Find a partner who can finance your business so you can truly take it to the masses.

When you learn to leverage the strengths of others, you truly can become the Rockstar in your industry.

Step #6: Audition.

Like a Rockstar, you need to constantly audition for the show. In the world of business, you audition by pitching yourself and pitching your business. Pitching your business once isn't going to cut it.

Entrepreneurship takes the ability to stand up and dust yourself off, time and time again. I succeed with about 25% of the projects I'm involved in. Not only have I given many pitches, I've actually taken over 50,000 pitches from every kind of person you can imagine. That being said, I know what investors look for because I am an investor who's pitched to all the time.

When you're creating the perfect pitch, it's important to include:

- An overview of your industry.

- An overview of your background and experience in your industry.

- The unique proposition that you have. (Include what niche you're targeting and highlight how you're different to competitors.)

- Highlight any multi-functionality that exists in your offer.

And last, but definitely not least, when you're creating your pitch you NEED to clearly highlight what's in it for the investor. Investors want to know they can make a large return on their investment because it's a huge risk investing in an idea or start-up business.

I've raised over $100 million and in one instance, I raised $20 million from 191 investors and one trend became very clear. When you can accelerate their payback, an investor is more likely to invest in your company. Get creative and make a pitch that's hard for an investor to say no to.

Here's an example of a pitch that screams confidence:

"If you invest $1 million in my company, 100% of company profits will be delivered to you until you receive your $1 million investment back. Then, once your investment is recuperated, you'll continue to receive 20% of company profits for the rest of your life."

If you want to launch a product or new business and you've never pitched to an investor, do not wait any longer. Investors can open doors for you that you never knew existed.

Start putting together your pitch today and follow the SIX simple steps to becoming a Rockstar in your industry.

Anyone can become a Rockstar when they're willing to get in the game and get going.

About Kevin

Kevin Harrington - Inventor of the Infomercial, Original Shark on *Shark Tank* and *As Seen on TV* pioneer - is one of the most successful entrepreneurs of our time.

In 1980 Harrington started The Small Business Center and Franchise America. Kevin, as a real estate and business broker, sold thousands of businesses and then offered one stop services from accounting to insurance to advertising to finance and more.

While watching television one night in 1984, Harrington noticed that sometimes the only thing on the screen were the color test bars that stations ran when they had nothing else to air, thus giving Kevin the idea to produce the industry's first 30-minute infomercial to fill that dead air space, which is what coined him the Inventor of the Infomercial.

Since then, he has been involved with over 500 product launches that resulted in sales of over $4 billion dollars worldwide and 20 products that reached individual sales of over $100 million. By 1990, Harrington was named one of the 100 best entrepreneurs in the world (by *Entrepreneur Magazine*).

In the mid-80's he formed Quantum International which grew to $500 million in sales selling products in 100 countries in 20 languages. He then formed HSN direct in conjunction with Home Shopping Network and soon after formed Reliant International Media. Kevin also founded As Seen on TV, Inc. and acquired AsSeenOnTV.com, the world's largest web site featuring as seen on TV products.

Harrington has worked with some of the biggest celebrities including Cee Lo Green, Kim Kardashian, Paris Hilton, 50 Cent, Jack LaLane, George Foreman, Frankie Avalon, Paula Abdul, Montel Williams, Chubby Checker, Hulk Hogan, Kris and Bruce Jenner, Tony Little, Billy Mays and many more.

In 2009, Kevin was selected as one of the original 'Shark Tank' Sharks on the ABC hit show. As an innovator and pioneer in the industry, Kevin has been featured on over 150 Shark Tank segments over the last five years on both ABC and CNBC.

Kevin is regularly featured as an industry expert in numerous media outlets including the NBC Today Show, ABC Good Morning America, CBS Morning News, The View, the Wendy Williams Show, CNBC, Squawk Box with Jim Kramer, the Bethenny Show, Bloomberg, Fox Business, CNN, MTV, *Entrepreneur Magazine, Fast Company, Fortune, Inc., The Wall Street Journal, New York Times* and many more.

He went on and founded two global associations – ERA (Electronic Retailers Association), which is now in 45 countries and Young Entrepreneur's Association (now EO - Entrepreneurs Organization) which boasts combined member sales of over $500 billion dollars.

Harrington is on the board of University of South Florida (USF) entrepreneur programs, and teaches regularly. He has also been involved with Moffit Cancer Research, and is constantly giving back to the community. Harrington's recent book, *Act Now: How I Turn Ideas Into Million-Dollar Products*, details his life and achievements in the direct marketing world, and his business was used as a class case study for 12 years at Harvard/MIT, illustrating the essential principles of grass-roots entrepreneurship.

"I believe that anyone with drive and vision – **anyone** – can achieve success"